I

What is a book?

1 Past, present, and future 6
2 Creating a book 13
3 Approaching the design 23

II

The book designer's palette

4 Format 30
5 Grids 42
6 Typographic palette 71
7 Type 86

III

Type and image

8 Editorial structure 101
9 Communicating through image 110
10 Layout 140
11 Covers and jackets 160

IV

Manufacture

12 Pre-production 172
13 Paper 191
14 Paper engineering 200
15 Printing 210
16 Binding 219

Additional material

Styling the text 240
Further reading 249
Glossary 251
Index 253
Picture credits, Acknowledgments 256

LAURENCE KING

Published in 2006 by Laurence King Publishing Ltd
e-mail: enquiries@laurenceking.co.uk
www.laurenceking.co.uk

Copyright © Text and design 2006 Andrew Haslam

A catalogue record for this book is available from
the British Library

ISBN-13: 978 1 85669 473 5
ISBN-10: 1 85669 473 9

Design and diagrams by the author
Photography by Martin Slivka
Printed in China

Frontispiece: *Blago* designed by Gordon Davey
Cover: photography by Martin Slivka

The images shown in this book are generally reproduced at one of five sizes: 100%, 66%, 50%, 33%,
and 25%. In cases where there are several images
on the page, I have generally used a common scale
so that the books can be effectively compared by
the reader.

Books are to be returned on or before
the last date below.

LIBREX–

Andrew Haslam

Book design

Laurence King Publishing

What is a book? I

What is a book?

The book is the oldest form of documentation; it stores the world's knowledge, ideas, and beliefs. In this first part I will briefly examine the origins of the book; consider definitions of the book; examine how a book is created, identifying the various roles within the publishing industry; clarify some of the terms used to describe the physical components of the book; and, finally, discuss a range of approaches to book design.

Past, present, and future

Books have a long history, stretching back more than 4,000 years; this chapter will provide a brief glimpse into their early origins. By examining the words we use to describe books, we gain an insight into the past as well as an understanding of books themselves.

The origins of the book

The English word 'book' is derived from the Old English word *bok*, itself linked to the word for 'beech tree'. Beech boards were written on by Saxons and Germans, and a literal definition of the book is 'a board for writing'. The word *codex*, used to describe very early books such as manuscripts of the Bible or ancient literature, has a similarly woody origin: the Latin for 'tree trunk' is *caudex*, planks of which were used as a writing surface. When we refer to the *leaves* of a book, the reference picks up on the organic material of the writing surface used by early Egyptian scholars. The broad flat leaves of Egyptian palms were used for writing on, and later, papyrus stems were crushed, woven, and dried to make a writing surface suitable for ink.

The first book designers were Egyptian scribes, who wrote in columns and illustrated their scrolls with drawings. Egyptian writing was not bound in the form of a book but rolled - papyrus sheets were glued edge to edge and then rolled up into a scroll. Papyrus continued to be used throughout the ancient world as the principal writing material, although samples of Egyptian, Greek, and Roman writing have also been found on leather and dried animal skins. It was probably Eumenes II, the king of Pergamum in Asia Minor, who first investigated the use of animal skins as an alternative to papyrus. His scholars produced for him a two-sided animal skin that had been stretched on a frame, dried, whitened with chalk, and smoothed flat with a pumice stone. This material is what we now call *parchment*.

The origins of the bound parchment codex can be seen in the earlier Greek and Roman practices of fastening wax-filled wooden tablets together along one edge. The material properties of parchment were a spur to the development of the codex. Parchment was made in larger sizes than the brittle papyrus and could be folded without damage. The codex broke with the tradition of the scroll, in that the sheets were joined edge to edge and folded, then piled and bound along one side. Folding the large parchment sheets in half created two *folios* (the word we now use to number pages, deriving from the Latin word for 'leaf'); by continuing to fold the sheet in half, four pages were created, known as a *quarto* or quaternion; folding in half again made eight pages – an *octavo*. All three terms are used today to describe paper sizes derived from folded sheets. Roman and Greek scribes followed the principle of the Egyptian scroll for the codex by writing on each page in columns. The word *page*, describing one side of a book leaf, comes from the Latin *pagina*, meaning 'something fastened', reflecting its bookbinding rather than scroll origins.

Paper, a word derived from 'papyrus', was developed in China around 200 BC, although official Chinese history states that paper was discovered by Tsai Louen, director of the imperial workshops, in AD 104. Early Chinese paper was made from mulberry or bamboo bark pulped into fibres, spread over a woven cloth, and allowed to dry. By 751 paper-making had spread to the Islamic world and by 1000 paper was being produced in Baghdad. The Moors transported their knowledge of paper-making to Spain, and the first European paper mill was founded at Capellades in Catalonia in 1238.

Johannes Gutenberg, a German from Mainz, produced the first European printed book using movable type in 1455. Gutenberg's Bible, which was printed in Latin, was the product of several diverse technologies. Gutenberg had a knowledge of metalwork and he was familiar with the presses that were used for crushing grapes in the wine-making process. He owned and read codex

Above Johannes Gutenberg produced the first printed edition of the Bible in 1455. The Bible went on to become the most published work ever, disseminating throughout Europe and the rest of the world the beliefs on which both Jewish and Christian cultures were based.

bound books and was aware of paper. Gutenberg's unofficial status as 'the father of printing' derives from a somewhat misleading and Eurocentric view of history. Sand-cast movable type had been used in Korea as early as 1241; a Korean book of *c.* 1377 states that it was printed using movable type. The Chinese had used woodblock printing since the seventh century to produce playing cards and paper money, which were in circulation as early as AD 960, while in AD 868 a book of the Theravada Buddhist canon, the *Tripitaka*, was printed on paper in China, and involved the cutting of 130,000 woodblocks.

Despite academic arguments over the precise date of the invention of printing, the impact of the printed book on the development of Western European history is less debatable. Since Roman times, a 22-letter Western alphabet had been used for handwriting, and each letter, word, and sentence of a handwritten book was created individually: one artisan, one artefact. Movable type and its offspring, the printed book, enabled a single printer, having set a text, to produce multiple copies. The early printers were responsible for setting the type and designing the layout of the pages as well as for the text's reproduction. The printed book industrialized the production of language. Printing was faster than calligraphic copying and, as a consequence, words became inexpensive and widely available.

The search for a definition: what is a book?

Having established the origins of the words 'book' and 'codex' and some of the associated terms, I feel that a clear definition of a book would be helpful. The *Concise Oxford Dictionary* presents two simple alternatives:

1 'Portable written or printed treatise filling a number of sheets fastened together.'

2 'Literary composition that would fill a set of sheets.'

These simple definitions identify two key elements: the physical description of a portable printed set of bound sheets, and a reference to writing and literature. The *Encyclopaedia Britannica* offers:

3 '... a written (or printed) message of considerable length, meant for public circulation and recorded on materials that are light yet durable enough to afford comparatively easy portability.'

4 'Instrument of communication.'

Encyclopaedia Britannica 1 1964, vol. III, p. 870

These definitions introduce the ideas of readership and communication. In *The Encyclopedia of the Book* (1996), Geoffrey Ashall Glaister puts figures to the notions of expense and extent:

5 'For statistical purposes the British book trade once assumed that a book was a publication costing sixpence or more.'

6 'Other countries define a book as containing a minimum number of pages; a UNESCO conference in 1950 defined a book as "a non-periodical literary publication containing 49 or more pages, not counting the covers".'

These definitions are clearly born out of legal concerns and tax regulations. While the physical descriptions of sheets and fastening may be accurate, none of the above definitions seems to capture the influence or power of a book. It may prompt further discussion if I put forward a definition of my own:

7 Book: A portable container consisting of a series of printed and bound pages that preserves, announces, expounds, and transmits knowledge to a literate readership across time and space.

Publishing as business: the commercial value of the book

Publishing today is an enormous business. The world's largest publisher in 1999 was Bertelsmann AG, whose German-based group made a profit of nearly 27 billion marks (more than 14 billion dollars) - more than the entire economy of many countries. The number of printed books published throughout the world increases annually, although this is an elusive figure to pin down as many publications do not use ISBN numbers, the method of numbering and thus tracking books. No one knows how many books have been printed since 1455, nor even the number of books currently held in the world's libraries, as many remain uncatalogued. The Great Library of Alexandria, found in the third century BC by the Egyptian king Ptolemy II, and destroyed by fire in 640 AD, held between 428,000 and 700,000 scrolls and was the most extensive library of the ancient world. Today, the United States Library of Congress catalogue runs to 119 million items in 460 languages, while the British Library claims 150 million items in 'most known languages'. The acquisition rate for the British Library is 3,000,000 items per year. It keeps a copy of every book published in English and has huge international and specialist collections. The largest bookshop in the world is Barnes and Noble, 105 Fifth Avenue, New York, which contains 207,000 metres of shelving.

The power of print: the influence of books

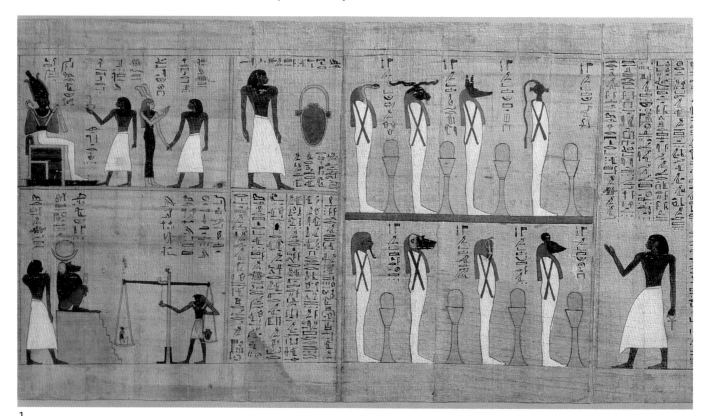

1

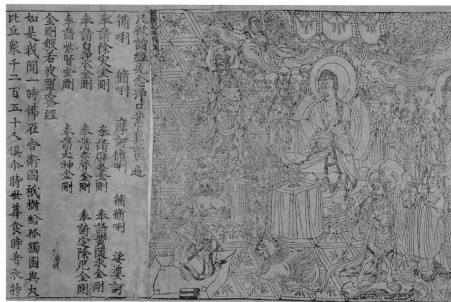

2

1 The Egyptian royal scribe Hunefer wrote the *Book of the Dead* in around 1300 BC when in the service of Seti, king of Egypt. The text runs vertically in narrow columns divided by rules. The imagery of the frieze breaks across the columns and is enlarged to illustrate the most important scenes. The books on this spread are not shown at a common scale.

2 The *Diamond Sutra* is often cited as the world's oldest and most complete dated book; it is dated 868 AD. For centuries it was hidden in a sealed cave in northwest China. The word *sutra* comes from Sanskrit, an ancient sacred language of India, and means 'religious teaching' or 'sermon'. The text, written in Chinese, is considered one of the most important writings of the Buddhist faith. The text reads vertically and the illustrations were printed using wooden blocks.

3 Adolf Hitler in his 1925 *Mein Kampf* (*My Struggle*) presented an alternative to the ideas of the Left in the form of extreme nationalism. This combination of unreliable autobiography, ill-considered political philosophy, and overt racism was bought by 9,000,000 Germans during Hitler's lifetime and was widely translated. It crudely laid out the principles of National Socialism and established the platform for Hitler's dictatorial fascism.

3

4

4 The thoughts of Chairman Mao Zedong were brought together in his famous 'Little Red Book' (*Quotations from Chairman Mao Zedong*). This collection of inspirational thoughts, moral guidance, and dictatorial precepts was distributed across China to all workers regardless of their level of literacy. Mao sought to bond together a huge rural population with a sense of national pride and extend the ideas of collective ownership, presenting a radical alternative to capitalism.

New technology: the future of the book

The sheer extent of knowledge preserved in libraries and the number of the publications produced annually make it impossible for us to imagine a world without books. Their influence and effect is immeasurable; in the year 2000 Gutenberg was voted the most significant individual of the last millennium by the readership of the British newspaper *The Times*. His invention of movable type, which led to the multiple production of printed books, created the first form of mass media. In the late nineteenth and early twentieth centuries, a new form of media arrived with the development of audio-based communication systems: the telephone, the radio, and sound-recording devices. Later, film and television combined sound and the moving image. But the printed book, together with its offspring - newspapers, periodicals, and magazines - remained the principal written form of mass communication.

With the invention of digital technology and the creation of the Internet, the end of print was predicted and the death of the book was hailed as imminent. To date, digital technology has revolutionized the way we write, design, produce, and sell books, but the World Wide Web has not replaced them. The optimistic book enthusiast takes heart from the yearly increase in book sales since the advent of the Internet. By contrast, pessimists cite the gradual decline in newspaper sales, a decline that they predict will eventually be mirrored by book sales. Yet this is countered by the increase in the number of titles and overall sales of magazines and specialist periodicals. The market for information would seem to be ever-expanding, and the new reading technology of the Internet is at present augmenting rather than replacing its older cousin, the book. Reading off a computer monitor continues to be less pleasurable than reading from the printed page. However, as technology improves screen-reading, and new electronic papers offer the possibility of downloading books, it may be that the MP3 model of music distribution that has been so successful will become the future of the book.

The power of print: the influence of books

The printed book has been one of the most powerful means of disseminating ideas that have changed the course of intellectual, cultural, and economic development. An insight into the influence of all printed books can be gained by considering the power of only a handful: the Bible, the Koran, *The Communist Manifesto*, *Quotations from Chairman Mao Zedong* (the famous 'Little Red Book') and Hitler's *Mein Kampf (My Struggle)* (see page 11). If it is impossible to quantify the collective influence of these books on the lives of millions of people throughout history, it is clear that they laid down many of the religious and political foundations of much of the modern world. A similar shortlist of books could be drawn up as the foundations of medicine, science, psychology, literature, drama, and so on - in fact, for every intellectual discipline. Such books are known globally, both their ideas and their authors revered or derided, but without the work of the largely forgotten book designer and printer, the influence of the ideas they contain would have been transient.

Creating a book

This chapter will examine who creates a book by identifying roles within the publishing and printing industry and looking at simple models of book creation. Job titles and what is expected within a particular role may vary from one publishing house to another, as will the actual process of creating a book.

The major roles within publishing

A printed book is the product of a collaborative process. The designer's task may vary from book to book, but it will always involve working with others as part of a team. A basic knowledge of the roles within publishing provides the working context for the designer.

Author, writer

The author of a novel or of a non-fiction work has 'an idea for a story', and may write the book and present a finished manuscript to an agent or publisher. A published author may consult his or her existing editor first about the themes a potential book is to explore. One way of sounding out enthusiasm, for both published and unpublished fiction and non-fiction authors, is to create a synopsis that will then be discussed by agents and publishers. If the response is positive and the publisher offers a contract, the author begins to write the full-scale work. A designer will not necessarily meet with an author before working on a book.

Agents: literary, illustration, design, and photography

Agents represent the work of their clients to potential employers. Agents generally develop specialisms for particular genres of book, such as historical biographies, children's fiction, or science. The literary agent's role is to represent the work of the writer to the publisher and to broker deals on his or her behalf. For this service, the literary agent charges a fee or receives a percentage of the author's fee or royalty. To the author this service is often invaluable, as a good agent has a working relationship with a number of publishers. Agents work in a similar way on behalf of illustrators, designers, and photographers, presenting portfolios or books to publishers who require specialist freelance work for particular projects.

Publisher

A publisher is an individual or a company prepared to invest in the production of a book. This involves paying for the writing, production, printing, binding, and distribution of a book. Usually, the publisher makes an agreement with an author in the form of a contract. This model continues today, though publishers also make financial deals with overseas publishers to produce co-editions and foreign-language books. A printed book is a publisher's product and the contractual agreement made with authors and other publishers defines how, where, and at what price that product is sold. Publishers take a significant financial risk in producing a book, as they rely on sales to recoup their initial outlay and make a profit. The relationship between publisher and author is very close: publishers need authors to write books, and authors need publishers to produce and distribute them; neither can communicate their ideas or make a living without the other. In recognition of the mutual benefits of the author–publisher relationship, contracts are usually written so that both parties benefit financially from the sale of the book. Most publishers offer the author an advance as payment for the time spent writing a book plus a royalty (a percentage of the book sales profits after the production costs have been recouped). Some publishers prefer to pay authors and writers a flat fee, though this practice is disliked by the majority of professional writers.

Publishers are responsible for marketing their books. A publisher's catalogue is made up of lists of books that have a common subject-matter or approach, for example crime novels, gardening, architecture, or children's fiction. Careful building of a list is very important to publishers as the quality and nature of the books begin to define retailers' perception of the publishing house. A publishing house is a brand associated with a type of book and a set of design and production values. Most small publishers focus on a particular type of book or market. Some large publishers create or buy 'imprints', which are smaller brands associated with specific types of book.

Book packager

Book packagers are commissioned by publishers to create books. They are companies that combine editorial, design, and production and sometimes marketing specialists to put together or 'package' a book, but they do not take the financial risk of paying for all of the production and distribution.

Commissioning editor

The commissioning editor is responsible for selecting the books to be produced each season. This selection process is often undertaken in consultation with the publisher and an editorial board. It is a vitally important job for the success of a publisher; a commissioning editor who rejects a potential bestseller is passing over a huge income. The commissioning editor's role involves talking to potential authors, encouraging ideas, and building up a network of writers, designers, illustrators, and photographers. The editor needs to have a clear focus and a keen eye for new developments in readers' interests as well as to watch carefully the lists of other publishers. In addition, the editor has managerial responsibilities, establishing schedules and publishing dates and supervising teams of editors working on individual titles. The book designer works closely with the commissioning editor.

Editor

The editor works with the author to shape the content of the text, offering both encouragement and objective criticism, to which the wise author responds. Editors may work on a freelance or an in-house basis, and often work on several books simultaneously. Much of their time is spent reading and correcting copy, identifying text that they find unclear, and setting up questions for the author to consider. A good editor is likely to suggest ways of restructuring a text, perhaps breaking chapters into more logical elements. Having scrutinized, questioned, structured, and corrected the copy supplied by the author, the editor passes it on to the designer. The editor has to have excellent writing skills, be familiar with typographic and grammatical conventions, and be able to offer objective advice to the author, as well as manage schedules and sometimes commission artwork, illustrations, photographs, and so on. Editors may on some books write captions and organize the detail of footnotes and acknowledgments and permissions pages. Digital technology has enabled the editor to work with the designer on finished pages. Changes to the copy can now be made in the layout immediately before going to press. Senior editors responsible for many titles may be helped by assistant editors, who are often responsible for proofreading. Copy editors are editors who concentrate on the text side of the process as outlined above without being responsible for the management or administrative aspects.

Proofreader

Originally, proofreading, as the name suggests, was the reading and checking of the final printer's proofs. Today, the term may be used to describe the correction of copy at virtually any stage in the editing process. Proofreaders comb through an author's text, usually after it has been edited, checking for grammatical and spelling errors (traditionally referred to as 'literals' when made by the author, or 'typos' when made by the compositor or typesetter). Specialist proofreaders traditionally were responsible for signing off the corrected copy of every book that a publisher produced prior to its final print run; today, this task is often undertaken by the editor.

Consultant

Consultants offering a wide range of specialist expertise are frequently used by publishers developing non-fiction books. A publisher planning a gardening series might have selected a garden writer but might also seek the help of a consultant with specialist knowledge of vegetable- or rose-growing. Consultants contribute ideas and read through synopses and first drafts to see what additional information can be added to a book. Consultants are usually freelance and work on a specific book or series.

Reader

Readers or reviewers, like consultants, have a specialist knowledge of a book's subject but do not work directly with the author to create the text. They are employed on a freelance basis by a publisher to offer an objective view of the manuscript, commenting on the text's accuracy and quality, identifying omissions and assessing its appropriateness for the anticipated readership. Readers' comments are fed back to the editor, author, and designer, who respond by making amendments to the text.

Art director

Art director is a title that refers to a specific role within a publishing house, and also describes a designer working with an illustrator or photographer. The art director, in the first sense, usually has a design training, having responsibility for the visual appearance of a publishing house's entire book list. The appearance, production values, and list combine to form the readership's impression of the publisher's brand. Most progressive publishers consider the visual identity of their books to be extremely important. The art director will establish guidelines for series, such as typographic conventions, covers, common formats, the use of logos, and so on.

Designer

The designer is responsible for shaping the physical nature of the book, its visual appearance, the way it communicates, and for positioning all the elements on the page. In consultation with the publisher and editor, the designer selects the format and size of the book and decides how it is to be bound. Designers devise grids, select type styles, and lay out the page. They also work with picture researchers, illustrators, and photographers, art-directing and commissioning images. A designer receives a brief from an editor and passes on artwork, usually in digital form, to the production manager or direct to a printer. The designer and editor work together to oversee the proofing process. Today, many non-fiction books are visually led, and it is often designers who propose a book or a series idea to a publisher.

Picture researcher

Illustrated books feature images from many different sources and the picture researcher is responsible for tracking down pictures, and usually securing permission from the copyright owner for their reproduction in a book. Picture researchers typically use picture libraries or commercial image banks together with museum archive material and private collections. They may also work with photographers to record artefacts.

Permissions manager

For a publisher to use an extended piece of text or an image owned by someone else, written permission has to be agreed with the copyright owner prior to publication. The copyright owner may charge the publisher a fee for usage covering specific markets, such as English language, or may offer 'world rights', allowing the publisher to use an image in a book that is to be translated. Other elements affect the price for usage, such as promotional or editorial use, reproduction size (specified as spread, page, half- or quarter-page), and number of copies printed. The permissions manager is also responsible for controlling the usage of text and images owned by the publisher: if another publisher, advertiser, or design group wishes to use material from a book, it is the permissions manager to whom the potential user applies.

Image-makers: illustrator, photographer, cartographer

Specialists responsible for creating imagery used within books usually work on a freelance basis and are employed by a publisher to produce a set of images for a particular title. They may be paid a flat fee per illustration or photograph or, where the book is visually driven, offered a fee-plus-royalty option, which offers the potential of additional income if the book is a success. In some books, the images are the most important element, and the image-maker is responsible for the visual authorship, with the writer, editor, and designer working around the vision of the image-maker. Many illustrated children's books work in this way, with the illustrator being responsible for the creation of a character and a story that is then developed with the writer. Some book designers create illustrations themselves or art-direct a photographer.

Rights manager

The rights manager is responsible for the contractual agreements between a book's creators - authors, illustrators, photographers, and so on - and the publishing company. They also control the way in which material owned by the publisher is reproduced in different markets such as overseas editions. Rights managers usually have a business or legal background and seek both to protect the rights of a publisher and to maximize the market potential of the books produced. Rights managers work closely with the publisher and marketing department to identify co-publishers that will print or distribute books in other countries or through specialist book clubs.

Marketing manager

The marketing manager works with the rights manager and is responsible for promoting and selling books to other publishers and retailers, while overseeing distribution. Developing appropriate strategies for marketing a series or an entire list are the concerns of the marketing manager. The marketing manager will also be responsible for briefing the sales representatives and promoting sales of books at national and international book fairs. It is here that publishers meet other publishers to make deals to sell their books into overseas markets. The largest annual book fair takes place in Frankfurt, Germany.

Print buyer, production manager

The print buyer, or production manager, is employed by a publisher and works with the designer to oversee the production of the book. He or she is responsible for overseeing the quality and costings of the book's production. This involves liaising with printers to establish costs for each book and organizing production and delivery schedules.

Printer

The printer receives artwork or a digital file from a designer or a production manager. On any book the printer has pre-press work to do, scanning high-resolution images and preparing the plates for imposition prior to proofing. The proofing process may be undertaken by the printer or contracted out to a specialist proofing firm. Publishers work with printers all over the world, responding to competitive production costs and reputations for quality.

Print finisher

The print finisher is responsible for any activity in the production process after the printed sheet has been produced, including collating or binding. Print finishers often have specialized machinery for processes such as perforating, embossing, gilding, die-cutting, and folding printed sheets. They organize fiddly jobs that can only be done by hand; for example, most pop-up books require hand-construction, as folding and gluing individual elements to printed pages is too complex for machinery.

Binder

The binder deals with the 'book block', the collated printed pages, and secures the pages between covers. Binders offer designers, production managers, and printers specific knowledge of paper qualities and suggest tolerances and appropriate binding techniques for books of different extents (numbers of pages). Most binders will provide a publisher with a bulking dummy (a blank unprinted book bound using the correct stock and covers) as a sample before the print run is begun. From the binder, books are shipped to a warehouse, often situated close to the principal market rather than close to the publisher.

Distribution manager

The distribution manager keeps a stock record and oversees the movement of books from the warehouse to the retailer. This is a process that presents many logistical problems, as frequently a balance has to be struck between moving small quantities of books over large distances, which is costly and inefficient, and less frequent distribution, which is more economical but may lead to a shortage of books at the retailer.

Sales representative

Large publishers employ teams of sales representatives to contact retailers, book clubs, and other publishers. Smaller publishers often contract this work out. An enthusiastic sales representative builds a working relationship with retailers and gets to know their buying habits and tastes. Many sales representatives are paid on commission, their salary increasing in direct proportion to the number of books they are able to sell.

Retailer

The number of channels through which books are sold is continuing to expand. The number of independent booksellers, owning a single shop, was for many years in decline as owners were forced out of business, unable to compete with the huge discounts offered by chains of book stores or newsagents stocking a limited range of bestsellers. Today, as the book market fragments into smaller parts and publishers develop specific lists, independent retailers with quirky interests are able to focus their stock list and target a particular readership. The development of specialist markets has also presented opportunities for the growth of direct-mail marketing. Book clubs offer members reduced rates if they agree to buy so many books annually from a range of titles offered through club magazines (essentially catalogues). Specialist book clubs for children, cooks, gardeners, travel, art, history, and so on sell millions of books to readers who never enter a bookshop. It is estimated that 20% of the American book market operates through book-club sales. Another expanding market is the Internet, where Amazon, which specializes in book sales, is the most successful online retailer.

The components of a book

The various parts of a book have specific technical names that are used throughout publishing. Familiarity with some of these basic terms will support a better understanding of the chapters that follow. Other terms will be introduced and explained in the context of the design process, while a helpful glossary can be found on page 251. I have organized the basic components of the book into three groups: the book block, the page, and the grid.

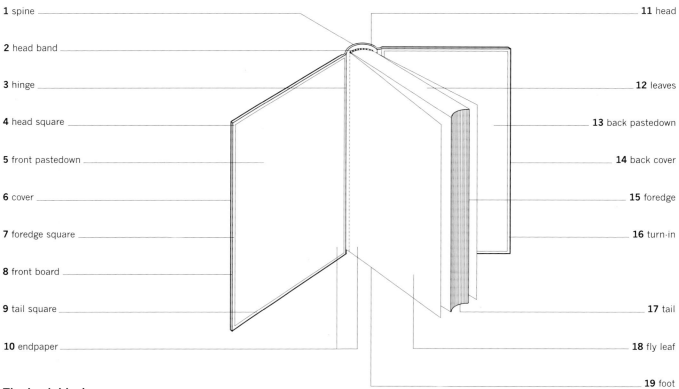

1 spine — — — — — — — — — — — — — — — — — — **11** head

2 head band — — — — — — — — — — — — — — — — — — **12** leaves

3 hinge — — — — — — — — — — — — — — — — — — **13** back pastedown

4 head square — — — — — — — — — — — — — — — — — — **14** back cover

5 front pastedown — — — — — — — — — — — — — — — — — — **15** foredge

6 cover — — — — — — — — — — — — — — — — — — **16** turn-in

7 foredge square — — — — — — — — — — — — — — — — — — **17** tail

8 front board — — — — — — — — — — — — — — — — — — **18** fly leaf

9 tail square — — — — — — — — — — — — — — — — — — **19** foot

10 endpaper — — — — — — — — — — — — — — — — — —

The book block

1 spine section of book cover that covers the bound edge.

2 head band narrow band of thread tied to the sections that is often coloured to complement the cover binding.

3 hinge fold in endpaper between pastedown and fly leaf.

4 head square small protective flange at the top of the book created by the cover and back boards being larger than the book leaves.

5 front pastedown endpaper pasted down to the inside of the front board.

6 cover thick paper or board that attaches to and protects the book block.

7 foredge square small protective flange at the foredge of the book created by the cover and back.

8 front board cover board at the front of the book.

9 tail square small protective flange at the bottom of the book created by the cover and back boards being larger than the book leaves.

10 endpaper leaves of thick paper used to cover the inside of the cover board and support the hinge. The outer leaf is the pastedown or board paper; the turning page is the fly leaf.

11 head top of book.

12 leaves individual bound paper or vellum sheets of two sides or pages recto and verso.

13 back pastedown endpaper pasted down to the inside of the back board.

14 back cover cover board at the back.

15 foredge front edge of the book.

16 turn-in paper or cloth edge that is folded from the outside to the inside of the covers.

17 tail bottom of the book.

18 fly leaf turning page of endpaper.

19 foot bottom of the page.

signature (*not illustrated*) folded sheet of printed paper bound in sequence to form the book block.

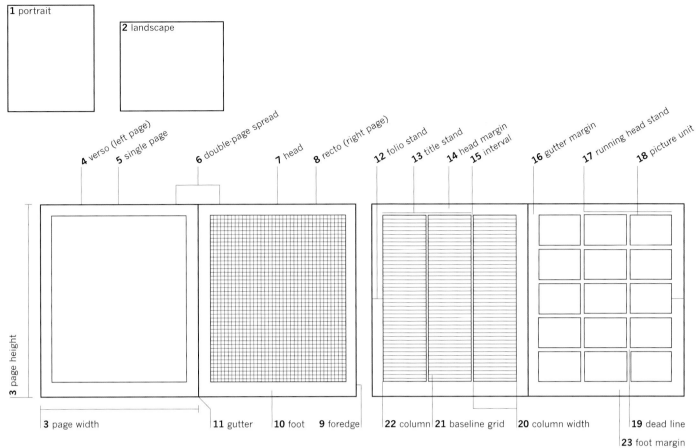

1 portrait

2 landscape

4 verso (left page)   5 single page   6 double-page spread   7 head   8 recto (right page)   12 folio stand   13 title stand   14 head margin   15 interval   16 gutter margin   17 running head stand   18 picture unit

3 page height

3 page width   11 gutter   10 foot   9 foredge   22 column   21 baseline grid   20 column width   19 dead line   23 foot margin

The page

1 portrait format in which the height of the page is greater than the width.

2 landscape format in which the height of the page is less than the width.

3 page height and width size of the page.

4 verso left-hand page of a book usually identified with even folio numbers.

5 single page single leaf bound on the left.

6 double-page spread two facing pages in which the material continues across the gutter, designed as if they were a single page.

7 head top of the book.

8 recto right-hand page of a book usually identified with odd folio numbers.

9 foredge front edge of the book.

10 foot bottom of the book.

11 gutter binding margin of the book.

The grid

12 folio stand line that defines the position of the folio number.

13 title stand line that defines the grid position of the title.

14 head margin margin at the top of the page.

15 interval/column gutter vertical space that divides columns from one another.

16 gutter margin/binding margin inner margin of the page closest to the bind.

17 running head stand line that defines the grid position of the running head.

18 picture unit modernist division of a grid column divisible by the baseline and separated by a dead or unused line.

19 dead line the line space between picture units

20 column width/measure width of the column determining the length of individual lines.

21 baseline line on which the type sits. The base of the x rests upon it; descenders hang from it.

22 column rectangular space on a grid used to arrange type. Columns within a grid may vary in width but are taller than they are wide.

23 foot margin margin at the foot of the page.

shoulder/foredge (*not illustrated*) margin on the foredge of the page.

column depth (*not illustrated*) height of the column defined in points, millimetres, or by the number of lines.

characters per line (*not illustrated*) average number of characters set in a point size to a specific measure.

gatefold/throwout (*not illustrated*) bound page with additional width that is folded into the book, usually along the foredge.

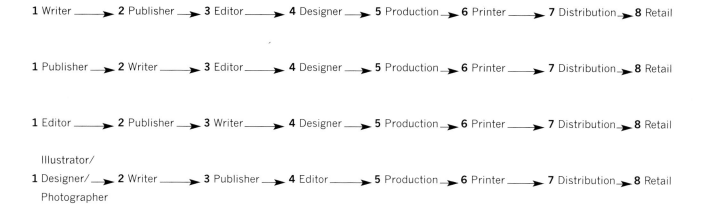

1 Writer ⟶ 2 Publisher ⟶ 3 Editor ⟶ 4 Designer ⟶ 5 Production ⟶ 6 Printer ⟶ 7 Distribution ⟶ 8 Retail

1 Publisher ⟶ 2 Writer ⟶ 3 Editor ⟶ 4 Designer ⟶ 5 Production ⟶ 6 Printer ⟶ 7 Distribution ⟶ 8 Retail

1 Editor ⟶ 2 Publisher ⟶ 3 Writer ⟶ 4 Designer ⟶ 5 Production ⟶ 6 Printer ⟶ 7 Distribution ⟶ 8 Retail

1 Illustrator/ Designer/ Photographer ⟶ 2 Writer ⟶ 3 Publisher ⟶ 4 Editor ⟶ 5 Production ⟶ 6 Printer ⟶ 7 Distribution ⟶ 8 Retail

Above Four simple models of book creation. The first, traditional model, places the author first, but the subsequent approaches place the publisher, editor, or illustrator/designer/photographer as the start of the book-creation chain.

Where do books begin?

The conventional model of a book's creation places the author at the start of the production chain. The author has an idea for a book and begins to write either a synopsis or the text itself, hoping that eventually the finished manuscript will be accepted by a publisher and become a printed book. This traditional approach to authorship remains the predominant model for works of fiction and is also used throughout non-fiction publishing. Authors identify, sometimes with the help of an agent, a publisher that they think would be interested in their book, submit the manuscript, and hope for a contract. The model of a book's development is often referred to by publishers as the critical path. It identifies the order of the key stages and is often accompanied by a detailed production schedule.

Non-fiction publishers have become more proactive in the authorship process, developing a variety of alternative models. Progressive and forward-thinking publishers view their role not only as the the conduit for great literature or quality information, but also as the producer of a commercial product. The publisher has become a brand offering a range of book products. The growth of this overt commercialism and its accompanying market strategies has not always been well received by traditional publishers concerned with quality literature and critical acclaim. Nonetheless, the most financially successful publishing companies today are well aware of their brand status.

Authorship within publishing has come to mean more than just the writing, and can be applied to those responsible for a concept or idea as much as the written text. Publishers, commissioning editors, or art directors may have a concept for a series of books. They search out writers who have expertise in a particular subject and ask them to write to a set length and for a specific readership. For the publisher, this product-based model has many advantages; although the up-front costs are higher, the potential market is far bigger. The costs are predictable, and the copyrights are held by the publisher as opposed to the writer. The publisher has effectively applied a mass-production model to the creation of the series as well as to its print reproduction. The product's range and profit margins have been increased and the volume of sales is expected to rise. The reader now begins to build a relationship with the series brand rather than with the writer.

Approaching the design

This chapter will examine the early stages of a book project in three sections, first looking at broad approaches to design, then at the design brief, and finally identifying the nature and components of the content. The chapter will explore the ways in which a designer may approach a text or book, his or her first thoughts, what he or she should be looking for when faced with the material, and how to consider the best way to translate it into a book - with the readership and market in mind.

Experienced designers develop a range of approaches to book design. These approaches are common to graphic design and can be simply broken down into four broad categories: documentation, analysis, concept, and expression. These categories are not mutually exclusive; it is unlikely that a single design job can be based entirely on one approach. Most design work includes an element of each approach, though not necessarily in equal measure. In addition, there is a part of the design process that is personal to the individual designer and is less easily defined by practical analysis. Design is a mixture of rational, conscious decisions that can be analyzed, and subconscious ones that are less easily defined, stemming as they do from an individual designer's experience and creativity. For this reason, some designers are slightly embarrassed and evasive when questioned about their working process, suggesting that any detailed examination restricts their creativity. Phrases such as 'personal expression' and views about individuality are put forward, along with a desire 'not to be closed down by systems', or the idea that 'it is important to preserve the mystery'. Like many creative activities, design has an undefinable 'X-factor', and to examine it too closely is to risk its destruction. The subconscious clearly has an influence on the layout of a page and we often position elements out of our experience or instinct rather than as a result of a conscious decision. The subconscious element of design becomes part of our visual and kinetic memory in the manner of walking or riding a bike. These are skills honed through practice that have become so ingrained that we are hardly aware of them as part of the process. By examining these four rational starting points, however, I hope to provide an insight into features of the design process that can be examined and that through practice can be implemented.

Documentation

All graphic design involves working with documentation. Documentation records and preserves information through text and image, though it may take many forms: a brief, a manuscript, a listing, a set of figures, a photograph, a map, a sound recording, a video. Documentation is at the root of writing and image. It is fundamental to typography, illustration, graphic design, cartography, graphs, charts, tables, diagrams, photography - in fact, all the components of a book. Without documentation there is no graphic design: there are no books, magazines, newspapers, posters, street signs, packaging, websites; there is no preserved visual language; there is merely gesture.

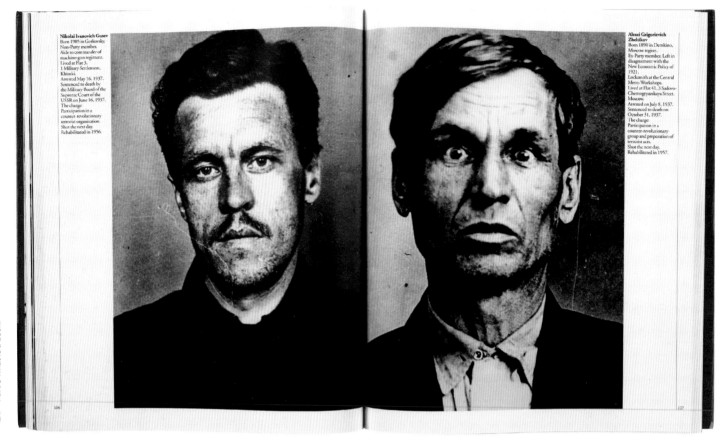

Nikolai Ivanovich Gusev
Born 1905 in Gorkovsky.
Non-Party member.
Aide to commander of
machine-gun regiment.
Lived at Flat 3,
1 Military Settlement,
Khimki.
Arrested May 16, 1937.
Sentenced to death by
the Military Board of the
Supreme Court of the
USSR on June 16, 1937.
The charge:
Participation in a
counter-revolutionary
terrorist organisation.
Shot the next day.
Rehabilitated in 1956.

Alexei Grigorievich
Zheltikov
Born 1890 in Demkino,
Moscow region.
Ex-Party member. Left in
disagreement with the
New Economic Policy of
1921.
Locksmith at the Central
Metro Workshops.
Lived at Flat 41, 3 Sadovo-
Chernogryazskaya Street,
Moscow.
Arrested on July 8, 1937.
Sentenced to death on
October 31, 1937.
The charge:
Participation in a
counter-revolutionary
group and preparation of
terrorist acts.
Shot the next day.
Rehabilitated in 1957.

Above David King's book *Ordinary Citizens, the Victims of Stalin* (2003) uses documentary photographs of victims of the Soviet regime. The premise of the book was to record the portraits of those who were killed.

Documentation is fundamental to the modern world; it preserves ideas and allows them to live long beyond human memory and speech. Documents give an external form to internalized thought. They can be reproduced and published, allowing the author's ideas to transcend time, unrestricted by life span and geography, and be presented simultaneously across the world years or even centuries after the author's death.

Documentation is the starting point for a book. In its raw state, it is the manuscript that is to be manipulated, organized, and arranged. Documentation can also be used as the principal editorial and design approach within book design. A collection of reportage photographs, for example, documents an event, situation, or group of people: the photographs are visual documents that a designer orchestrates within a book.

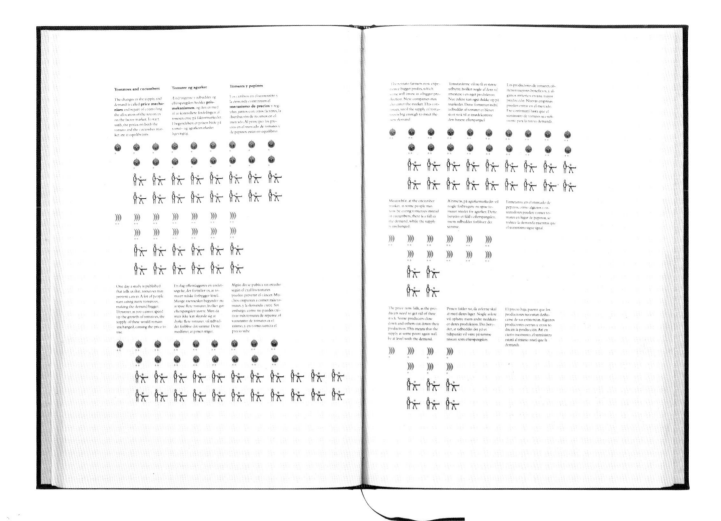

Analysis

Analytical thinking is involved in all book design. The books that lean most heavily on this approach are those that deal with complex factual information. Books that have maps, charts, diagrams, tabular matter, complex indexing, or cross-referencing are designed to allow the reader to compare and contrast elements of data. An analytical approach seeks to find structure within content, data, or documentation. Where this is not possible it imposes a structure upon the data so that it is more intelligible. Analysis is born of rationalism: it is the search for a discernible pattern within a mass of information. This approach is much championed by modernists. Designers operating in an analytical way seek either to break the totality of the content into many smaller units, or, by examining the many parts, seek to understand the whole. Either way, the designer is attempting to find a pattern to classify the various elements. Having made segregated groups of information, the designer seeks to prioritize and order the groups to give the content structure, sequence, and hierarchy. This process may involve working closely with an author and editor. When a book has been through this form of editorial analysis, the designer looks to reinforce the editorial structure visually through sequence and hierarchy.

Above Annegeret Mølhave's book *For Sale: an Explanation of the Market Economy* (2003) is an explanation of how free-market economics works. The book is produced in three languages – Danish, English, and Spanish – and is illustrated throughout by symbols. The approach to the book is a combination of documentation and very precise analytical thinking.

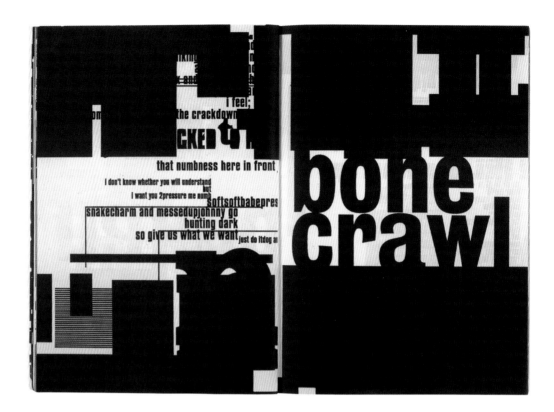

 (within image) I feel;
the crackdown
CKED
that numbness here in front,
i don't know whether you will understand
but
i want you 2pressure me numb softsoftbabepres
snakecharm and messedupjohnny go
hunting dark
so give us what we want just do itdog a

bone
crawl

Above Designed by Tomato, *Mmm...Skyscraper I Love You: A Typographic Journal of New York* takes an expressive approach in which the content of the words and the form of their typographic presentation combine to evoke the emotional heart of poetry about New York.

Expression

An expressive approach to design is motivated by visualizing the emotional position of the author or the designer. It is driven by the heart or in some cases the gut; it is visceral and passionate. It strives through colour, mark-making, and symbolism to emotionally 'reposition' the reader. The reader picks up on the emotional position within the design while absorbing the content. Expressive design is rarely definitive or entirely rational. It is often lyrical, not intended to deliver meaning to the mind, but rather asking questions and inviting reflections. This approach views content as a starting point from which an interpretation is to be made. It parallels the relationship in music between composer and performer, casting the writer as composer and the designer as performer - the designer brings to the piece his or her own personal interpretation. For some designers, this approach is suspect, as it lacks objectivity and can be prone to self-indulgence.

A tension exists between the need to honour the author's original text and the designer's individual ideas; consequently, many designers who enjoy this approach have become authors themselves in order to control both the content and the form of the book.

Concept

A conceptual approach to graphic design seeks out the 'big idea' – the under-pinning concept that encapsulates the message. Within advertising, cartoons, promotion, and branding, conceptual thinking forms the basis of communication. The approach is often referred to as 'ideas graphics' and is defined by reductive rather than expansive thinking: complex ideas are distilled into succinct, pithy visuals, often working in relation to clever titles, strap lines, or marketing premises. A conceptual approach frequently uses two or more ideas to throw light on a third. It makes use of pun, paradox, cliché, metaphor, and allegory. It is often clever, witty, and entertaining, but it has to be delivered with precision as it relies on designer and target audience sharing a subtle understanding of image and word-play.

The term 'conceptual' can also be used to describe a more expansive approach than that of ideas graphics, when an art director is responsible for the visual appearance of a series of books or even the output of the whole publisher. A series of books may be linked by a common concept, which defines an approach to the nature and use of text, photography, and illustration, the number of elements on the page, the extent and form of the books, and so on. The art director working with an editor may create strategies of explanation that form the guidelines for the series writers and designers.

Above I devised three series of non-fiction children's books based on a conceptual premise. The *Make it Work!* Science, History, and Geography series were based on the idea that children could understand the world around them through making and experimenting. The concept of learning through active engagement with a book's subject, as opposed to merely reading about an experiment, historical event, or geographic feature, encouraged children who were less excited by reading to learn through making. Here, a spread from *Make it Work! North American Indians* shows a model Plains Indian camp. This very time-consuming conceptual approach required me to make thousands of models over the course of a decade for 27 books, but the series was very well received: the books were published in 14 languages and sold in 22 countries.

The design brief

The designer should try to gain an overview of a book's content at the editorial briefing meeting, seeking an insight into the author's, the editor's, and the publisher's vision. The designer needs to establish the relationship between text and image, but it is unnecessary for him or her to be an expert in a book's content - a certain objective distance is often helpful when searching for structure within a manuscript. Some briefings are delivered with great clarity and the designer is aware of the publisher's intentions for a specific audience; other briefings are consultations in which opinions are sought, reviewed, and contemplated. Some initial meetings are exploratory and open-ended, working on the basis that if able minds come together with an embryonic book they will bounce ideas off one another, resulting in an approach that would not have been conceived by a single person. If the brief is woolly and ill-informed, the designer may need to turn interrogator, peppering the commissioner with questions in search of the book's essence. Is the book organized in discrete chapters, or as a single unbroken text? Has the author written to a specific brief? Is the text intended to be illustrated? Are the illustrations marked within the main body of text, or to be found in a separate appendix? Has the author written extensive captions that need to be integrated with the text? Are some extended captions sufficiently large to be presented as separate side stories? Is the organizational structure alphabetical, chronological, or thematic? Are the images or the text leading the reader? What is the extent? What is the intended retail price? What are the production values?

The designer usually leaves the initial briefing meeting with many questions that require more extensive answers but having absorbed sufficient information to gain an overview of the project. A period of reflection is helpful, allowing contemplation of the book's external form in relation to its internal structure.

The book designer's palette II

The book designer's palette

In a previous book, *Type and Typography* (2005), Phil Baines and I divided into ten elements the typographic palette in relation to a simple text page. This approach first focused on the nature of the type and then examined the broader context of the page, from the micro to the macro. Within *Book Design*, a more extensive discussion is required, and it seems appropriate to reverse the order of description, moving from the page to the type, from the macro to the micro. The typographic palette presented in Part 2 is organized into four chapters, covering the following areas: format; defining the text area and constructing a grid; typographic arrangement; and type size and typeface.

4 Format

The format of a book is determined by the relationship between the height and the width of the page. In publishing, the term 'format' is sometimes used misleadingly, with reference to a particular size. However, books of different size may share the same format. Books are characteristically designed in three formats: portrait, in which the height is greater than the width; landscape, in which the width is greater than the height; and square. A book can be of virtually any format and size, but for practical, production, and aesthetic reasons, careful consideration is required to design a format that supports the reading experience. A pocket guide must fit in a pocket, whereas an atlas is studied at a table and its detailed content requires a large page. In practical terms, choosing the format of a book determines the shape of the container that holds the author's ideas. From the designer's perspective, it is far more: book design is to the written word what stage design and theatrical direction are to the spoken word. Authors provide a score and the designer choreographs the performance.

Designers tend to develop idiosyncratic ways of making decisions about proportion, but it is helpful to begin by becoming familiar with a range of approaches to format.

Portrait format

Landscape format

Golden section, the Fibonacci series, and its derivatives

The German typographer Jan Tschichold (1902–1972) dedicated many years of his life to analysing Western printed books and manuscripts, and discovered that many books were printed in a golden-section format. The golden-section rectangle can be divided so that the relationship between the smaller and the larger is the same as that between the larger and the whole. An approximate decimal value defines the proportion as 1:1.61803, which can be expressed in algebra as a:b = B (a + b). A golden-section rectangle can be drawn from a square (see diagram on page 31). The square and the rectangle have a consistent relationship: if a square is added to the long edge of the rectangle, or formed within the rectangle, a new golden section is created. The consistent relationship between square and rectangle creates a logarithmic spiral sequence. Each square relates to the next as part of the Fibonacci series (in which each number is the sum of the two preceding numbers: 0, 1, 1, 2, 3, 5, 8, 13, 21, etc). The adding together of two successive figures in the series will create golden sections infinitely.

Square format

Golden section

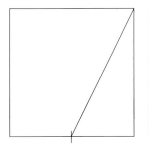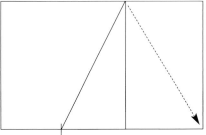

Left To form a golden-section rectangle from a square, the square is divided in half. The diagonal of the half-square is rotated to the horizontal, defining the length of the rectangle.

Fibonacci series

3	**1**	3	3	3	3	4	4	4	4	4	5	5	5	5	6	6	6	7	7	8
4	**1**	6	7	8	9	5	6	7	8	9	6	7	8	9	7	8	9	8	9	9
7	**2**	9	10	11	12	9	10	11	12	13	11	12	13	14	13	14	15	15	23	17
11	**3**	15	17	19	21	14	16	18	20	22	17	19	21	23	20	22	24	23	32	26
18	**5**	24	27	30	33	23	26	29	32	35	28	31	34	37	33	36	39	38	55	43
29	**8**	39	44	49	54	37	42	47	52	57	47	50	55	60	53	58	63	61	87	69
47	**13**	63	71	79	87	60	68	76	84	92	73	81	89	97	86	94	102	99	142	112
123	**21**	102	115	128	141	97	110	123	136	149	120	131	144	157	139	152	165	160	229	181
199	**34**	165	186	207	228	157	178	199	220	241	193	212	233	254	225	246	267	259	371	293
322	**55**	267	301	335	369	254	288	322	356	390	313	343	377	411	364	398	432	419	600	474
521	**89**	432	487	542	597	411	466	521	576	631	506	555	610	665	589	644	699	678	971	767
843	**144**	699	788	877	966	665	754	843	932	1021	819	898	987	1076	953	1042	1131	1097	1571	1241

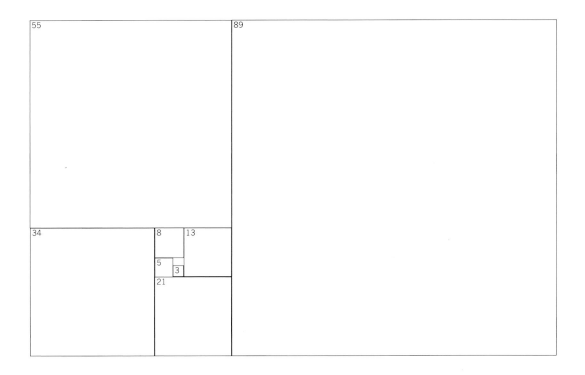

Above A table showing Fibonacci sequences (columns) in which each number is the sum of the two preceding numbers. The golden-section series is shown in bold.

Left The consistent relationship between square and golden-section rectangle creates a logarithmic spiral sequence. Each square relates to the next as part of the Fibonacci series.

Above The chambers of a nautilus show the logarithmic spiral of a Fibonacci sequence.

The proportions of the golden section have embodied a mystical sense of beauty for some artists, architects, and designers. The golden section is found in nature; the chambers of the nautilus and the growth patterns of many leaves share the logarithmic spiral. Designers in the classical tradition believe that the natural proportion is the definitive source of truth and beauty. Others of a relativist persuasion, more sceptical of the idea of a definitive truth, argue that notions of beauty are constructed through experience rather than discovered and unveiled. The golden section, for them, has been elevated by repetition to a position of cultural importance in the West; they argue that what appears to be instinctive, natural, and truthful is in fact memory in disguise.

Bringhurst's chromatic scale

In his book *The Elements of Typographic Style* (1996), Robert Bringhurst compares the proportions of the page to the chromatic scale of Western music. Both page proportion and the chromatic scale are defined by numeric intervals. For example, Bringhurst equates the octave with the double square, both sharing the proportions 1:2.

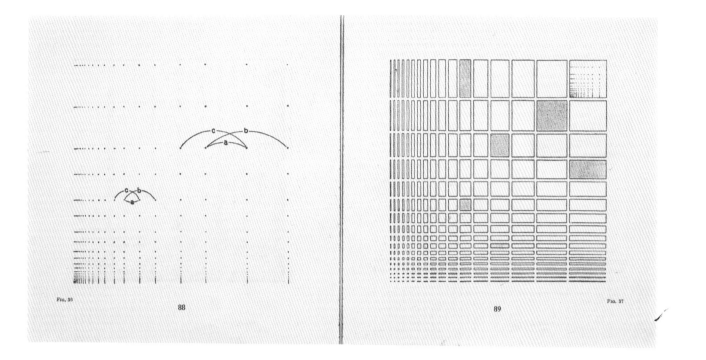

Le Corbusier's Modulor, derived from the golden section

The French architect Le Corbusier devised a modern version of the golden section that subdivided the format in relation to the proportions of the human figure. He termed the system of proportion 'Modulor' and saw it as a universal design tool for determining the proportions of buildings, furniture, and print. He used the system to design his books *Le Modulor* (1950) and *Modulor 2* (1955).

Rational and irrational rectangles

Rectangles are either rational or irrational. Rational rectangles are those that can be subdivided by squares and have an arithmetical basis; irrational rectangles can be subdivided only into rectangular units and are derived from a geometrical basis. The formats: 1:2, 2:3, and 3:4 are all rational rectangles, as they are divisible by a square unit, whereas the golden section is an irrational rectangle. Ideas of classical proportion are derived from geometrical rather than arithmetical relationships. Greek, Roman, and Renaissance mathematicians took considerable delight in geometry as a way of determining proportion. By constructing regular polygons with three, four, five, six, eight, and ten sides using a circle, the proportions of familiar irrational rectangles are formed.

Above A spread from *Le Modulor* shows Le Corbusier's proportional division of space based on the measurements of the human body.

1:4

1:3.873

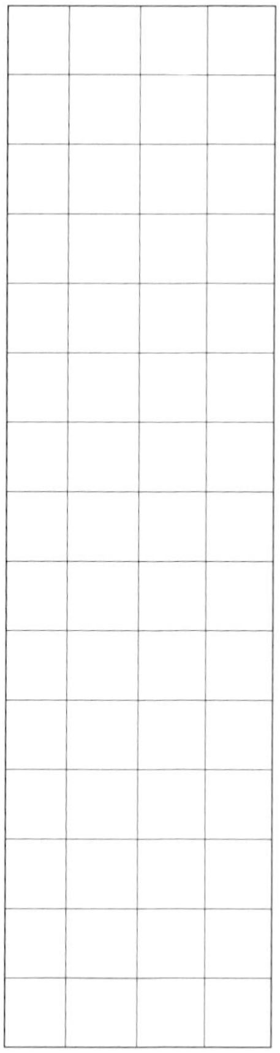

1:3.75

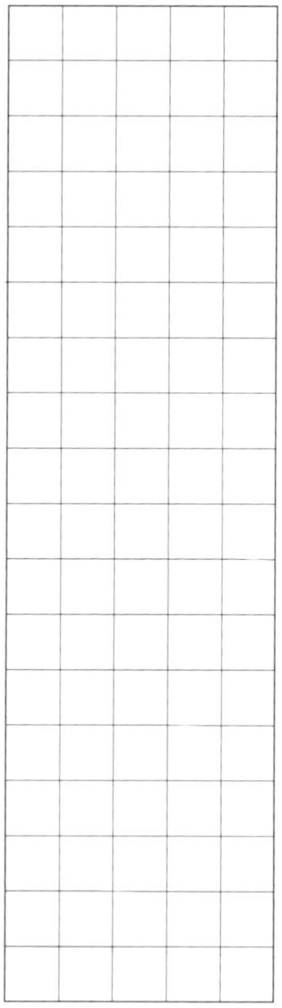

1:3.6

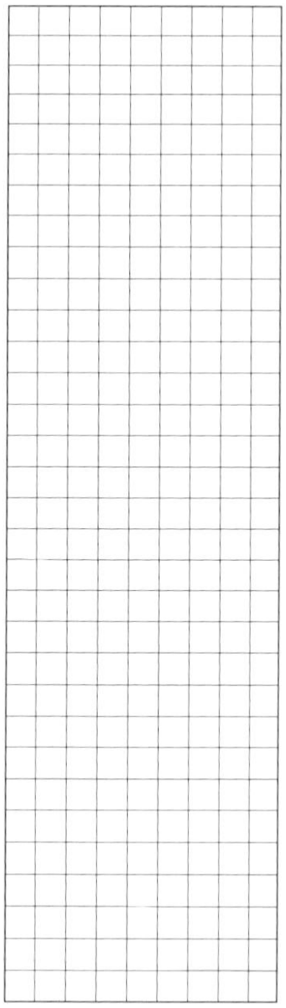

1:3.556

1:3.162

1:3.142

1:3.078

1:3

1:2.993

1:3.464   1:3.414   1:3.333   1:3.236   1:3.2

1:2.828   1:2.753   1:2.718   1:2.667   1:2.646

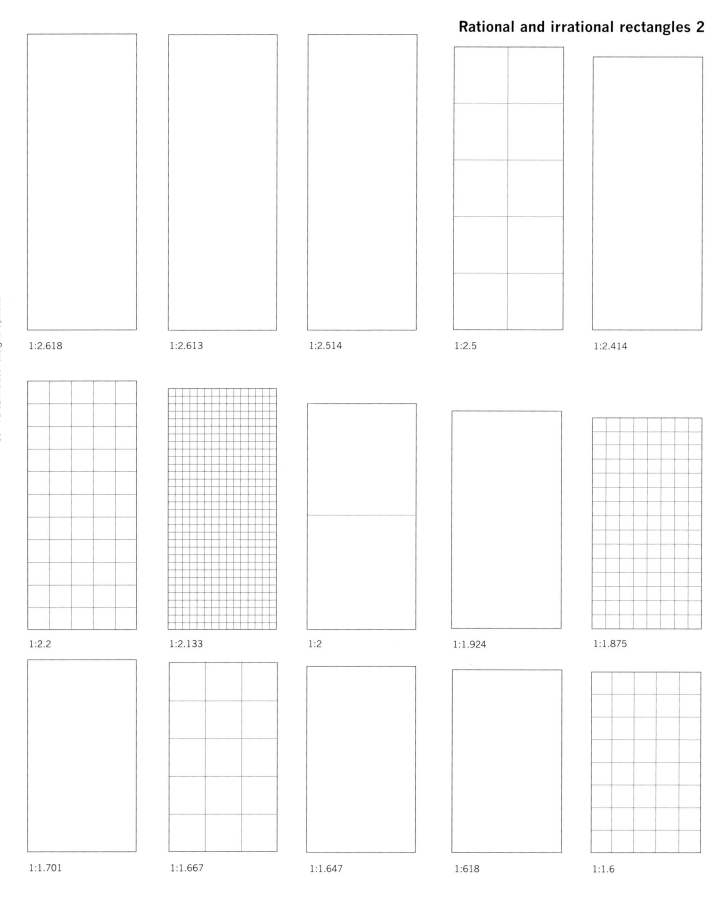

1:2.618

1:2.613

1:2.514

1:2.5

1:2.414

1:2.2

1:2.133

1:2

1:1.924

1:1.875

1:1.701

1:1.667

1:1.647

1:618

1:1.6

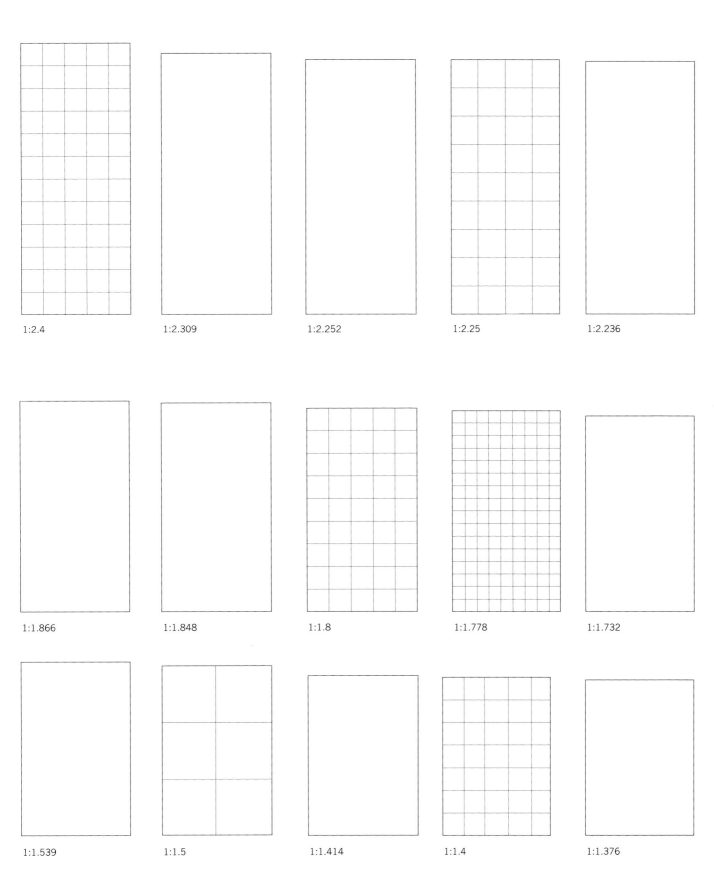

1:2.4   1:2.309   1:2.252   1:2.25   1:2.236

1:1.866   1:1.848   1:1.8   1:1.778   1:1.732

1:1.539   1:1.5   1:1.414   1:1.4   1:1.376

Part 2 The book designer's palette

1:1.333

1:1.307

1:1.294

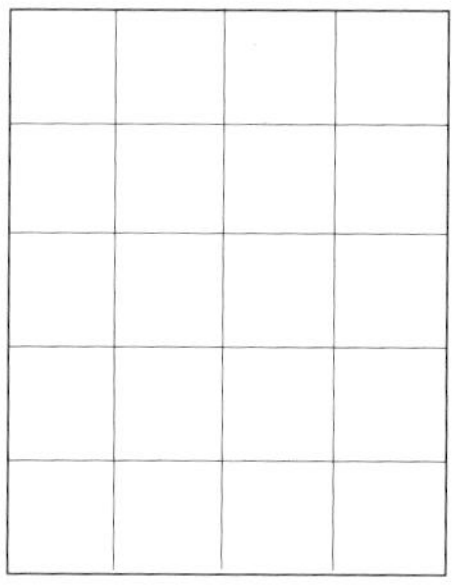

1:25

1:1.207

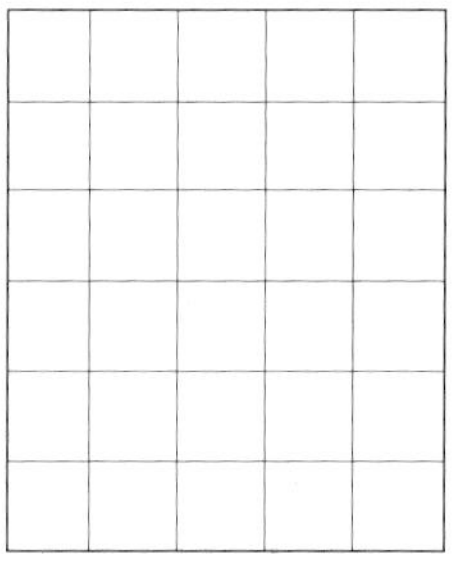

1:1.2

1:1.176

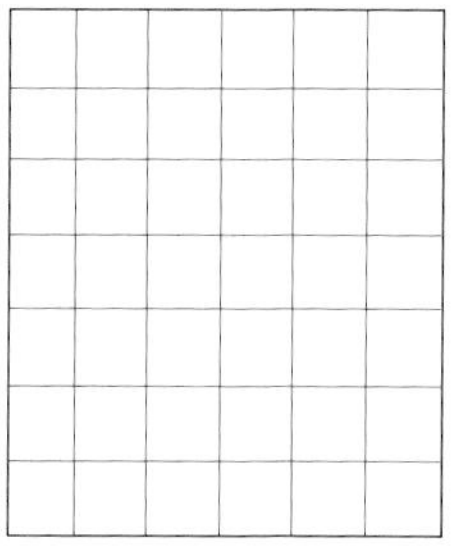

1:1.167

1:1.156

1:1.155

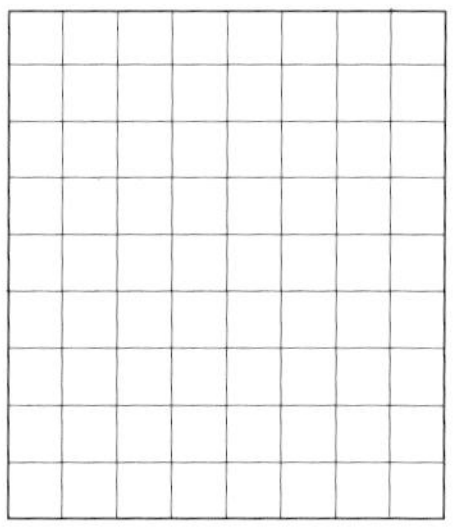

1:1.125

1:1.082

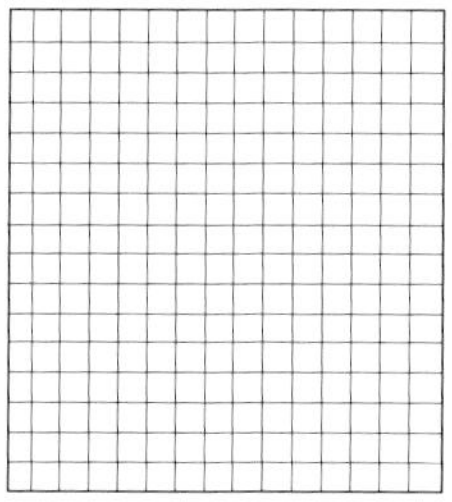

1:1:067

1:1.051

1:1

1:1:0951

1:1:0.924

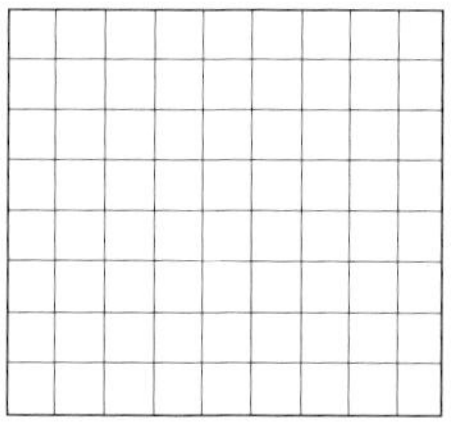

1:0.889

1:0.866

1:0.829

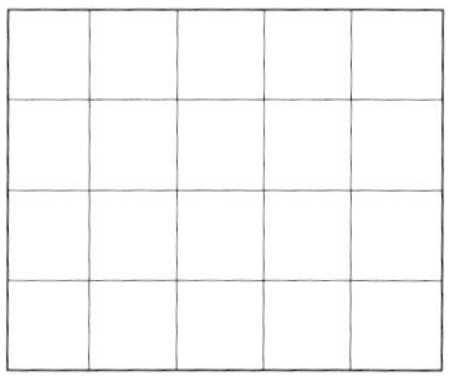

1:0.8

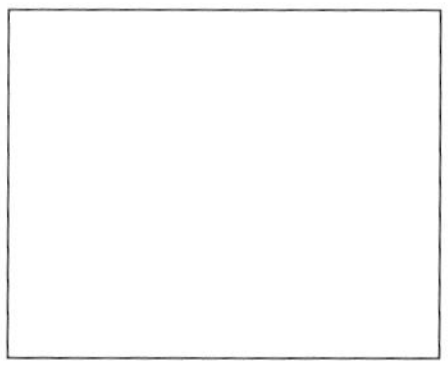

1:0.773

Previous pages and above A series of rectangular formats redrawn from Hans Bossard's book *Raster Systems* (2000).

Paper sizes: imperial and A sizes

Another approach to establishing the format of a page is to make use of a simple division of an existing paper size. This approach is extremely economical, as wastage is kept to a minimum. Imperial size paper, as traditionally used in Britain and the United States, uses formats specified in inches. Some of the formats are regular rectangles – for example, 30 x 40-inch poster sheets, but most are irregular. The metric DIN (Deutsches Institut für Normung) or ISO (International Organization for Standardization) format rectangle is unique in that it is the only rectangle that when divided in two creates a format with exactly the same proportions of length to width. A-size papers are based on this format, and each size is therefore half of the preceding size: A0 is halved to form A1, A1 is halved to form A2, A2 is halved to form A3, and so on (see page 191).

Formats determined by the internal elements of the page

Often a designer will have established a working format before deciding on the exact height and width of the page. The working format and size are often refined in the process of constructing a grid, influenced by decisions about type size, the height of the type's body (see page 86), and leading – the space between lines (see page 83). Designers may do this to ensure that the page height is exactly divisible by the number of baselines. Some designers are unconcerned by a mismatch of baseline grid and format, arguing that if the foot margin is large enough then the slight inconsistency will go unnoticed. For others, this incongruity is an unbearable irritant, niggling away at their aesthetic values and presenting a problem to be solved. Some designers shorten or lengthen the page to the nearest line; others subdivide the shortfall into the existing line count and in so doing attempt to create baseline grids with points specified digitally in hundredths.

The root of this problem often lies in the use of two separate scales for defining the dimensions of the page, for example millimetres for the page and points for the internal baseline grid. A way of resolving the mismatch is to use a common scale for specifying the page's internal and external dimensions.

A similar problem of fit concerning the width of the page may occur when subdividing the text area into columns. Some designers are ill at ease with margins or gutters defined by many decimal points and resort to horizontal subdivisions of the page that are calibrated in whole numbers.

Derivative and non-rectangular formats

Some formats are resolved not by geometry or internal grid structures but directly by the nature or proportions of the content. For example, many photographic books reflect the format of the original negative.

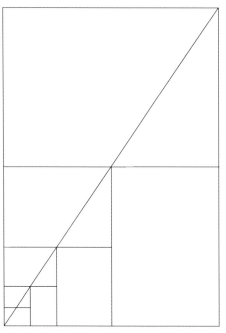

Above The ISO or A-size formats are based on a rectangle that can be divided in two yet retains the original format.

Books with formats derived from content

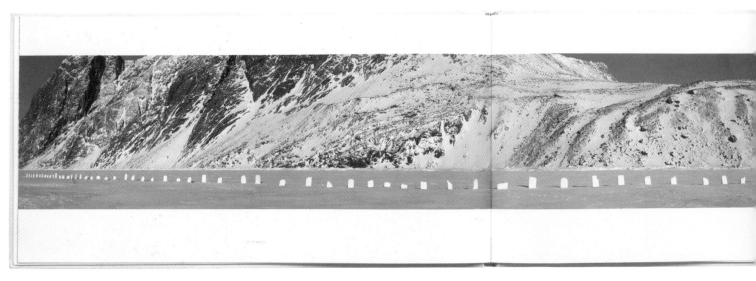

1

2

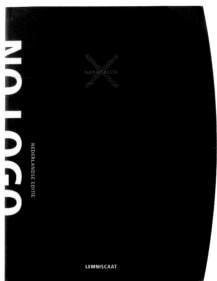

3

1 Sculptor Andy Goldsworthy's book *Touching North* (1989) features photographs of sculptures made of snow above the Arctic Circle. The format reflects the landscape's wilderness and constant-ly visible but distant horizon.

2 *The Silence* (1995), a book by Gilles Peress, features a series of photographs taken during the 1994 genocide in Rwanda and has a format based on the film negative. The photographs are uncropped and not retouched. This decision about format reinforces the notion of authenticity – appropriate for reportage photography.

3 The Dutch edition of Naomi Klein's *No Logo* (2001) has a curved foredge that gives the impression that the book format is linked to the arc of a circle.

4 The children's book *Witch Zelda's Birthday Cake* by Eva Tatcheva takes the shape of a pumpkin – the main ingredient of the witch's birthday cake.

5 The irregular die-cut format of the book *Chicks on Speed* reflects the layout of the content, which is layered and purposefully disjointed.

Grids

The format of the book determines the external proportions of the page; the grid determines the internal divisions of the page; and the layout determines the position of the elements. The use of a grid gives a book consistency, making the whole form coherent. Designers who use grids believe that this visual coherence enables the reader to focus on content rather than form. Each of the elements on the page, be they text or image, have a visual relationship with all the other elements: the grid provides a mechanism by which these relationships can be formalized.

Recently, some designers have begun to challenge the conventions of the grid and in some cases to question the need for it at all. To their minds, the grid is an unnecessary contrivance that, far from supporting content, stands between the reader's experience and the author's intentions. The consistency is not an asset but a deficit, limiting the layout of the page to a predictable set of mannered gestures.

The exploitation and the rejection of the grid form the two poles between which stand a variety of approaches. Some of these lean towards formal and attenuated rationalism; others veer towards the expressive and evocative. The historical development of book grids is a story of augmentation rather than replacement, the new ideas of successive generations having added to rather than replaced those of a previous era. Today, some designers are making use of medieval conventions, whereas others favour approaches derived from the modernism of the 1920s. Basic grid systems determine margin widths; the proportions of the print area; the number, length, and depth of columns; and the width of intervals between them. More complex grid systems define the baseline grid upon which the type sits and may determine the format for images as well as the position of headings, folios, footnotes, and so on.

Symmetrical or asymmetric

The first decision concerning the text area of a double-page spread is to ask the question, is it to be symmetrical or asymmetric? Most bound but unprinted books have symmetrical format around the central gutter. The symmetrical grids that were favoured by medieval scribes reinforced the natural symmetry of the book. The left-hand page of the manuscript was a mirror image of the right-hand page. Asymmetric pages, as the name indicates, have no line of symmetry in relation to the text area.

Grids based on geometry

Many early printed books have grid systems based on geometric construction rather than measurement. Europe in the fifteenth and sixteenth centuries had no accurate standardized system of measurement; measuring sticks were rudimentary and type sizes were devised by individual printers. The next section will examine grids developed through geometry.

Top Symmetrical text or image area.

Bottom Asymmetric print area. Most asymmetric text areas and grids share a common first and last line so that, while the side margins vary between left- and right-hand page, the head and foot margins are the same.

Defining the text area with a simple frame

Perhaps the simplest way to create a symmetrical print area is to define equal margins all around the page, forming a simple frame. This functional approach is favoured by such designers as Derek Birdsall, who frequently uses internal and external margins with the same width. The quantity of paper and style of binding must be considered carefully to avoid the equity of the frame being pinched on the inner bound margin.

Common proportions for format and text box

A rectangular text area that shares the proportions of the format is easily created by drawing two diagonals across the page and creating a new rectangle with corners that intersect the diagonals. A portrait page designed in this way has an equally deep head and foot margin and a matching narrower foredge and back margin. Designers opting for this approach usually make visual refinements by moving the text box towards the back margin and lifting it towards the top margin. By working in this way, four margin dimensions are created and the designer makes an assessment of their appropriate lengths by eye.

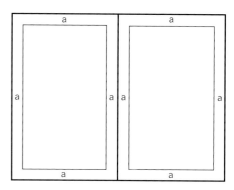

Above A simple text box with even head, foot, inner, and outer margins, *a* sits in the centre of each page. If the book has many pages, the margin will be pinched at the binding and the text area will appear to be drawn into the gutter, disrupting the equilibrium of the spread.

Drawing a grid with consistent format and text-box proportions

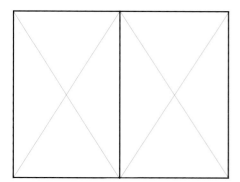

1 To create a text area that shares the same proportions as the page format, draw two diagonal lines across each page.

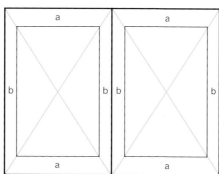

2 Select the depth of the top margin and draw a line parallel with the top of the page that intersects each of the diagonal lines across the page. The sides of the box are drawn with lines that emanate from the point at which the top margin intersects the diagonal and run parallel to the edge of the page. Two distinct margin widths are established: *a* head and foot margin; *b* inner and outer margin.

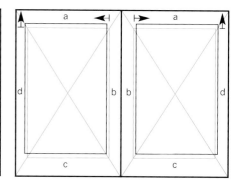

3 The text box can be moved slightly up the page and away from the gutter to allow for the pinch in binding. This refinement ensures that text box and page share a common proportion, but establishes four distinct margin widths. In this example, the foredge margin *d* is smaller than the gutter margin *b*; the head margin *a* is smaller than the foot margin *c*.

Villard de Honnecourt's diagram

The early architect Villard de Honnecourt (*c.* 1225–*c.*1250) devised a method of geometrically dividing space, which differs from the Fibonacci scale in that any chosen page format can be subdivided. This approach when used with a golden-section format effectively divides the page height and width by nine, creating 81 units, each of which has the same proportion as both format and the text box. The margins are determined by the height and width of the unit. This division into ninths can be used equally effectively as a landscape format.

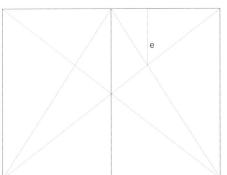

1 Select the format and size of the double-page spread. In this example, the proportion is 2:3.

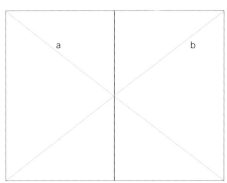

2 Draw diagonal lines from corner to corner *a* and *b* across the spread.

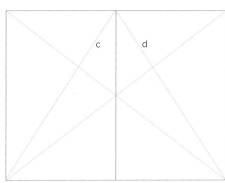

3 Draw diagonal lines from the bottom corners *c* and *d* of the spread to the gutter.

4 From the point at which the two diagonals intersect on the right-hand page, draw a line vertically to the edge of the page *e*.

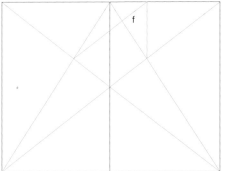

5 From the point established at the top of the right-hand page, draw a line to the intersection of the two diagonals on the left-hand page *f*.

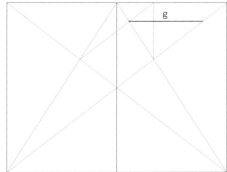

6 Draw a horizontal line *g* across the page from the intersection point on the right-hand page one-ninth of the page width from the gutter.

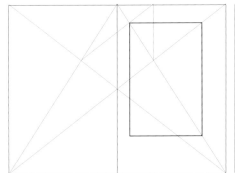

7 The top of the text box has been established. The sides can be drawn in by drawing lines parallel with the edge of the page, and the bottom is defined by the page diagonal.

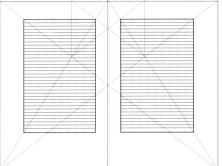

8 The process is repeated to establish the text area on the left-hand page. The baseline grid can now be drawn in.

9 Four margin widths are all relating to the proportions of the unit, which has divided the page width and height into ninths.

1	
2	
3	
4	
5	
6	
7	
8	
9	
10	
11	
12	
13	
14	
15	
16	
17	
18	
19	
20	
21	
22	
23	
24	
25	
26	
27	
28	
29	
30	

Left The division of the page has been achieved through geometric construction as opposed to measurement. The drawing was traditionally made with a straight edge and not a ruler. At the time of its devising at the beginning of the thirteenth century measurements of length were not standardized across Europe, and measuring sticks were inaccurate.

Paul Renner and the use of units

Paul Renner in his book *Die Kunst der Typographie* (1948) describes how to subdivide a rectangular format into units that retain the proportions of the original and are used to define the text box position and margin widths. This is achieved by dividing both the width and height of the page by the same number. A variety of text-box positions and margin widths can be drawn by dividing the width and height of the page into increments of: 13, 14, 15, 16, and so on. Digitally, this is fairly easy but may require many decimal points.

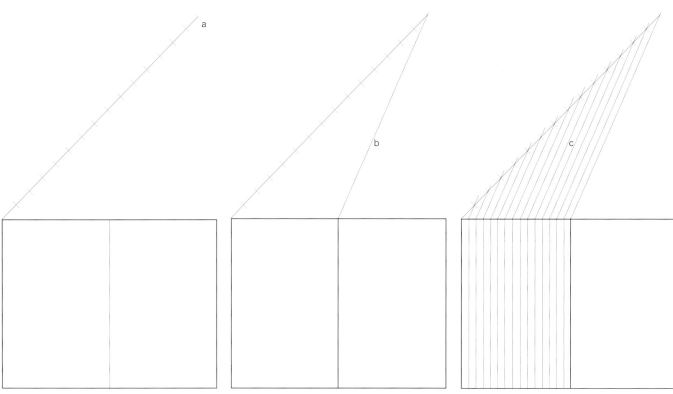

1 Having selected the page format and size, draw a line *a* at approximately 45° from the top left corner of the spread. Measure off 16 increments along the line.

2 This measure is transposed to divide the width of the page. Draw a transposition line *b* from the furthest increment to the top right-hand corner of the page.

3 Draw lines from each of the increments *c* running parallel to the transposition line until they intersect the top of the page, and then draw in the vertical columns.

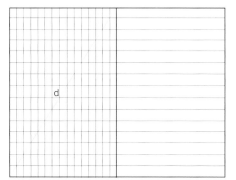

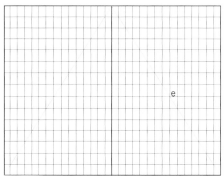

4 Draw a line *d* diagonally across the page. At the points at which the diagonal intersects the vertical divisions, draw horizontal lines across the spread. The page is divided into 256 units.

5 By drawing a diagonal *e* across the right-hand page, the horizontal lines are intersected. From the intersections, parallel vertical divisions can be drawn. The spread now has 512 units.

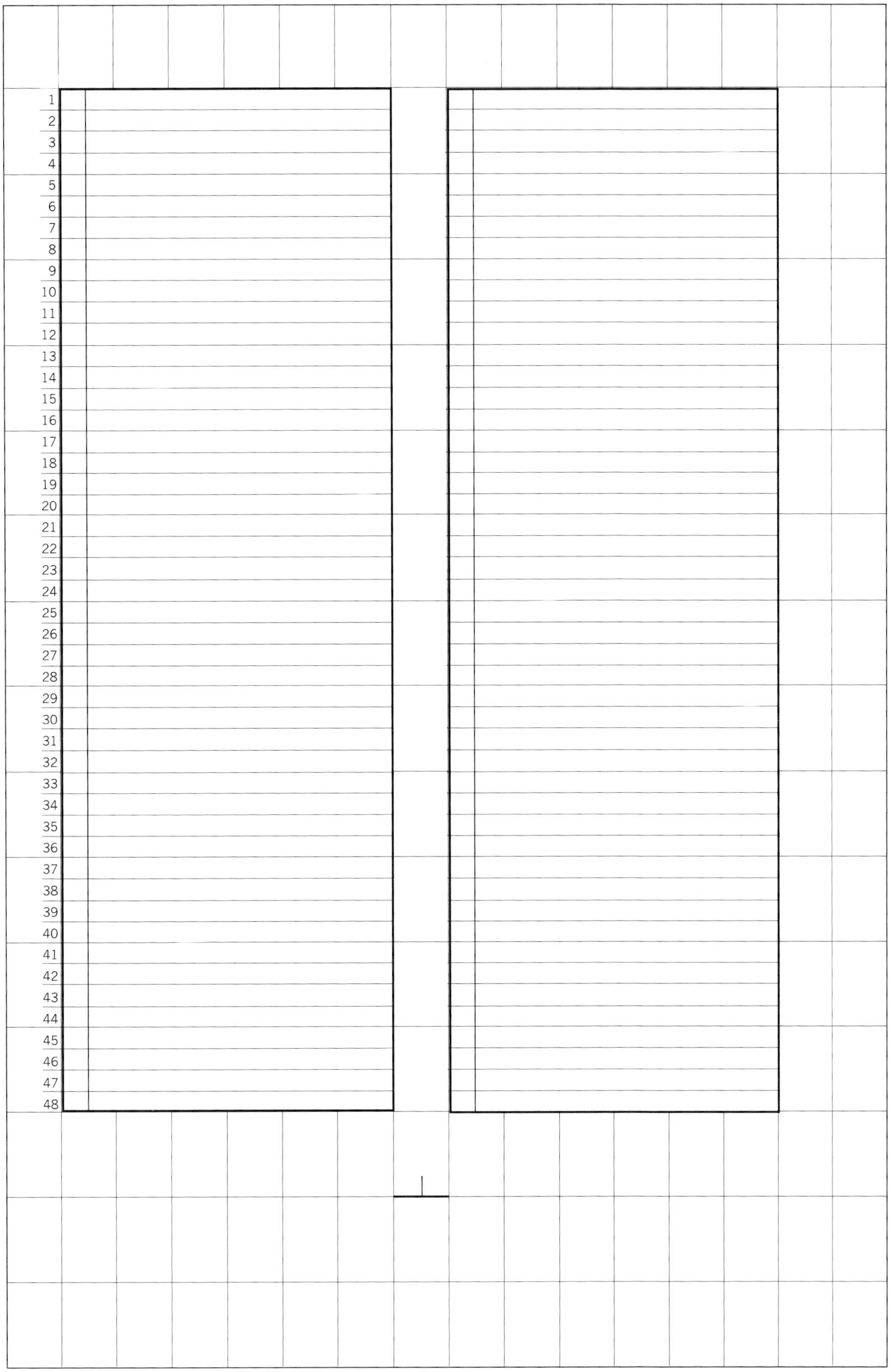

1
2
3
4
5
6
7
8
9
10
11
12
13
14
15
16
17
18
19
20
21
22
23
24
25
26
27
28
29
30
31
32
33
34
35
36
37
38
39
40
41
42
43
44
45
46
47
48

Left The geometric division of the format into 512 units that share the same proportion as the page can be used to create a variety of different margin and column proportions. Here, the two-column grid has a head margin 1 unit tall, and a foot margin 3 units tall, while the gutter margin is 1 unit wide and the foredge margin 2 units wide. The interval between the columns uses the width of a single unit.

Root rectangles

Another method of dividing the page is to make use of root rectangles – rectangles that can be subdivided into smaller rectangles that retain the height-to-width proportions of the original. For example, a two-root rectangle can be divided in two and a three-root rectangle in three, each new rectangle having the same proportions as the original. The width of margins and the position of the text box can be drawn from the intersection of the diagonals and the circles whose diameters are determined by the width of the rectangles.

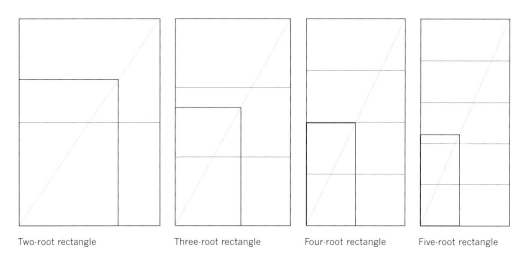

Two-root rectangle   Three-root rectangle   Four-root rectangle   Five-root rectangle

Constructing a grid using a three-root rectangle

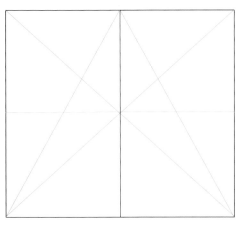

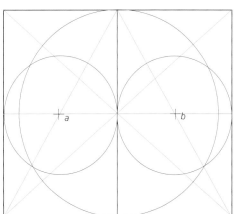

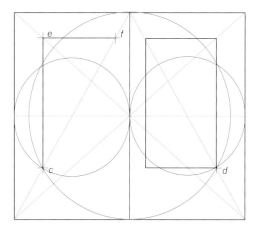

1 Draw out the spread and divide it into two pages. Draw two lines diagonally across the spread and a further two lines across each page from the outer corners to the gutter. At the intersection of the spread diagonals, draw a line across both pages, dividing the spread in two horizontally.

2 Use the intersection point of the page diagonal and page horizontal division on the a left-hand page and b right-hand page, as the centre for two circles (shown in magenta). Draw a large circle with its centre point at the intersection of the spread diagonals.

3 At the point on either page where the large and small circles intersect the page diagonal c left-hand page and d right-hand page, draw a line vertically up the page until it intersects with the spread diagonal. This line is the same width as the page width; it forms the side of the text box and defines the margin. At the point where this line meets the spread diagonal e, draw a line parallel with the top of the page to the intersection of the page diagonal f. The top of the text box is clearly defined. The inner and foot margin can now be drawn in.

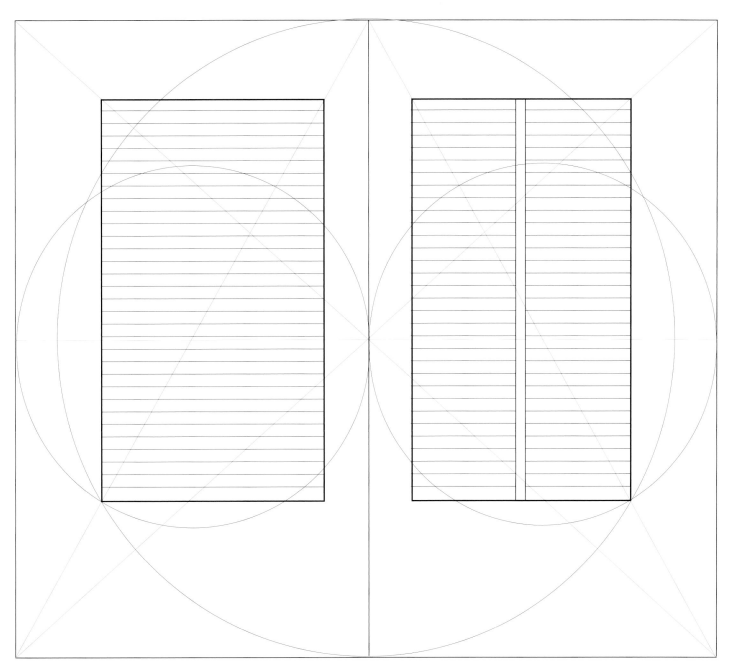

Above The elegant geometrically constructed three-root rectangle grid can be divided into a range of columns.

Grids based on measurement

The following approaches to the construction of a grid were made possible by the standardization of units of measurement and type size during the seventeenth and eighteenth centuries.

Proportional or modular scales

I have described the way in which designers have made use of the Fibonacci series when making decisions about format (see page 30). Modular scales of this type can also be used to design grids. They provide a very flexible approach to grid construction, which can reflect the content: for example, the grid for a book on natural history could be derived from a scale based on a leaf or a shell. Such an approach to creating the grid may be lost on all but a few of the book's readers, but for those who appreciate its subtlety it enhances their appreciation. For the designer, it allows the grid structure to be derived from content rather than being imposed arbitrarily on it. The approach can be used with any unit of measurement – millimetres, inches, points, or didots. Some designers consider this derivation of proportion from content a contrivance, particularly when dealing with subject-matter without physical properties – for example, a political memoir – as there is no obvious basis for the construction of the scale.

Constructing a grid using a proportional scale

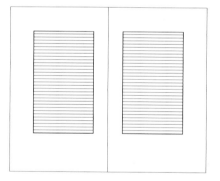

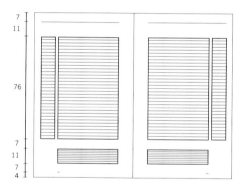

1 Select the numeric basis for the proportional scale and develop the scale by adding successive pairs of numbers to create the next number in the series. Decide the basic format – landscape or portrait. Roughly draw out the proportions and approximate size of the page and spread (here shown in cyan).

2 Select the nearest figure to the width and weight of the rough drawing from the scale. Draw the page and spread. Select a figure from the scale to determine the head margin and depth of the text box. Draw in the head and foot of the text box. The foot margin is created by the depth of the text box and will automatically be a figure from the scale. In the same way, select a figure from the scale to determine the inner margin and then the width of the text box, bearing in mind the type size and line length you anticipate using. The outer margin will be a figure off the scale determined by the inner margin and text-box width.

3 Having established the text box/position and area, make decisions about the type size, leading, and baseline grid. Choose figures off the scale to determine the other elements of the grid, *eg* width of shoulder column, interval, position of footnotes, folio, and running head. Digital setting, which allows type to be of any size, supports the fluid use of this approach.

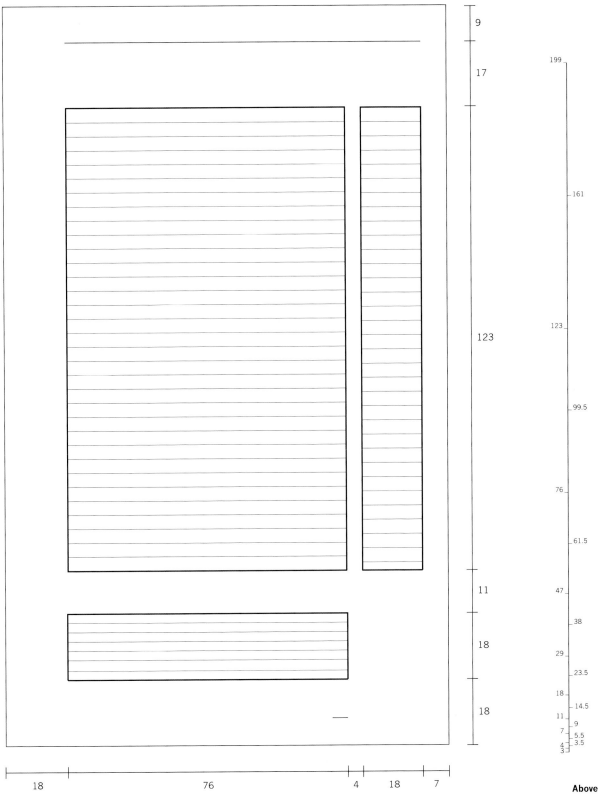

Above
Proportional scale (left)
and half-scale (right)
using a Fibonacci series.

Table of modular scales

The modernist grid

Jan Tschichold, like many artists and designers of the early twentieth century, questioned the relevance of old type forms, grids, and layouts with regard to modern messages. In his book *The New Typography* (1928), he rejected all that had gone before and cleared the ground for a radical, rational, and invigorating new approach to modernist book design. The influence of modernist thinking on the development of the book grid had two key phases. The first began with the Bauhaus and constructivism during the 1920s and 1930s. The second phase began after the Second World War, when a new generation of designers extended the ideas of Tschichold and the early typographic pioneers of modernism. In Switzerland and Germany, Max Bill, Emil Ruder, Hans Erni, Celestino Piatti, and Josef Müller-Brockmann began to make extensive use of systematic grids in which the position of all elements – text and image – were determined by a rational structure.

In his book *Grid Systems in Graphic Design: a Visual Communication Manual for Graphic Designers, Typographers and Three-dimensional Designers* (1961), Müller-Brockmann explains his approach to the grid: 'In a sophisticated grid system not only the lines of text align with the pictures but the captions and the display letters, titles and subtitles.' His A4-format book both explains in text and demonstrates through design his rational approach: Müller-Brockmann engineers rather than crafts the design of the page. His calibrations are exact and all elements of the grid can be expressed mathematically in whole numbers: columns are subdivisions of format; margins and units are subdivisions of columns; baselines are equal and exact subdivisions of units.

Opposite The table of modular scales is based on Fibonacci sequences, arranged from smallest successive numbers on the right (3, 4) to pairs of greater value on the left. The horizontal rule at the base of the table links the scales by the lower number in the initial Fibonacci pair, *eg* 4 with 5, 6, 7, 8, and 9. If the divisions of a single scale do not provide sufficient usable lengths for the required grid and margins, they can be divided in two to create a half-scale or by 3 or 4 to create third- and quarter-scales respectively. Any unit of measurement – points, didots, millimetres, etc – can be used with a modular scale, making the system extremely versatile.

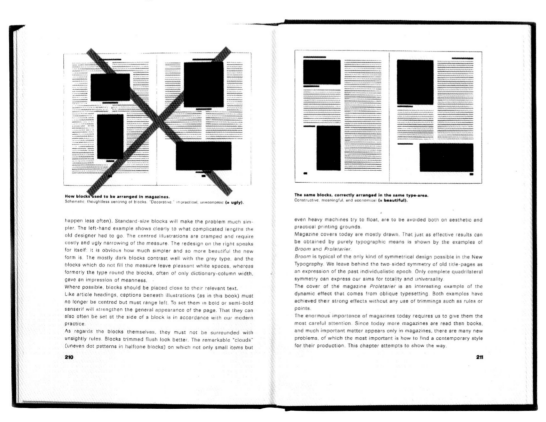

How blocks used to be arranged in magazines.
Schematic; thoughtless centring of blocks. "Decorative," impractical, uneconomic (**= ugly**).

The same blocks, correctly arranged in the same type-area.
Constructive, meaningful, and economical (**= beautiful**).

happen less often). Standard-size blocks will make the problem much simpler. The left-hand example shows clearly to what complicated lengths the old designer had to go. The centred illustrations are cramped and require costly and ugly narrowing of the measure. The redesign on the right speaks for itself: it is obvious how much simpler and so more beautiful the new form is. The mostly dark blocks contrast well with the grey type, and the blocks which do not fill the measure leave pleasant white spaces, whereas formerly the type round the blocks, often of only dictionary-column width, gave an impression of meanness.
Where possible, blocks should be placed close to their relevant text.
Like article headings, captions beneath illustrations (as in this book) must no longer be centred but must range left. To set them in bold or semi-bold sanserif will strengthen the general appearance of the page. That they can also often be set at the side of a block is in accordance with our modern practice.
As regards the blocks themselves, they must not be surrounded with unsightly rules. Blocks trimmed flush look better. The remarkable "clouds" (uneven dot patterns in halftone blocks) on which not only small items but

210

even heavy machines try to float, are to be avoided both on aesthetic and practical printing grounds.
Magazine covers today are mostly drawn. That just as effective results can be obtained by purely typographic means is shown by the examples of *Broom* and *Proletarier*.
Broom is typical of the only kind of symmetrical design possible in the New Typography. We leave behind the two-sided symmetry of old title-pages as an expression of the past individualistic epoch. Only complete quadrilateral symmetry can express our aims for totality and universality.
The cover of the magazine *Proletarier* is an interesting example of the dynamic effect that comes from oblique typesetting. Both examples have achieved their strong effects without any use of trimmings such as rules or points.
The enormous importance of magazines today requires us to give them the most careful attention. Since today more magazines are read than books, and much important matter appears only in magazines, there are many new problems, of which the most important is how to find a contemporary style for their production. This chapter attempts to show the way.

211

Left This spread from Jan Tschichold's *The New Typography* illustrates his feelings on traditional book layout. The left-hand page caption reads: 'How blocks used to be arranged in magazines. Schematic, thoughtless centring of blocks. "Decorative", impractical, uneconomic (= ugly).' The right-hand page caption reads: 'The same blocks, correctly arranged in the same type-area. Constructive, meaningful, and economic (= beautiful).'

The modernist grid and postmodern experimentation

1 A spread from Josef Müller-Brockmann's *Grid Systems* (4th edition 1996) shows his approach to dealing with irregular-shaped images. 'To give a cut-out photograph greater optical stability it can be underlaid with a colour area like a blockout illustration.' For many designers today, this reinforcement of the grid, at the expense of the form of the content, is a triumph of a mechanical system over reader's appreciation.

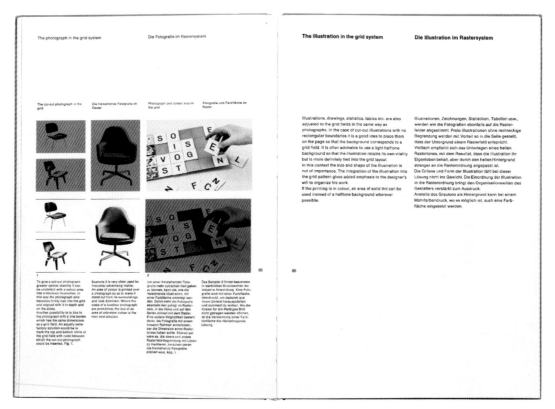

1

2 A spread from Emil Ruder's *Typographie* (7th edition 2001) shows a grid with nine square picture fields per page.

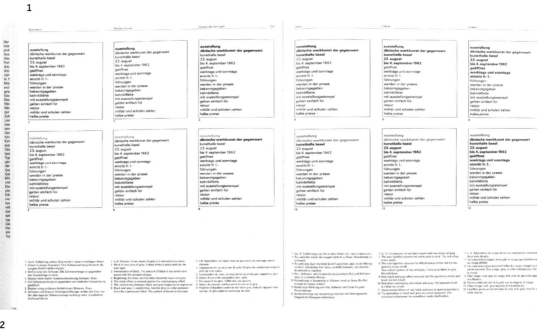

2

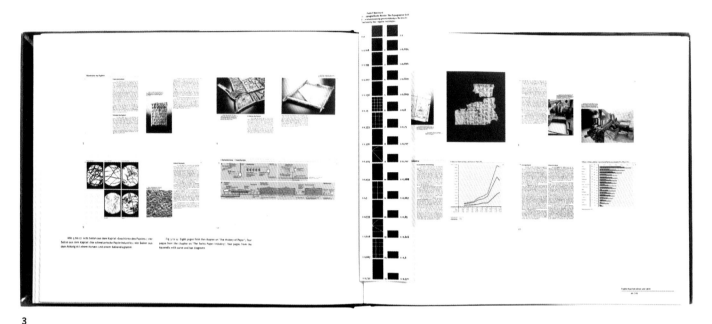

3

4

3 Hans Rudolf Bosshard in his landscape-format book *Der Typografische Raster* (*The Typographic Grid*) (2000) shows a range of pages based on a four-column grid. The text in the examples shown is justified, visually reinforcing the grid structure. The book comes with a very useful bookmark that shows a range of book formats.

4 A spread from Wolfgang Weingart's *My Way to Typography* (2000) shows examples of asymmetric layout, though the page is laid out on a formal four-column grid. The text is justified, reinforcing the column. Both folio numbers for the spread are printed two-thirds of the way up the right-hand page – useful when finding a page having consulted the index.

Grids using modernist principles

In a grid constructed using modernist principles, virtually any number of units could be formed within the column, but typically columns are divided between two to eight. The designer now seeks to draw a baseline grid and must therefore make decisions about font, type size, and leading. He or she then seeks to establish how many lines of type, including the leading, will fit into each module and each column. If the designer wants to create six units per column, and has a line count of 53 lines in the chosen size, the number of lines in the column (53) is divided by the number of units (six), minus the five empty lines that stand between the units. For example, a 47-line column − 5 lines = 42, divided by 6 = 7 lines per unit. If the page is four columns wide, a unit field of 24 units per page and 48 per spread has been created.

Constructing a modernist grid

1 Select the format (landscape or portrait) and a size, characteristically based on the metric A sizes.

2 Make approximate decisions about margin widths in relation to content and define the text area (shown in cyan).

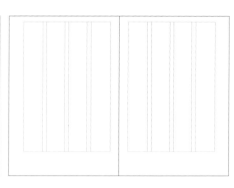

3 Divide the rough text area by the anticipated number of columns, drawing in intervening gutters.

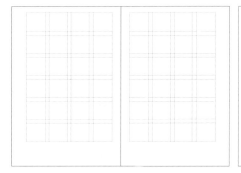

4 Rough out the column divisions into even picture fields, separating them using an empty line.

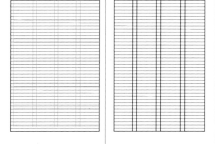

5 Make decisions about the size of the type and the leading so that the precise measurements of the rough grid can be finalized (shown in black, right-hand page). All the fields and spaces relate to the baseline grid. This example creates 6 units per column and has a line count of 41 lines in the chosen size. The number of lines in the column (41) is divided by the number of units (6) minus the 5 lines termed *empty lines* by Müller-Brockmann, which stand between the fields. 41-line column − 5 lines = 36 lines divided by 6 units = 6 lines per field. The exact margins can now be considered.

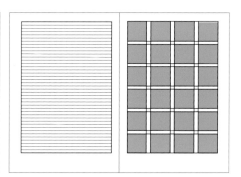

6 The horizontal baseline grid and vertical columns overlay the fields (marked in yellow). The ascenders of the first line align with the top of the picture field; the descenders at the bottom of the column align with the bottom of the last picture field. Type of different sizes can be used within the layout providing baselines can be established that relate to the picture field.

The neatness of this example is unlikely to be achieved at the first attempt. It is more likely that the final division will end in a line being divided into several decimal points. To overcome the half-line problem the designer must look for the nearest whole number divisible by 6, as this is the number of units per column. For example, 47-line column − 5 lines = 42, divided by 6 = 7 lines per unit.

These calculations will probably involve minor changes to type size or the amount of leading to adjust the number of lines per column, or alternatively minor changes to the depth of the text area and as a consequence the margin and possibly the format. Some designers working with modernist principles prefer to have the whole page divisible by the baseline grid.

Once the basic grid is largely constructed, the designer considers how to incorporate type elements other than the main text, which may include headings, captions, folios, footnotes, labels, and annotation. For Müller-Brockmann, this process relates directly to the established baseline grid. He uses the baseline grid to determine the sizes and leading of all the other type elements on the page. The smallest type on the page − perhaps a caption, for example − might be 7pt with 1pt of leading; the main body copy might be 10pt with 2pt leading; and the larger titles might be 20pt with 4pt leading. All three type sizes plus their respective leading are factors of 24.

Below Each of the grid fields within Müller-Brockmann's system is divisible by the baseline grid. A range of type sizes can be positioned on the grid, but the combination of type size and leading always relates to the depth of each line. The visual structure is preserved by varying the leading.

Relating the type to the grid fields

Different type sizes can be used within a modular grid. Swiss/German modernism dictates that the type and leading combined must be an exact subdivision of the height of the picture unit and relate directly to the baseline grid. In this example, the baseline grid is 20pt, the type is 5/10pt News Gothic, and the field is 120pt deep and accommodates 12 lines of type. The number of characters per line is approximately 48. The empty line between the fields also relates directly to the baseline grid.	**Larger type sizes** can be used but work better with a wider column. Here the baseline grid is 20pt, the type is 10/20pt News Gothic.	**Chapter Titles** might use large sizes; here 16/20pt, again strictly adhering to the picture units. Large numerals used as section openers relate directly to the baseline grid.

Body copy is made to work in a range of column widths. In this example, the baseline grid is 20pt, the type is 8/10pt News Gothic, and the field is 120pt deep and accommodates 12 lines of type.	Here 10pt News Gothic type is used across the wider column. The number of characters per line is increased to approximately 54. When the type moves up to 12pt/20pt the leading is further reduced.	7

Grid fields

The modernist approach to the construction of a grid provides the designer with exact page positions for type and image. The grid fields offer a wide variety of picture formats: the larger the number of fields in the grid, the greater the number of potential picture formats. Images within the unit field are cropped to the whole units or multiples of whole units and not, as with other approaches, to the nearest baseline.

Multiple grids within a single format

All but the most simple books are likely to contain more than one grid. A largely text-based non-fiction book, for example, may have one grid for the chapters and perhaps two for glossary and index. The text area characteristically remains the same, though the number of columns and type size may vary.

Multi-layered grids

The more complex a grid system, the greater the number of possible variations in layout. In 1962, Karl Gerstner, a Swiss designer working on the magazine *Capital*, designed a grid system based on a square text area within a portrait rectangular format. The single text square per page can be subdivided into multiples of two, three, four, five, and six units, creating picture units of one, four, nine, 25, and 36. As the text area is square, vertical and horizontal space can be divided using the same increment. Fifty-eight vertical and horizontal units can be subdivided in this way.

Ideas of multiple-layered grids have begun to move away from some of the early modernist principles of simplicity equating with clarity. Today, many designers familiar with modernist principles have begun to explore more complex decorative grid structures that often become a kind of geometric baroque. The grid, historically an essential tool in letterpress production, has progressively become a space for the development of experimental work independent of content.

For some designers, the extremes of this approach are to be derided as entertainment, an elevation of the designer's importance over that of the author's message. For such purists there are many examples to be vilified, where the complexity of the grid leads to visual saturation.

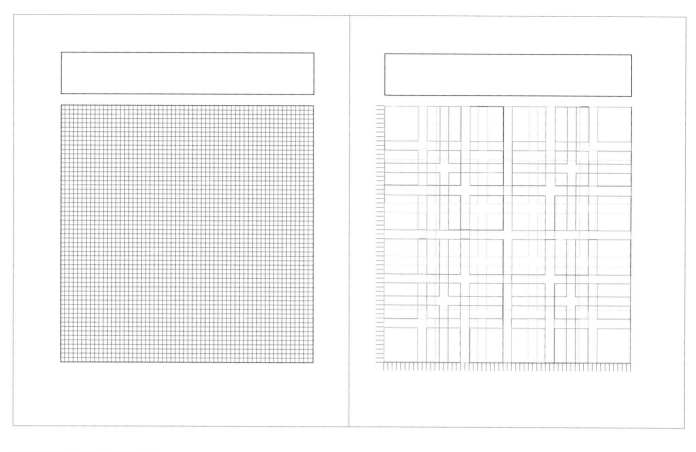

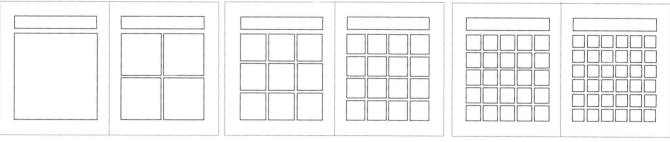

1 unit field
58

4 unit field
28 + 2 + 28 = 58

9 unit field
18 + 2 + 18 + 2
+ 18 = 58

12 unit field
13 + 2 + 13 + 2
+ 13 + 2 + 13 = 58

25 unit field
10 + 2 + 10 + 2
+ 10 + 2 + 10 + 2
+ 10 = 58

36 unit field
8 + 2 + 8 + 2 + 8
+ 2 + 8 + 2 + 8 + 2
+ 8 = 58

Above Karl Gerstner's grid for the magazine
Capital is extraordinarily flexible, supporting
different column widths while retaining the
same interval margin. A designer using a grid
of this type characteristically crops the pictures
strictly to the grid, but the number of variables,
picture formats, and sizes ensures variety within
a coherent structure. The matrix, as Gerstner
referred to the grid, is based on a unit field of
58 by 58.

Grids based on typographic elements

The grid systems already examined have been devised from the *outside in* – from format to the detail of the type. A variety of strategies and approaches to divisions of a chosen format have been used to establish the text area and relative width of the margins. The text area has then been subdivided into the required number of columns. Conversely, many designers, particularly those with experience of letterpress composition and hand-setting, prefer to develop a grid from the *inside out*, identifying the number of columns required to accommodate text and pictures in relation to the characteristics of the content before setting the exact widths of margins.

Factorial grids

Many grid systems are based on factorial relationships between the width of the page and the number of columns and intervals between the columns. In mathematical terms, factors are numbers divisible by whole-number divisions; for example, 16 is divisible by two, four, and eight. This principle is often referred to as 'partitioning'. It is used within many grid systems to divide space. The designer is able to see the number of units required to support a wide range of columns within the grid. The factorial grid table describes the mathematical relationships between numbers rather than exact lengths. Having identified the number of units required to support a range of columns, the designer can then select the width of the individual unit, millimetres, points, and so on.

Factorial grids: establishing columns using interval sequences

The table of interval sequences opposite can be used to determine the number of columns and gutters on any given page. Each row of the table shows a solid block (a potential column width) followed by space (the interval between columns). The black figures on the right edge of the table show the number of units used on each row. The first row in each sequence has the narrowest column; for example, top of the page first row, the columns are 2 units wide and the interval 1 unit wide. The second row shows columns 3 units wide but the interval remains 1 unit wide. The cyan blocks show where 2 or more rows share a common width. The cyan number identifies the units divisible by the columns and intervals. For example, in the first interval sequence the number 71 is divisible by: 2 units (24 columns, 23 intervals), 3 units (18 columns, 17 intervals), 4 units (12 columns, 11 intervals), 7 units (9 columns, 8 intervals), 8 units (8 columns, 7 intervals), and 11 units (6 columns, 5 intervals). If 71 is selected as a page width, 6 sequences can be used to divide it into columns. The unit of measurement can be specified in whole points, picas, didots, millimetres, or divisions of any of those measurements, but the factorial relationship will remain the same. For example, if the unit width is 2mm, then the text area will be 142 mm wide (2 x 71mm), the interval will be 2mm wide (2 x 1mm), the narrowest column 4mm (2 x 2mm), and the widest column 22mm wide (2 x 11mm). Interval sequences with even-numbered columns can produced double-width columns; for example, 11 units + 2-unit interval + 11 units, 24-unit column.

Single interval sequence

Double interval sequence

Triple interval sequence

Quadruple interval sequence

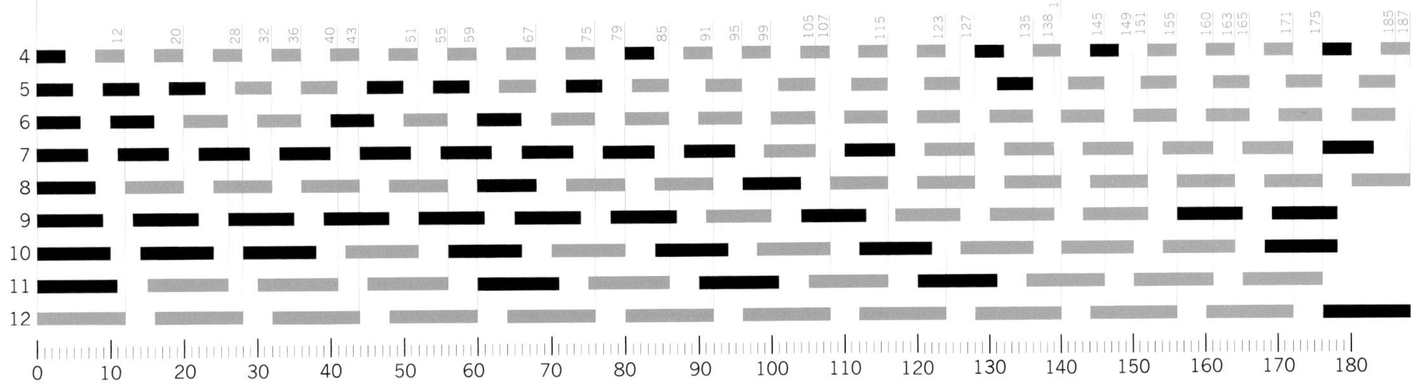

The point quadrat grid system

In metal setting, grids were easily devised by taking the square of a type size, known as the *em* or *quad*, to set the column width and interval (the name *em* is derived from a time when the letter M was cast on a square body). By alternating the em and the interval and building up a pattern of 12-quad columns, a simple division of space is achieved. The em quad was used as the standard for width of lines or measure, which is described as being so many ems wide. Grid structures based on 12 quads were commonly used by compositors in Britain and the United States, as the system derives from imperial measurements. The number 12 is divisible by one, two, three, four, and six columns, whereas ten, based on the metric system, is divisible only by one, two, and five.

The designer using the quad grid system usually has a notional page format and approximate size in mind. Selecting the appropriate quad, the designer can easily develop a multiple-column grid. All the elements of the page can be specified in quads: baseline grid, line length, column depth, margins, and format. Designer Derek Birdsall has adapted this basic imperial system to what he describes as the metric quad grid system.

The metric quadrat grid system

We have already discussed some of the implications of the mismatch of metric and imperial measurement systems when devising a format (see page 39). The same problems arise in developing a quad grid system. The page's external dimensions are frequently specified in millimetres, while the internal dimensions of the quad grid are based on points. Derek Birdsall in his excellent book *Notes on Book Design* (2004) explains how through 50 years of practice he has adapted the quad system to work with metric measurements. The adaptation that Birdsall proposes is something of a hybrid between the imperial and metric systems, but has the advantage of retaining the best features of both. The approach establishes a common measure for the external and internal dimensions of the page. The em squares and the intervals are replaced by metric squares; for example, 4mm x 4mm, 5mm x 5mm. The metric squares, also termed quads, are built up in twelves as opposed to tens as this allows for a greater number of columns to be developed. The system makes use of 12 basic columns but can be adapted to support virtually any number.

Having established the basic column and interval divisions of the grid, the designer selects the margins around the text box, so defining the format. In a similar way to the point quad system, all the elements of the page can be specified in metric quads. The vertical and horizontal divisions of the page are determined by millimetres and therefore the baseline grid, leading, and type sizes are specified in millimetres, although it is still possible to use points. European and younger British and American designers are often most familiar with specifying type in millimetres, although some older designers continue to use points. It is clear when working with this approach that the grid is being constructed from the inside out, from quad square to page format and size.

Right Twelve-point em quads with eleven-em intervals 276 points wide, set in letterpress, show the basis for a quad grid system derived from cold-metal composition. Fourteen-point quads with 1-point quad intervals give a measure of 322 points and 18-point quads 414 points.

Developing a grid using the metric quad system

1 Decide on the approximate format and size and make decisions about the number of columns required to support the content, eg 2, 3, 4. Consider the type style, weight, and size to establish a line length.

2 Select one of the metric quad divisions: here 10mm/4mm intervals x 12 = 164mm. The quads define the width of the text area and the number of columns and their width. Here: a single column 164mm wide

two columns 80mm wide (6 quads x 10mm + 5 x 4mm intervals

three columns 52mm wide (4 quads x 10mm + 3 x 4mm intervals)

four columns 38mm wide (3 quads x 10mm + 3 x 4mm intervals)

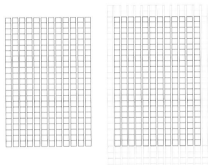

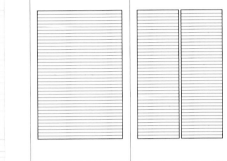

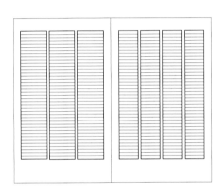

3 Decide on the depth of the columns in quads: here 22 = 220mm depth left-hand page. Define the margins in quads; Birdsall prefers 'equal side margins, ... I like left- and right-hand margins to have the same basic grid.' The quad system supports any approach to margin widths and can be used in relation to formats derived at by subdivisions of paper size. In the example right-hand page, one quad plus one interval have been added to inner and outer margins: 10mm + 4mm x 2 = 28mm. When the margins are added to the width of the text area, the page width is established as 248mm. Two quads have been added to the top margin and four to the foot adding an additional 60mm to the depth of page, which is now 280mm deep.

4 Left-hand page: a single column 164mm wide (12 quads, 11 intervals); right-hand page two columns 80mm wide (6 quads x 10mm + 5 x 4mm intervals).

5 Left-hand page: three columns 52mm wide (4 quads x 10mm + 3 x 4mm intervals); right-hand page four columns 38mm wide (3 quads x 10mm + 3 x 4mm intervals). The quads in the system are often used to form the baseline grid for the text, but can merely be used to establish the page format, size, and the required number of columns.

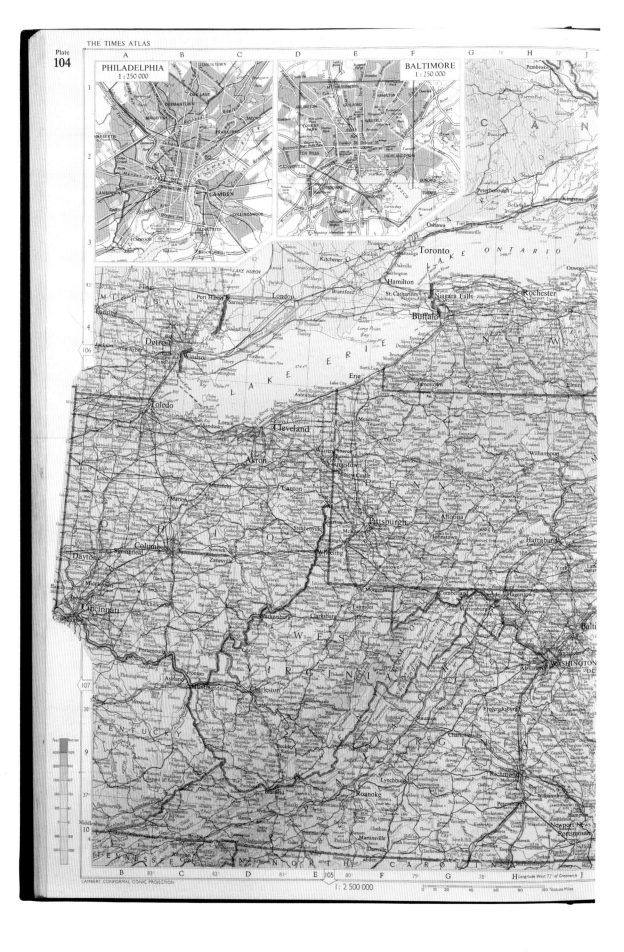

Incremental grid squares: area, cartography, and maps

It is not only books designed to carry text that have made use of grid systems based on squares. Cartographers use the square as the basis for the creation of maps. In cartographic grids, the square grid structure has two principal functions: it delineates the scale of the geographic area being recorded, and serves as the basis for a coordinate-based indexing system.

Incremental grid squares: time

In an atlas, the grid structure is based on increments that relate to area, but grids based on other incremental systems can be used to support different narratives through a similar process of plotting. Books that have a sequential chronology may be based on a grid structure plotted in relation to increments of time. For example, these might be decades or centuries when telling the story of ancient civilizations or the history of costume, or months, weeks, and days in relation to the story of a baby's development. The use of time increments running as vertical divisions allows stages of development to be plotted accurately against one another. When a book has a single developmental narrative, these simple columns combined with a baseline grid provide an appropriate grid structure upon which the narrative can be plotted. A more complex narrative enabling direct comparisons between objects or ideas that occur simultaneously may need to make use of horizontal divisions of space running across the page. The grid now takes on the form of a matrix, with time being plotted on the horizontal axis running across the page and a classification structure running down the page. The designer of this sort of incremental time-based grid works in much the same way as a cartographer who uses a scale grid to record landscape. Grid structures of this type have layouts determined not by the designer's sense of composition but by the plotting of the relative positions of the content in time as opposed to space.

Opposite The *Times Atlas* uses a square grid to represent geographic space and as an indexing system to identify specific places or features through a system of coordinates.

Appropriation: the derivative grid

The notion of the appropriated grid takes the principle of basing a system on the book's content more literally. If the content of the book has a visual basis, it is possible to construct a grid determined directly by the content. A book on theatre design may use the proscenium arch; an architectural book the façade of a building. In the case of the latter, the right-hand page might be determined by the front façade, while the rear elevation could be used for the left-hand page. This idea can be extended, if a book has several chapters, by developing grids for each chapter based on a series of elevations, floor plans, or cross-sections. By working in such a way, the book grid locks the content into the architect's orthographic drawings. The form of the building determines the grid of the book. This approach is at odds with the early modernist concept of the neutral modular grid devised as an organizing device to bring clarity, efficiency of production, and order to complex information. The appropriated grid is not a passive device upon which content is arranged, but an active element within the design signifying the relationship between the form of the content and the form of the book. Aspects of this approach if applied too literally may box the designer into a grid structure within which it is tedious to work. The consequence for the reader may be distracting, with the grid standing between the eye and the information.

Developmental and organic grid systems

Most of the approaches to creating a grid system discussed so far have presented the grid as a static, neutral device upon which information is laid out. By contrast, developmental grids change through the pages of a book; as a consequence, the layout of the information changes. A simple developmental grid might involve moving headings and page numbers progressively through the book, but more complex structures might involve moving virtually all the grid elements. This approach is similar to animation, in which successive cells may contain essentially the same image but its position within the frame has moved fractionally. The grid structure for each page is unique to the page, but makes use of common elements throughout the book.

This approach opens up a world of possibilities for some designers. Each chapter of a book can be given a slightly different starting point, from which developmental grids unique to each page can be designed. The depth of the page might be divided by the number of chapters and then the position of the folio and heading determined by the number of pages within the chapter.

Many designers would question the mathematical arbitrariness of this playful approach, which has little relation to the content of the book. For others, though, this approach is as valid as any stable static grid, which is often equally unrelated to content. For readers, the approach may at first be a little disconcerting but after a few pages they learn to anticipate the progressive rhythm of the grid and perhaps even enjoy its subtle development.

Books without grids

A great many illustrated books are designed without the use of a grid. Once the format and the extent of the book have been decided, the images are drawn or painted in proportion to the page and the illustrator or designer works on composing the elements. Lettering or type may be applied to the illustration but often does not have to be formalized within even a rudimentary grid structure. Type or calligraphic letterforms may be used but baselines and inter-character spacing may be considered as part of an integrated image and treated in much the same way as marks within a drawing.

Above This spread has nothing to do with grids; it is composed as a painting in relation to a canvas the width of a spread. The painterly illustration is from *On ne copie pas* by Olivier Douzou and Frédérique Bertrand, published by Editions du Rouergue.

Above The Cranbrook Academy of Art 2002 book designed and illustrated by Catelijne von Miiddlekoop and Dylan Nelson uses pages of fluid type without resorting to a grid. This approach seems appropriate for an art institution determined to claim its place in the vanguard of the new.

With the advent of digital composition, it is possible to set text without using a geometric grid. Digital technology has closed the split between text and image that occurred when Gutenberg invented type in 1455. The handwritten letterforms of the medieval calligrapher were individual and could be arranged fluidly. Today the letterforms are identical, making them type, but their arrangement can be either fluid or formally structured by a grid.

Typographic palette

Considerations of the way to arrange type on the page within a grid structure force the designer to look at how meaning is articulated through paragraphs, how the text is aligned within the grid, and how vertical and horizontal space are used within the book. It is important that the reader gains confidence from whatever system of arrangement is used, as this enables smooth progress through the text.

Column depth

In book design, the depth of page column can be considered in two ways: the linear depth measured in points, picas, didots, or millimetres (determined by the grid, as described in the previous chapter); and the number of lines to the column, determined by the size of the type and the depth of the leading. The depth of the column should also be considered in relation to its width, the interval, the gutter, and the proportions of the format, particularly where the designer is anticipating an extended period of reading. Although we have grown used to reading long newspaper columns, the way we read articles is not the same reading experience as the book. We have learned to read newspaper columns of 96 lines deep, though often the column depth of an individual article may be made shorter by running the content over several columns. We tend to be selective when reading the newspaper and dip in and out of spreads attracted to various articles by the headline or the writer. Therefore our reading patterns and exposure to very long columns is broken into short intense periods rather than the extended periods of concentrated reading associated with reading a novel. Many books celebrated for their fine printing and cited as examples of distinguished design have approximately 40 lines to a column, as do many novels designed for continuous sustained reading. Johannes Gutenberg produced both a 42-line and 38-line Bible, and books using a similar number of lines for continuous reading have formed a tacit convention through Western printing history. Non-fiction books may well have longer columns, but the reading experience is broken down into smaller passages through the use of subheadings. Works of reference where the reader is dipping into information also have deeper columns: dictionaries often have 68 lines, thesauruses 70, and telephone directories 132. Encyclopedias designed for extended periods of reading often have many lines to the column – the *Encyclopaedia Britannica* has 72 lines – but the columns are usually broken by subheadings within extended entries. Column depths for book indexes often contain far more lines because space is at a premium; the *Times Atlas* has 134 lines. To support the reading of long columns of continuous text, adding additional leading makes the reading experience more pleasurable.

moi. Il faut manger. » L'Arabe secoua la tête et dit oui. Le calme était revenu sur son visage, mais son expression restait absente et distraite.

Le café était prêt. Ils le burent, assis tous deux sur le lit de camp, en mordant leurs morceaux de galette. Puis Daru mena l'Arabe sous l'appentis et lui montra le robinet où il faisait sa toilette. Il rentra dans la chambre, plia les couvertures et le lit de camp, fit son propre lit et mit la pièce en ordre. Il sortit alors sur le terre-plein en passant par l'école. Le soleil montait déjà dans le ciel bleu ; une lumière tendre et vive inondait le plateau désert. Sur le raidillon, la neige fondait par endroits. Les pierres allaient apparaître de nouveau. Accroupi au bord du plateau, l'instituteur contemplait l'étendue déserte. Il pensait à Balducci. Il lui avait fait de la peine, il l'avait renvoyé, d'une certaine manière, comme s'il ne voulait pas être dans le même sac. Il entendait encore l'adieu du gendarme et, sans savoir pourquoi, il se sentait étrangement vide et vulnérable. A ce moment, de l'autre côté de l'école, le prisonnier toussa. Daru l'écouta, presque malgré lui, puis, furieux, jeta un caillou qui siffla dans l'air avant de s'enfoncer dans la neige. Le crime imbécile de cet homme le révoltait, mais le livrer était contraire à l'honneur : d'y penser seulement le rendait fou d'humiliation. Et il maudissait à la fois les siens qui lui envoyaient cet Arabe et celui-ci qui avait osé tuer et n'avait pas su s'enfuir. Daru se leva, tourna en rond sur le terre-plein, attendit, immobile, puis entra dans l'école.

L'Arabe, penché sur le sol cimenté de l'appentis, se lavait les dents avec deux doigts. Daru le regarda,

puis : « Viens », dit-il. Il rentra dans la chambre, devant le prisonnier. Il enfila une veste de chasse sur son chandail et chaussa des souliers de marche. Il attendit debout que l'Arabe eût remis son chèche et ses sandales. Ils passèrent dans l'école et l'instituteur montra la sortie à son compagnon. « Va », dit-il. L'autre ne bougea pas. « Je viens », dit Daru. L'Arabe sortit. Daru rentra dans la chambre et fit un paquet avec des biscottes, des dattes et du sucre. Dans la salle de classe, avant de sortir, il hésita une seconde devant son bureau, puis il franchit le seuil de l'école et boucla la porte. « C'est par là », dit-il. Il prit la direction de l'est, suivi par le prisonnier. Mais, à une faible distance de l'école, il lui sembla entendre un léger bruit derrière lui. Il revint sur ses pas, inspecta les alentours de la maison : il n'y avait personne. L'Arabe le regardait faire, sans paraître comprendre. « Allons », dit Daru.

Ils marchèrent une heure et se reposèrent auprès d'une sorte d'aiguille calcaire. La neige fondait de plus en plus vite, le soleil pompait aussitôt les flaques, nettoyait à toute allure le plateau qui, peu à peu, devenait sec et vibrait comme l'air lui-même. Quand ils reprirent la route, le sol résonnait sous leurs pas. De loin en loin, un oiseau fendait l'espace devant eux avec un cri joyeux. Daru buvait, à profondes aspirations, la lumière fraîche. Une sorte d'exaltation naissait en lui devant le grand espace familier, presque entièrement jaune maintenant, sous sa calotte de ciel bleu. Ils marchèrent encore une heure, en descendant vers le sud. Ils arrivèrent à une sorte d'éminence aplatie, faite de rochers friables. A partir de là, le plateau dévalait, à l'est, vers

Above Pages from Albert Camus' *L'exil et le royaume* show the characteristic column depth of a novel.

Articulating meaning: paragraphs

The sentences that make up a paragraph are linked by a common idea. The designer seeks to articulate the writer's ideas within a text by delineating the paragraphs using typographic conventions. Through time and different writing traditions, a range of conventions has developed for clarifying running text. These include line breaks, paragraph pilcrow, indents, hanging indents or exdents, run-on with symbol, and drop lines.

Line breaks

The line break is the basic typing convention for a paragraph, although when used within extensive narratives such as novels this tends visually to fragment the text and uses considerably more paper. Within technical non-fiction writing, where the reader may require more time to reflect on complex ideas contained in a paragraph, this approach serves to divide a set of themed ideas into short, readable passages.

A priest says

Almighty God, the Father of our Lord Jesus Christ,
who desireth not the death of a sinner,
but rather that he may turn from his wickedness and live;
and hath given power, and commandment, to his ministers
to declare and pronounce to his people, being penitent,
the absolution and remission of their sins:
he pardoneth and absolveth all them that truly repent
    and unfeignedly believe his holy gospel.
Wherefore let us beseech him to grant us true repentance,
    and his Holy Spirit,
that those things may please him which we do at this present;
and that the rest of our life hereafter may be pure and holy;
so that at the last we may come to his eternal joy;
through Jesus Christ our Lord.

All **Amen.**

or other ministers may say

Grant, we beseech thee, merciful Lord,
to thy faithful people pardon and peace,
that they may be cleansed from all their sins,
and serve thee with a quiet mind;
through Jesus Christ our Lord.

All **Amen.**

All **Our Father, which art in heaven,
hallowed be thy name;
thy kingdom come;
thy will be done,
in earth as it is in heaven.
Give us this day our daily bread.
And forgive us our trespasses,
as we forgive them that trespass against us.
And lead us not into temptation;
but deliver us from evil.
For thine is the kingdom,
the power and the glory,
for ever and ever.
Amen.**

¶ *Morning Prayer*

*The introduction to the service (pages 62–64) is used on Sundays,
and may be used on any occasion.*

These responses are used

O Lord, open thou our lips

All **and our mouth shall shew forth thy praise.**

O God, make speed to save us.

All **O Lord, make haste to help us.**

Glory be to the Father, and to the Son,
and to the Holy Ghost;

All **as it was in the beginning, is now, and ever shall be,
world without end. Amen.**

Praise ye the Lord.

All **The Lord's name be praised.**

Venite, exultemus Domino

1 O come, let us sing unto the Lord :
    let us heartily rejoice in the strength of our salvation.

2 Let us come before his presence with thanksgiving :
    and shew ourselves glad in him with psalms.

3 For the Lord is a great God :
    and a great King above all gods.

4 In his hand are all the corners of the earth :
    and the strength of the hills is his also.

5 The sea is his, and he made it :
    and his hands prepared the dry land.

6 O come, let us worship, and fall down :
    and kneel before the Lord our Maker.

7 For he is the Lord our God :
    and we are the people of his pasture, and the sheep of his hand.

Paragraph pilcrow

The origin of the paragraph indent may lie in the writing conventions of the ancient Greeks, who devised a graphic symbol to represent a new string of connected thoughts. Although some sources maintain that it is a medieval invention (it appears in manuscripts as early as the 1440s), the pilcrow, or paragraph symbol ¶, was initially used in running text and often inserted in red. Over time, the paragraph was afforded a new line, so that the pilcrows aligned along the left of a column. The black text of each paragraph was indented to allow for the red pilcrow to be inserted by hand after printing, but the space then made the pilcrow redundant. With the advent of hand-composition and advances in the speed of printing, calligraphic insertions of red pilcrows became a contrivance. The mark is retained in many fonts and has been used by typographers interested in reviving medieval calligraphic design traditions, as it supports the creation of perfectly delineated justified text blocks. It is also used within the Invisibles facility in word-processing programs as an aid to editors and designers.

Above Derek Birdsall was commissioned by the Liturgical Commission of the Church of England to design the new Anglican prayer book *Services and Prayers for the Church of England* published to celebrate the millennium in 2000. Birdsall selected the typeface Gill Sans; a decision described by designer and writer Phil Baines as 'wearing its Englishness on its sleeve'. Birdsall made use of paragraph pilcrows in a manner that would surely have gained approval by Eric Gill (1888–1940), the font designer, who frequently used them in his own work.

Indents

Indents, derived from the absence of the pilcrow, are today the most frequently used form of articulating paragraphs. Most traditional compositors have grown up with the convention of using the em (square of the type size) as an indent. This is an extremely practical convention for hand- or machine-setting. In a digital age, however, specifying any value is equally easy and so designers have begun to develop a range of approaches. The em-square indent does not account for any leading, so the visual appearance of this form of indent is of a white portrait rectangle. Many designers prefer to retain a square by devising an indent that reflects the baseline-to-baseline distance. Other designers prefer to link this kind of decision to their approach to the construction of the grid. A designer using a golden section for both format and text box might apply the same strategy to the micro-spaces within the page and create golden-section indents between the baselines. A designer making use of proportional scales or the Fibonacci series might choose one of the smaller values on the scale to form the indent, while the arch-modernist might devise an increment based on the division of a single grid field.

Hanging indents or exdents

Hanging indents reverse the conventional relationship between the first line of a paragraph and the remaining lines, so that the first line runs out to the left visually appearing to occupy the margin, which appears to be established by the majority of lines in the paragraph. The size of the exdent varies, but designers will usually find a rationale that relates to the approach they have used for the selection of format or grid construction or that is pertinent to the type size.

Run-on with symbol

This approach does not use white space to signify the start of a new paragraph but places a symbol after the full point of one paragraph's final sentence and before the first word of the next paragraph. It was used in many early calligraphic books where the text block was solid and both left and right margins were clearly delineated. During the incunabula period of printing (*c.* 1455–1500), when printers justified type as a facsimile of the calligraphic form, this approach continued to be used. The symbol could be: ¶ a pilcrow, perhaps printed in a second colour; | a vertical line, again in a second colour; Ω a pictorial element relating to the content of the text – in this instance omega, symbolizing the end – or a decorative lozenge; **6.7** a numeral in a different weight; **6.7** a numeral in a different font or colour. This approach suits short chapters, or sections that could be identified by the use of a decimal point, as used in the margins of reports or minutes of meetings. It can also be used effectively within the body of the text, but the symbol has to be carefully considered in relation to verse numbers and foot- and source notes.

Some early modernist typographers at the Bauhaus questioned nineteenth-century written and typographic conventions. Determined to minimize the number of decorative elements and reduce the internal hierarchy within a typographic page, in the belief that type, like people, should all be of equal value, they stripped away the number of signifiers. thissortofexperimentis usefultodayasitforcesustoconsiderwhatpurposethesymbolicelementstrapped withinthephoneticcodeserve.*this sort of experiment is useful today as it forces us to consider what purpose the symbolic elements trapped within the phonetic code serve.*inter-word space clearly supports the identification of words and hugely improves the readability of text.a full point signifies the end of one sentence and the beginning of another. Some modernists dispensed with the space after the full point and removed all capitalization.this approach reduced the sentence signifiers to one. other approaches made use of two conventions, the full point and the space.Others removed the space but retained the capital, though this was less popular as it retained the visual hierarchy.

paragraph articulation was simplified to a line break. **e**xperiments in running text included emboldening the first letter.colour was used to signify the first letter of the paragraph, but with letterpress setting this was slow and inefficient and not in keeping with the modern machine age.today with lithographic printing this presents fewer problems though multilingual publishing prevents its extensive use as each new colour requires an extra plate.

Drop lines

Another approach to signifying the paragraph break is to make use of drop lines.

Here, as the term implies, the first word of a new paragraph is immediately below the last word of the previous paragraph, on a new line.

The reader finds this transition very smooth, though the visual appearance of the text in relation to the white space block is dependent on the length of the preceding paragraph's final line. If the paragraphs are short and the text extensive, far more lines will be required than with other conventions (apart from line breaks) and the visual appearance of the text block is fractured by white intrusions from the margins.

Alignment of text

The four basic alignments of text are: ranged left, ranged right, centred, and justified. A book may make use of several forms of alignment for the title page, contents, chapter openers, body copy, captions, and index. Each alignment has strengths that support the reading of different information or the visual appearance of the page. Readers have, through time, been conditioned to anticipate certain styles of alignments with specific elements of a book's design. Nineteenth-century books often have centred title pages, while indexes were characteristically ranged left. The former was the consequence of style; the latter the consequence of function.

Ranged left

The alignment shown here is referred to as 'ranged left' in the UK and 'ragged right' or 'flush left' in the United States. The adoption of this convention came relatively late in the history of the printed book. The type aligns along the left-hand margin; lines on the right-hand margin can look very ragged when it is used with narrow columns. It is a style that often makes use of hyphenation to limit the visual effects of irregular line lengths (see page 81).

Ranged right

The alignment shown here is known as 'ranged right' in the UK, or 'flush right' in the US. The arrangement does not support the comfortable reading of extended passages, as the start of each line on the left of the page is variable. The eye has no way of accurately anticipating the beginning of each new line, and there is a momentary confusion that disjoints the reading experience. The effects of this problem can be limited, but not solved, if the interline spacing (leading), is increased and the column is wide enough to support between 45 and 70 characters. Hyphenation can be used to adjust visually the unevenness of the left edge of the text, but this approach still leaves the eye searching between lines and introduces another level of reading complexity. The concerns about readability make this arrangement largely unsuitable for those learning to read and it is therefore rarely appropriate for the body text in children's books.

Linking text and image

Ranged-right alignment is often used for short passages of text or captions, where its inadequacies are less glaring. It has certain visual advantages when placing a caption to the left of a square-cropped image, as the right edge of the text and the left edge of the image abut neatly. Type ranged right in this situation leaves a white meandering river.

Centred

The alignment here is centred and is often used for title pages. The type is aligned along a central axis and, although not strictly symmetrical (one side of the axis exactly mirroring the other), presents the appearance of symmetry, a feature much treasured within the classical traditions of book design and used extensively in traditional title pages. The lines often appear to create the form of a vase. The approach, although easily created, is difficult to master, as careful crafting of the internal text hierarchy must be considered in relation to reading, line length, type size, and weight. The modular nature of type naturally supports this form of alignment, whereas calligraphic pages required several drafts of each line to establish length before being arranged around the central axis. A line of metal type or digital setting can have the same number of spacing units added at either end to establish the central axis. Centred type is rarely used for body text as, like type ranged right, the eye finds the start of the next line difficult to locate.

Justified

This alignment is justified: like centring, it presents the text symmetrically with a central axis. It has been the principal approach to setting text in books since 1455 and is derived from the earliest columns on Egyptian scrolls. The convention remained largely unchallenged within book design until modernism began to question ideas of symmetry and unpick classical notions of beauty. The right and left edge of each page run parallel. Justification differs from left, right, and centred alignment in that text has irregular inter-word spacing. Most text fonts, excluding those of mono-width designed for typewriters, contain characters of several widths. When lines of type are set with consistent inter-character and word spacing they run to a different length, which destroys the parallel appearance at the edge of the column. There are only two ways of retaining the parallel appearance of justified text: hyphenation, and varying the width of inter-word spacing. In hand-setting, this process relied on the skills of the individual compositor, who determined the word breaks and inserted spacing elements evenly between words to retain the common line length. Today, digital typesetting programs have built-in default settings that determine the inter-word spacing, but these should not be relied on without careful consideration. Designers should seek to edit hyphenation and inter-word spacing through H&J settings in relation to the typeface and line length.

Tapered centring

Some justified type in early printing makes use of tapered centring. Somewhat surprisingly, this is more easily read than simple centring: the eye is given a visual prompt by the black shape of the text against the white ground of the page, in which a recognizable pattern can be identified and used to anticipate the position of the following line. Successive lines contain fewer characters while retaining their central alignment. This approach has historically been used as a conclusion to a section. Symmetrical double-page spreads featuring justified text that tapers to the base of each page present three lines of symmetry, one major and two minor: the spread is divided by the major central axis

of the book, and each page is divided by a minor axis from which the text
is centred. The tapering of centred text explored by early printers in the
printing of incunabula was revived by the Englishman William Morris
(1834–1896), a prime mover in the Arts and Crafts Movement.
Today tapered centring is rarely used within commercial
publications, though some poetry may be set in this way.
Many modern calligraphers use this form of alignment,
particularly for books of remembrance. The simple
triangle standing on its point, inverted
Gothic arch, or copula transcends
decoration, the white space
cherishing the text as
though the words
were borne
up on
angels'
wings.

†

ΩΩΩΩ

Forced

Forced alignment is a version of justification. Offered in typesetting programs, it
does what the name implies, dividing up the inter-word space evenly, forcing the
words to fit the line until a minimum default is reached or until the designer hits
the   return   key;   it   is   evident   that   this   can   have   disastrous   visual
c   o   n   s   e   q   u   e   n   c   e   s
and   has   little   place   in   text   setting   for   book   design.

Horizontal space

For the book designer there are six principal considerations when manipulat-
ing horizontal space within type: line length, characters per line, inter-word
space, set width, tracking, and kerning.

Line length or measure

This is determined by the width of the column. Headings, chapter openers,
and quotations may, however, be used in ways that break the grid. The line
length may be specified in points, picas, or ciceros, which relate to the typographic elements of the page; or in inches, centimetres, or millimetres, which
relate to the external proportions of the page.

Characters per line

For continuous reading, 65 characters per line is considered optimum,
although anything between 45 and 75 characters can be made to work in a
book. In non-technical English this works out at about 12 words per line. In
other languages, such as German, which makes use of many compound words,
65 characters will amount to fewer words per line. Extremely long lines usually

require more leading and are tiring to read regardless of the alignment, as the eye must travel a long way to pick up the new line.

Short lines in extended text are tiresome, but we are accustomed to reading them in newspapers and on digital phones, GPS, and so on. Short lines usually destroy the phrasing of a

sentence;

however,

if the writing

is short,

pithy,

& to the point,

and

the designer

& writer,

work together,

phrasing &

meaning

can be

retained

or even

emphasized.

Inter-word space: metal type

Inter-word space using metal type was determined by spacing units derived from the typeset em. This square unit gained its name from the space occupied by the capital M of any given typeface and size. The em square in 6pt is 6pt x 6pt; the em square in 8pt is 8pt x 8pt, and so on. The inter-word space was determined by the designer or compositor, who, in running text copy, would generally select spacing elements called thicks, thins, or mids, depending on the weight and width of the face, which were usually approximately the width of the lower-case i.

The set em, which is proportional to the size of the type, is not to be confused with the pica em, which is a fixed 12pt square. The traditional spacing units within metal type are:

em square: of the point size
This   line   is   inter-word   spaced   using   em   squares.

en: 1/2 the em square, or 2-to-em
This line is inter-word spaced using en spaces.

thick: 1/3 the em square, or 3-to-em
This line is inter-word spaced using thicks or 3-to-em.

□ 6
□ 8
□ 10
□ 12
□ 14
□ 18
□ 24

□ 36

□ 48
□ 60

□ 72

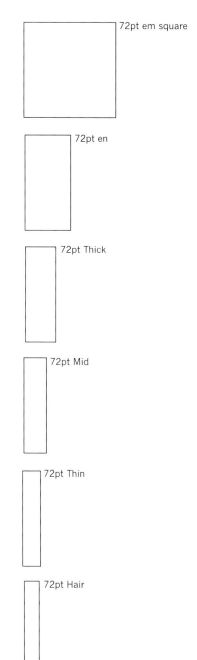

72pt em square

72pt en

72pt Thick

72pt Mid

72pt Thin

72pt Hair

Above Spacing divisions of a 72pt em.

mid: 1/4 the em square, or 4-to-em
This line is inter-word spaced using mids or 4-to-em.

thin: 1/5 the em square, or 5-to-em
This line is inter-word spaced using thins or 5-to-em.

The hair space in a pre-digital age varied according to the size of the body. In sizes under 12pt, it is 1/6 to 1/10; in 12pt or above it is 1/12. This variation is largely notional, as a hair space in lead (a narrow piece of metal) 1/12 of 6pt would be extremely thin, difficult to pick up and inclined to bend or break.

hair: 1/6 the em square, or 12-to-em
This line is inter-word spaced using hairs of 12-to-emin6pt.

hair: 1/10 the em square, or 10-to-em
This line is inter-word spaced using hairs of 10-to-em in 9pt.

hair: 1/12 the em square, or 12-to-em
This line is inter-word spaced using hairs 12-to-em in 12pt.

These spacing units can be used in multiples to provide a wider range of inter-word spacing that remains proportional to the type size. In metal type, spacing can be added only between characters and words as the minimum distance is determined physically by the width of the shoulder or the side bearings. The type designer and type founder, therefore, controlled the minimum distance for typesetting in each of the manufactured sizes. A designer could add space only between elements.

Inter-word space: digital type
The inter-word spacing of digital type is determined by the type designer, who assigns a set distance that is proportional to each type size in a font. The word space is approximately a quarter of the point size: for example, 10-point type has a word space of 2.5 point, which is about the width of the lower-case i. Digital inter-word space, like metal inter-word space, is determined by divisions of the em square of the type size. However, rather than divide the em into six fractions, digital setting divides the em into equal units. Some digital programs divide the em into 200 units, whereas others are capable of divisions into 1,000 units. As the em is always proportional to the type size the inter-word space of 40 units (of a 200-unit em) in 6 point occupies the same space proportionally as it does in 8, 10, 12, or 72 point.

6 point with 40-unit inter-word space

8 point with 40-unit inter-word space

10 point with 40-unit inter-word space

12 point with 40-unit inter-word space

Digital type, unlike metal type, can be set in virtually any size, from 2pt to 720pt, in QuarkXPress software. The unit spacing relating to the em allows the designer to specify what used to be termed 'bastard sizes' (sizes such as 13pt that are not basic letterpress sizes) while retaining the inter-word space proportions.

The digital inter-character space set by the type designer can be overridden. Space can be added to or subtracted from the default through the use of Hyphenation and Justification (H&J). H&J settings in digital typesetting allow the designer to control the way words are spaced and how they are broken between lines. The software with which books are designed allows the designer to make four key amendments to the default settings determined by the type designer:
1 Should hyphenation be used? 2 How are words broken? 3 What are the maximum and minimum inter-word spaces in justified setting? 4 What is the consistent inter-word space in ranged-left setting?

Should hyphenation be used?

Hyphenation does not reflect the way we speak, nor honour the integrity of words, nor in most cases support fluid reading. It is a contrivance and in some typographers' minds it constitutes poor crafting. It breaks words into elements without meaning, forcing the reader to suspend comprehension between the end of one line and the beginning of the next, though we learn to anticipate words from the context of the sentence. The counter-argument is concerned, not with issues of reading and comprehension, but with the visual appearance of the layout. If no hyphenation is used the right-hand edge of the line may appear messy in ranged-left text when the text block is considered as a visual element within the spread. The deficiencies of the visual layout without hyphenation weighed against the deficiencies of the reading experience with hyphenation present a dilemma; in practice, designers must use experience to make a judgment determined by the nature and extent of the content in relation to the anticipated readership. For children's books, where reading abilities may vary considerably, hyphenation is not helpful. For the more experienced reader, however, it may not present a problem, though an excessive number of breaks is distracting.

In justified setting hyphenation is important as it allows the designer to regulate the inter-word space between lines. This prevents rivers of white space running through a text and lakes, or pools, being formed within the text.

How are words broken?

Within justified setting, word breaks visually improve the appearance of text on a page. In metal-setting, the editor or compositor would determine the word breaks. In Britain these were determined by etymology (the way the meaning of a word is formulated) and in the US by pronunciation. A spelling dictionary offers guidance in these matters, and many publishing houses have internal house styles, or house rules, which determine where specific words should break.

The same justified text set to a wider column (35mm) has some of the same deficiencies, but the spacing issues are significantly reduced.

The necessity of the H&J settings is clearly illustrated when a justified alignment is used in combination with a short measure (here 20mm) or narrow column that contains few characters and no hyphenation. There are insufficient word breaks to compensate for the short line length and the inter-word spacing becomes irregular. The white space between words begins to form rivers or pools within the text, which is spotty at best.

The necessity of the H&J settings is clearly illustrated when a justified alignment is used in combination with a short measure or narrow column that contains few characters and no hyphenation. There are insufficient word breaks to compensate for the short line length and the inter-word spacing becomes irregular. The white space between words begins to form rivers or pools within the text, which is spotty at best.

H & J word space and character space work in combination; adjustments to one have a direct visual effect upon the other. Broad tolerances between maximum and minimum word space percentages present words as dark spots separated by white space, while extremely tight tolerances in word space make it difficult to identify the word shapes on each line. Large tolerances within the maximum inter-character space have the effect of tracking a word, destroying the word shape; if coupled with tight inter-word spacing readability of the setting can be severely compromised.

Digital typesetting programs have incorporated simplified dictionaries for commonly used words that automatically determine the break point of a word. These basic defaults within a program can be edited by the designer, who can select the shortest word to be broken, the minimum number of characters before the break, and the minimum number of characters to occupy the next line after the break. However, these parameters should be discussed with the editor, because editorial factors are a major concern when it comes to the correct use of hyphenation.

Regulating the inter-word space

The type designer has already determined the inter-character and standard inter-word space within a font, but the book designer can override the default setting to control the maximum and minimum inter-word space. The American type designer Jonathan Hoefler describes the process of type design as follows: 'When you're designing a typeface, you are really making a product. You're building a machine that will go to make other products.' The typeface machine has therefore to be adapted to the individual purposes of each book by adjusting the spacing while retaining the integrity of the font. The book designer is able to control the variations in white space between words. The maximum and minimum space between words is expressed as a percentage and an optimum can be set. It is unusual to use more than 100 per cent, as the lines become spotty; slightly tightening the spacing within justified text presents a more unified line. The decision to control H&J settings should be considered in relation to the nature of the chosen font, weight, size, and line length.

Regulating the letter space

H&J settings can also be used to control the letter or inter-character space within a justified setting automatically. As with word space, this is expressed as a percentage maximum, minimum, and optimum.

H&J word space and character space work in combination; adjustments to one have a direct visual effect upon the other. Broad tolerances between maximum and minimum word-space percentages present words as dark spots separated by white space, while extremely tight tolerances in word space make it difficult to identify the word shapes on each line. Large tolerances within the maximum inter-character space have the effect of tracking a word and destroying the word shape. If coupled with tight inter-word spacing, readability of the setting can be severely compromised.

These changes to word and letter spacing have another significant effect on the way type is presented on the page. The 'colour' of the page changes according to the relationship between the black type and the white page: the wider the spacing, the lighter the colour on the page; the tighter the spacing, the darker the colour.

Many word-processing and typesetting programs allow the designer to adjust the vertical (here by 150%) and horizontal (here by 150%) relationship of the typeface. The proportions of the typeface are completely changed, but this is not a feature appropriate for regulating the space within justified setting. It has the effect of forcing the type to occupy more or less space, but completely destroys the integrity of the face. The inter-word space is now even in the setting as the variable character width is taking up the space, but the type character is being changed line by line.

Vertical space

Vertical space in hand-setting was determined by the size of type and the thickness of lead strips placed between lines of type (the origin of the term 'leading'). Leading was made and specified in point or didot sizes, half point being the smallest size, and larger measurements being built up out of smaller units. Metal type can be set without leading, this being referred to as 'set solid'. The space below the face of the letter on the first line, known as the beard, and the small space above the letter on the second line forms the white space between the lines. Here the 10pt type is set solid, 10 points on 10 points, which can be expressed 10pt/10pt.

Most text faces require leading, as white space between the lines clearly aids readability. Here 10pt type is set with 2 points of leading, which can be expressed as 10 on 12, or 10pt/12pt.

Typefaces with tall x-heights and therefore relatively short ascenders and descenders, or longer measures and wide columns, generally require more leading to create sufficient white space between lines. Here the type is set 11pt/14pt.

Metal type can be set without leading, this being referred to as 'set solid'. The space below the face of the letter on the first line, known as the beard, and the small space above the letter on the second line forms the white space between the lines. Here 10pt type is set solid, 10pt on 10points, which can be expressed10pt/10pt.

Most text faces require leading, as white space between the lines clearly aids readability. Here, 10pt type is set with 2 points of leading, which can be expressed as 10 on 12, or 10pt/12pt.

Left 10pt metal type set solid 10/10pt and with 2pt of leading 10/12pt leading. Here, the text is set in Baskerville like the digital version of the same words below it. Note that the exact shape of the letterforms will vary depending on the cut, foundry, and time of manufacture.

How do we make decisions about type size?

Decisions about type size should be made in relation to the nature of the readership, material, book, purpose, and format. It is often easiest to consider the main body of a text first, as this forms the bulk of the reading experience. Novels set for adult readers are normally set in sizes from 8.5 to 10pt, as this allows the eye to capture groups of letters easily, smoothing the reading process. Having chosen a font and type weight and considered such elements as format, size, and columns, it is helpful to set a short passage, perhaps a double-page spread, to the anticipated line length and then produce several versions set in different sizes. Positioning the text on the chosen or approximate format is helpful before printing out the versions. Most book designers find it difficult to make appropriate decisions about type sizes on screen, so high-quality printouts are important. Printing black on white gives the clearest impression of the type size. I always cut the page to size, as merely using a keyline to delineate the edge of the page gives a false impression of the expanse of white space in relation to text. If the text is to be produced in a colour or reversed out, it is likely that slightly larger point sizes will be required to achieve the same visual impact, and these can printed out at a high resolution before a final decision is made.

Most book pages contain more than a single size of type. The selection of these additional sizes combined with grid, typeface, and weight determines the typographic hierarchy. By setting a range of type sizes for elements such as headings, captions, footnotes, labels, and folios in relation to the main text, the designer can evaluate the relative visual importance of the elements. Headings are conventionally larger and often bolder than the main body of text, but smaller headings can be used to establish a hierarchy through the use of space, position, weight, and colour.

Modular scales to determine type size

A designer using a modular scale based on the Fibonacci series to determine format and grid may continue with this approach when selecting a range of type sizes. If the increments are considered to be too great, a second proportional scale can be developed from the first using any fraction: for example, a half-, third- or quarter-scale. As proportional scales are based on a common unit selected by the designer, such as millimetres, inches, or points, the page has an internal harmony in much the same way as the combination of notes within a single musical chord.

A simple Fibonacci scale using type size:

3 4 7 11 18 29 47

In this scheme, headings at 18pt perhaps work for chapter openers but are too large for subheadings. The main body copy set in 11pt determined by the scale is also too large, particularly as the secondary text for captions according to the scale is likely to be 7pt. The scale needs further increments and this can be done by developing a half-, third-, quarter- or fifth-scale, which will inevitably run into decimal points but is easily achieved through digital setting.

Combined scale and half-scale:

3 3.5 4 5.5 7 9 11 14.5 18 23.5 29 38 47

Using sizes selected from the combined scale and half-scale:

Major headings could be established at 14.5pt
subheadings at 11pt
body text at 9pt
and footnotes at 7pt

Combined scale, half- and quarter-scale:

3 3.25 3.5 3.75 4 4.75 5.5 6.25 7 8 9 10 10.5 10.75 11 12.75 14.5 16.25 18 20.75 23.5 26.25 29 33.5 38 42.5 47

Using sizes selected from the combined scale, half-scale, and quarter-scale, a more refined type-size hierarchy can be established:

Major headings could be established at 12.75pt
subheadings at 10.5pt
body text at 9pt
labels at 8pt
and footnotes at 7pt

It is important to remember that most typographic hierarchies make use of type size and type weight but may also use a change of font:

Major headings could be established at 12.75pt
subheadings at 10.5pt
body text at 9pt
labels at 8pt
and footnotes at 7pt

Type sizes within picture fields

Strict modernist grid structures in which the picture fields are divisible by the baseline grid offer less flexibility than the almost infinitely divisible proportional scales. The key practical constraints are the number of columns, which determines the line length; the increment of the baseline grid; and the number of lines per picture field.

When using a proportional scale to select the type size, it is the type that is harmonious, although the leading may also be defined by the scale; in contrast, the unifying element within a modernist grid is multiples of the baseline, and the type sizes may be unrelated.

Many designers make their decisions about type sizes without reference to a particular system and through experience develop an eye for the relative sizes of headings and text.

Type families: weight and width

A type family is a group of typefaces that usually share a common name and pattern, although are not necessarily drawn by the same designer. A font is a set of characters within a family. A font is likely to include ISO (International Organization for Standardization) Set 1, which consists of 256 characters linked to a standard keyboard layout: these will include capital (upper-case) and lower-case letters and accented characters, figures, punctuation, diphthongs, ampersand, and mathematical and monetary symbols. Expert sets may include non-aligning figures, fractions, and small capitals. Far larger sets will be required for some multilingual publishing and many typefaces may not have all the required characters for this purpose.

Below ISO Set 1, consisting of 256 characters. Enigma by Jeremy Tankard shows the basic character set. Note the Euro symbol, which has had to be added to many older book faces.

ENIGMA REGULAR

ABCDEFGHIJKLMNOPQRSTUVWXYZ
abcdefghijklmnopqrstuvwxyz&0123456789
ÆÁÀÂÄÃÄÅÇðÉÈÊËÍÌÎÏŁÑŒÓÒÔÖÕØÞšÚ
ÙÛÜýŸŽæáàâäãåçŁéèêëfiflíìîïŠñœóòôöõøþ
Ýßúùûüµýÿž¤£€$¢¥ƒ@©®™aº†‡§¶*!¡?¿.,;:
'‘"" ,„… '" ‹›«»()[]{}|/\--—_•´^~˙˚˜˘˝¨˝ ‹›
#%‰¼½¾=−+×÷~<>±≤≥¬°∧/.¦¹²³

When designing books, it is useful to select a family that offers a range of weights. Roman, italic, and bold are basics, but a light, a demi- or semi-bold, and compressed or extended forms can also be useful. Most typefaces are developed from a roman version that is redrawn to create other weights. The relationship between the roman and the subsequent weights in most older type families is not systematic. There may be an enormous leap in the relative weight between bold and black, and often the forms change significantly between weights. Many of these older type families are not the product of a single hand but have been redrawn in different cuts for different foundries through time. Adrian Frutiger (b. 1928), when designing Univers, addressed this problem. He planned Univers in 21 weights on a matrix that related both weight and width and used a logical numbering system to identify common line widths. The type family was developed from Univers 55 and shares the same line weight with five other forms, all prefaced 5. Lighter weights are prefaced 4 and 3 and heavier weights are prefaced 6, 7, and 8. The use of numerals rather than words supported Frutiger's universal vision for his font, as they are understood more widely throughout the world.

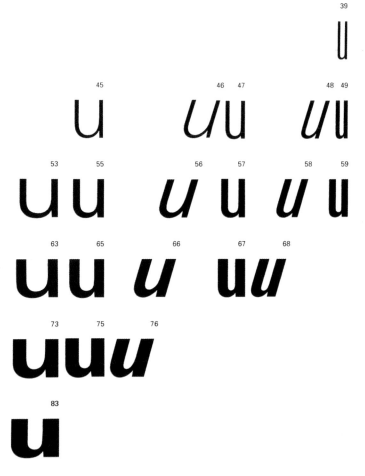

Left Univers Matrix by Adrian Frutiger, 1955. This example is taken from Willi Kunz's book *Typography: Macro- + Micro-Aesthetics*, in which Kunz explains why he consistently uses Univers.

Colour in book typography can refer to the colour of the ink used, or to the tonal values of a typeface, text often being referred to by printers as 'grey matter'. The tonal values of a face are determined by proportion and line weight; the more compressed or thick the line, the darker a font will look on the page. The tonal quality of the text is also affected by the horizontal space, the H&Js and the vertical space determined by a combination of x-height and the amount of leading. **Darker text blocks are brought forward, while lighter text blocks recede into the page. The tonal values separate the elements: for example, the main headings may appear slightly darker than body text, which in turn could appear darker than extended captions, or vice versa. The tone, or colour, of the type reinforces the hierarchy.**

Colour, contrast, and hierarchy

Colour in book typography can refer to the colour of the ink used, or to the tonal values of a typeface, text often being referred to by printers as 'grey matter'. The tonal values of a face are determined by proportion and line weight; the more compressed or thick the line, the darker a font will look on the page. The tonal quality of the text is also affected by the horizontal space, the H&Js, and the vertical space determined by a combination of x-height and the amount of leading. Darker text blocks are brought forward, while lighter text blocks recede into the page. The tonal values separate the elements: for example, the main headings may appear slightly darker than body text, which in turn could appear darker than extended captions, or vice versa. The tone, or colour, of the type reinforces the hierarchy.

Typeface

When choosing a typeface for a specific book, many issues influence the designer's decision, including the book's content, its origin or period when it was written, historical precedents, the readership, multilingual publishing, practical issues of legibility, the range of weights or small caps or fractions available in the font, and the anticipated production values.

Because of these variables, it is difficult to give definitive guidance on typeface selection, but it is worth examining a few positions that are frequently used to form the basis for a decision (and occasionally dogmatically clung to in periods of rationalization after the fact).

The type of nation

Many older composition manuals advise compositors to select type based on the nationality of the author – French type for French writers and so on. This historical throwback is derived from early printing when books were written, printed, and published in a single country. Typefaces became emblematic of nation and associated with the setting of a particular European language. Some designers continue to follow this tradition, sometimes through a sense of nationalism and sometimes merely embracing a historical precedent.

Type as ambassador of culture

Type designers through the ages have re-examined historical patterns from which to devise new forms. There are many examples of designers who have used the type within a book to promote and exemplify a set of cultural beliefs. In England, William Morris (1834–1896) and his associates in the Arts and Crafts Movement included book design, letterform, and typography in their revival of medieval craft-based traditions in opposition to what they regarded as dehumanizing industrialization. In 1890, Morris set up the Kelmscott Press, and book design and typography became the extension of his political and artistic vision: the selection of a typeface played an integral part as the visual embodiment of written ideas. For some designers today, the selection of a typeface is based on making visual that which is personal: the type is part of a canon of the designer's ideas.

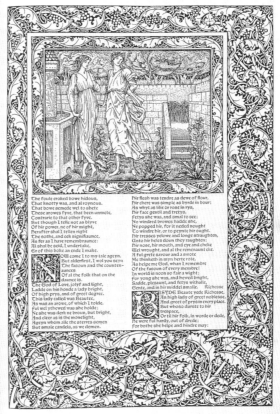

Type as historical plunder

William Morris's revival of medieval letterforms was born of an appreciation of early craft and a political ideology, and formed a lasting extension of his beliefs. Some designers today with a more irreverent sense of history make type selections of historical cuts purely on a visual basis. The plundering of historical letterforms may lead to the development of a book that is entirely in keeping with its subject. However, a designer who regularly adopts this strategy may be caught out through a lack of historical context, where an informed reader infers from the type a set of misleading associations. The plundering of historical forms has now become a quick fix against boring type for both book and type designers.

Type for today

For some designers, the revival of historical models is anathema; type should speak with the voice of today. Type, for them, is a product of the age and should reflect the new. This idea has occurred throughout the 550 years of type history. The Italian printer Giambattista Bodoni (1740–1813), for example, originally bought type from Pierre Fournier in France, but quickly sought to design forms that echoed the romanticism of his age, aiming for a light, sparkling effect that had many of the qualities of engraving. The new forms were visualized in Bodoni's *Manuale tipografico* (1818) and relied on significant

Above William Morris's *Kelmscott Chaucer* (1896) shows his interest in reviving medieval decorative traditions within book design.

new technical developments: improvements in casting, finer paper, new ink technology, and presses that offered greater pressure.

Today, many designers have adopted this principle and are constantly searching for the latest type developments. Designers' ever-growing demand for new forms, combined with the relative ease of digital type design and production and the online market, has promoted a flourishing of new fonts. The growth of type available on the Internet has increased the speed at which national barriers have broken down, and a kind of typographic globalization is under way. Old national stereotypes no longer apply when viewing type available online; a new geometric form is just as likely to have been drawn in Brasilia as Basle. The knock-on effect of this is seen in the design of books that can be difficult to place, in relation to cultural development, national identity, or design movements. Many type designers making their fonts available online have become tribal, forming like-minded clusters that transcend continents and exist independently of nation.

The type of internationalism

The German typographic pioneer Jan Tschichold believed that typography and book design should reflect the spirit of the age. In his ground-breaking book, *The New Typography* (1928) he encouraged designers to embrace new geometric forms that reflected the spirit of the machine age. Many early modernists, inspired by left-wing politics, saw design as a unifying agent that could aid in breaking down national divisions; typography that was an extension of national traditions was viewed as divisive. Ideas of internationalism re-emerged after the Second World War: typographically, this led to the development of fonts that sought a kind of visual neutrality, a typographic transparency. The designer became secondary to the information carried by font and book. Adrian Frutiger's Univers (1955) and the Swiss font Helvetica (1957) were examples of this new universal modernism. For some designers, such ideals of international modernism live on, and although the typefaces are far from literally modern (being 50 years old), they are chosen as emblems of modernism. Conversely, for many younger designers the fonts are perceived as belonging to another generation and no longer represent youthful modernist zeal. Typefaces, for them, do not have fixed meanings or associations.

The ideas the designer intends a typeface to allude to may not be shared by the reader, and certainly change through time. As books often outlive both author and designer, the reader may bring a set of ideas to both the text and the design from another decade or century. Book design is one of the few areas of graphics that shares with architecture a certain longevity: in choosing a font we make direct contact with every future reader of that edition, not merely the first buyer.

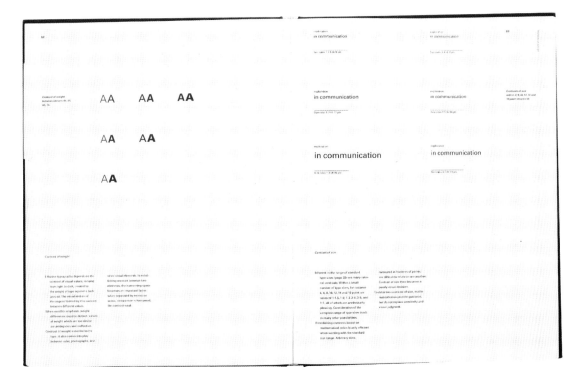

Unique message, unique font

The development of digital type combined with the search for the new has, over the last 15 years, prompted some designers to consider the possibility of developing type specifically for individual book or magazine projects. This requires a tremendous effort and long lead time; designing a typeface to reflect the specific content of a book is a time-consuming endeavour. Many designers and students in the early 1990s were inspired by this idea, although far more set out with this intention than ever realized a published book. However, it remains a possibility and seems to appeal to designers who are concerned by ideas of globalization. They wish to create each book with an individual voice derived from their interpretation of content. Type based on vernacular, regional letterform or on the author's handwriting has been used as the starting point for letterforms that resonate with content. The computer has become the servant of craft as well as a means of reassembling ready-made fonts. This approach has been most widely used in magazines about design issues such as *Emigre* and *Fuse*.

Above Willi Kunz's *Typography: Macro- + Micro-Aesthetics* (1998) uses Univers set on a rational grid, exemplifying the modernist vision of a common letterform for the whole world.

The type of content

Many designers link the choice of typeface with the subject-matter of the book, without seeking to impose a set of beliefs, national characteristics, or cultural or political ideals, nor buying into the most fashionable type. They consider such ideas an imposition on the book; for them, the typeface should reflect the content. This approach means that a designer may produce radically different books using a wide range of type. The designer who demonstrates adaptability through the body of work produced may not be instantly recognizable, but the choice of font, layout, and general feel of the book may more closely represent its content.

Type and the future

It is clear that type will continue to develop, and although we cannot accurately predict the form of fonts, some book types will continue to be based on historical patterns. A more radical vision for the type of the future is gained by extrapolating ideas based on combinations of technology. The computer provides a single platform on which books are written and designed, but it also has the capacity to process and edit sound. Speech-recognition systems are gradually improving, allowing sound to be transcribed directly into text. A sound interview can therefore become type without the use of a keyboard. Digital type for web and screen design can be animated in real time. Designers and programmers are increasingly looking to link speech with text in real time, not merely through frame-by-frame animation but through programming. A typeface can be adapted by an individual's voice pattern. While such technology is primarily designed for screen-based media, it could work equally well in books. The effect would be significant, as a typeface would reflect the expressive qualities of dialogue, accent, volume, speed, rhythm, and so on, and would visualize the author's or reader's interpretation of a text. This approach to text would significantly change our understanding of what typography is (modular lettering), returning the letterforms of a book to a calligraphic form in which no two letters were identical.

It is likely that keyboards and mice as we currently understand them will be superseded by voice-recognition systems linked to typesetting software, and this will ultimately change the way we write. The language codes of speech and writing will have meshed. Speech will directly influence the form of the written word. The potential for an author or an actor to set type through speech opens up new possibilities for the design of the book.

i was born in

manhattan

→ a really long time ago. incidentally, being born in **manhattan** is now OUT. manhattan isn't supposed to be hip any more. *

these **reverse** **snobs**

don't make tee shirts that say "manhattan." it's always "brooklyn."yeah, right! i say the hell with it. why pretend to be down to earth?

I feel sorry for people who come to new york and don't know anybody who lives here who could show them around.

manhattan is still what we think of when we say "new york."

i see them hanging around midtown, which is very **boring**, although that tour of radio city is pretty cool.

and you know it!

I WANT TO TAKE THEM TO THE PLACES I **REALLY** ♥ **LOVE** IN MY CITY.

THIS BOOK IS THE CLOSEST I COULD GET. a hundred guide books have ten thousand new york shops and restaurants. especially restaurants.

HOW CAN ANYBODY POSSIBLY TELL

?

and those

HIP

GUIDES are even worse.

all those TRENDY

design

all over the world, i

attract

you know, the museum cafe type.

i mean, WH

it's more fun to mix it up: and cheap places and hip ones a

this book is manhattan-cen and downtow

because that's what i know about. it isn't an accurate, fair, comprehensive guide at all. **it's personal.**

i once saw a poster from the 20s that said, "I HAVE FORGOTTEN TO FORGET-TOOTS PAKA." i have no idea what it was about but i have forgotten to forget it. i keep a list of everything i've forgotten to forget, plus addresses, telephone numbers and random thoughts that connect ...er in a right-brain, non-linear way. i ...ate my friends and keep track of appointments without using alphabetical order or page numbers, ...xplains a lot. i go by how the ...ok: the doodles and variations in ...g. i thought other people might want to ...rite in a book with stuff already in it. a ...s so scary! so i left out a few things to ...as of today, my list is 489 pages long ...doodles my father robert drew in ...and labels of all kinds, postcards or ...ed as rabbis, and the new york times ...georges de mestral, the man who ...ro. (what a sad day!)

NEW YORK

NotEbook

smushing IS AN INEVITABLE

TOGETHER

of a lifetime of living in new york plus juicy bits from these lists and different pieces of garbage i found particularly attractive. i hope you dig it. and if anybody knows anything about toots paka, please contact me at the earliest opportunity.

Type
Designers & programmers are wanting to link speech with text in real time.
a type of typeface :
in audio form (different voices !!!)
written printed on paper
screen based

The type of pragmatism: practical considerations

All of the approaches already identified form the context for pragmatic decisions. It is important to gain an insight into the book's content, although it is not necessary to read the whole book. Analysing the content in relation to a set of questions is helpful.

Questions to ask when selecting book type

- What is the book about?

- Who has written it?

- When was it written?

- Where is it set?

- For whom is it written; who will read it?

- Is it to be published in several languages?

- Is it a single text or are there several voices?

- Does the work include self-contained side stories?

- How are illustrations captioned?

- Is there significant quoted matter?

- Are there reference, foot-, shoulder- or source-notes?

- What is the hierarchy of chapters, headings, sections, and so on?

- Does the work include a foreword or introduction?

- Does the copy include extensive appendices?

- Is there significant tabular matter, or time charts?

- Is there a glossary of technical terms?

- How is it indexed?

- What are the production values, printing, paper stocks, binding?

- What tonal qualities has the type?

- What colour is the type to be reproduced?

- What is the anticipated retail price point?

Whatever the general approach to typeface selection, answers to these practical questions will prove extremely helpful. A designer starting out with the intention of designing a book using a single type family may find that the text includes many dates and fractions or lists of names. If the initial choice of font does not include an expert set or small caps, it may no longer be appropriate, forcing the designer to reconsider the choice of font or use a combination of faces.

Type and image III

Type and image

This section examines how text and image are used in a variety of ways to communicate a message to the reader. The discussion examines how the typographic palette and editorial structure link; how charts and diagrams are used to explain visual information; composition and page layout; and cover design.

Binding

Back cover
- Blurb (book description and promotion)
- Critics' quotes
- List of other titles in a series
- ISBN number
- Barcode
- Author's biography
- Image

Spine: Title, Author, Publisher's logo, Image

Cover
- Title
- Author's name
- Publisher's logo if not on back cover
- Blurb (book description and promotion)
- Critics' quotes
- Image

Endpapers
- Plain, printed flat colour, often decorative, sometimes with imagery or a motif derived from the book's content, sometimes typographic (as with atlases) used as a visual index

Frontmatter

Frontispiece (preliminary pages)
Right hand only;
Not always included in prelims
- Simple statement comprising author's name, title, publisher, and name of publication
- Image, often with no title

When appropriate: rights statement, copyright, Cataloguing in Publication CIP, *eg* British Library, Library of Congress, ISBN number, print details, *eg* printed in Milan (does not always name printer); these may appear in a separate entry following acknowledgments list; captions for cover and frontispiece if required

Title page (preliminary pages) Single right-hand page or working as a double-page spread
- Author's name
- Title and subtitle where appropriate
- Publisher
- Place of publication
- Year of publication
- Image

Contents page (preliminary pages)
- Title
- Contents
- Chapter numbers and titles
- Subsection titles and numerals
- Folio numbers: these may include preliminary pages making use of roman numerals, or occasionally letters
- All named elements of the book; may include preliminary pages but often starts the folios

---

Preface right hand
- Short statement of book's aims and origins or author's musings; may run over several pages

Foreword right hand
- Short statement of book's aims and origins or writer's musings; often written by someone other than the book's author

Possible **blank page** (particularly if foreword or preface finishes on a right-hand page)

Bibliography and recommended reading
- List of books, articles, papers, and websites
- To include author, title, publisher, date and place of publication, and sometimes ISBN
- Recommended reading; may give a short review of the subject

Appendix (endmatter)
- May include significant detailed information that relates to a specific chapter but is self-contained and is placed in the appendix so as not to disrupt the chapter flow

Index
- Credits and acknowledgments of picture sources, photographs, and illustrations
- Author's thanks to contributors, advisors, and editor
- Alternative position for dedication

Editorial structure

The elements of the typographic palette have specific functions within the layout of a book. This chapter examines how they are used in relation to the editorial content. Flatplans, such as the one shown below, are a useful device that help both editor and designer plan a book's layout and structure.

Blank page or pages (preliminary pages)
– Blind, unnumbered but frequently counted in the numbering scheme

Half-title (preliminary pages) Single right-hand page traditionally slightly understated as compared with title page, author's name in full, book title, subtitle where required, publisher's name, publisher's logo, place of publication, eg city: Berlin, London, New York, Sydney, volume number, traditionally may include decorative typographic elements, rules, etc. image, photograph, illustration, diagram, etc.

Title verso (left-hand page) (preliminary pages)
– May include the following when the title page is right-hand only, though the order of these elements varies: publisher's logo, publisher's name/co-publisher or in association with, etc date (year) of publication, copyright statement, publisher's postal address and postcode, publisher's contact details, eg telephone, fax, email, and website

Synopsis
– Rarely included in addition to a contents page; gives a breakdown of every page against a folio number

List of authors (may be found in endmatter)
– Often included in compilations of poetry or essays, usually listed alphabetically by surname

Dedication right hand
– Simple statement of the persons to whom the book is dedicated – often family or friends; may include dates for the deceased

Body of the book

Endmatter

Chapter opener right-hand page or double-page spread
– Chapter title; number sometimes roman
– Subheadings; sometimes with decimal numerals
– Quotation
– Image may include caption
– Folio number often omitted but actually very useful in finding chapter beginnings

Chapter close
– may include all of the previous elements
– single right-hand page/close on a left-hand
– double-page spread/close on the previous right-hand page:
– May include source-notes
– May include short bibliography
– May include picture lists, depending on editorial preference; alternatively these can be placed in the endmatter

Source-notes
– Sources and references may be positioned in the endmatter or at the end of each chapter

Above Individual books may have slightly different orders from this schematic flatplan, though the basic structure is likely to be similar.

Índice

Prólogo, por Alejandro Amenábar 7

El hombre que se negaba a amar, por Mateo Gil 9

Guión cinematográfico 11

Ficha artística 172

Datos de producción 172

Ficha técnica 173

Storyboard, por Sergio Rozas 174

Fotografías y bocetos 190

1   **2**

1 Contents page from *Mar Adentro* by Alejandro Amenábar and Mateo Gil. Numerals aligned right for the chapter headings are followed by a full point – a detail that contemporary practice might consider redundant. The chapter titles are then set in caps and small caps visually linked by evenly spaced dots aligned right like the page numbers.

2 The Spanish edition of Andreu Balius' *Type at Work: the Use of Type in Editorial Design* (2003), designed by the author. The contents page, or index as it is titled in Balius' book, takes the form of a flatplan or storyboard. The thumbnail spreads feature the section openers for each of the designers featured. Note that the folios for the spread are both on the right-hand page; *eg*, 10 · 11. This approach is appropriate for books that are visually led; one browses the contents as one browses the spreads, before dipping into the main text.

Contents

The contents page, or table, was traditionally a checklist for the printer as much as a guide for the reader. Signatures had to be collated in the correct order prior to stitching and case-binding, and the contents table enabled a printer to check the section order.

Conventionally, the contents occupies a right-hand page, although double-page spreads are often used, while works of reference may have an extended contents containing detailed chapter breakdowns.

Numerals or entry first?

Before laying out a contents page, a decision about the order of the headings and folios needs to be made. By putting the entry first, the emphasis is placed on the contents of the book, while putting the numerals first places the emphasis on the navigation system. Subheadings can be indented on separate lines beneath a main heading or run on in a different weight. Since all the chapter and section headings are likely to be of different line lengths, it is traditional to range right the folio numbers, possibly linking the two with a dotted rule or ellipsis points.

Contents and folios

Conventional numbering schemes for books use even numbers on the left-hand page and odd numbers on the right. Some publishers count the cover as page one and include endpapers and prelims in a single sequence through to the back cover, though the covers and prelims are 'blind' (folios not printed). Other schemes number from the right-hand half-title page. Many older books will have a separate numbering scheme for the preliminary pages making use

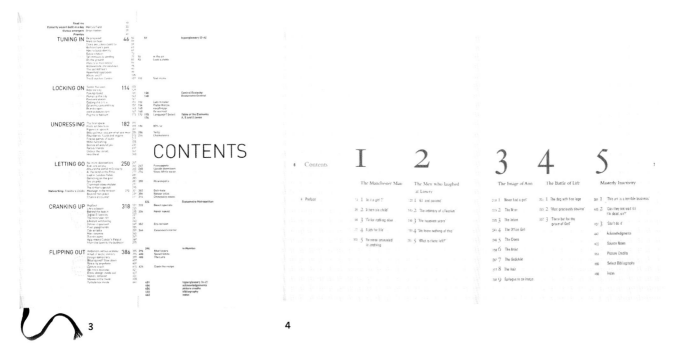

CONTENTS

Read me 17
Ecstacity wasn't built in a day Marcus Field 21
Status emergent Brian Hatton 29
Premise 41
TUNING IN Be prepared 46
Mark on heat
Class acts, class credit to
Architecture's pets
How to build identity
Ecco-criticism
Ten minutes to Landing
On the ground
Way's is in monastery'
Architecture, the volumes
The sacred heart
Hyperreal cityscapes
Whose job it?
The E-reaction Centre

LOCKING ON Tackle the town 114

UNDRESSING The final space 182

CONTENTS

LETTING GO No more decorations 250

CRANKING UP Redline 318

FLIPPING OUT 386

3   4

of Roman numerals or occasionally letters. This system is still used today by some publishers to allow editors, designers, and the production department to correct proofs while the indexer catalogues the contents and picture researchers finalize permissions.

Some technical books, manuals, and reports make extensive use of numeral coding and decimals as opposed to titles or headings to identify sections: for example, chapter five is 5, chapter five, part one is 5.1, and chapter five, part one, section three is 5.1.3. It is important that folio numbers are not confused with the section numerals.

Folios

Folios are generally found on every page of a book, the numbering sequence starting from 'one' on a right-hand page with 'two' and 'three' forming the first double-page spread. This pattern of even-numbered left-hand pages and odd-numbered right-hand pages continues throughout the book. Some designers number the right-hand pages only but retain the numbering sequence; others choose to print both numbers on the right-hand page. The initial signature may often make use of letters or Roman numerals. Folios can be placed anywhere on the page, though the outer margins are most often used. The placing of the folio should be in relation to the nature of the book and the scheme of the design. If the book has a single column of justified type, centring the folio at the base of the page is a convention but not a rule. If the book has many pages and is frequently accessed via the index, placing the page number adjacent to the heading may help the reader access information. Using a position half-way up the foredge margin allows readers to flick the pages and focus on the folio immediately above their thumb.

3 A complex layering system is used in the monograph *Guide to Ecstacity* (2003) featuring the work of architect Nigel Coates and designed by Why Not Associates. The page has many elements and may initially appear to have the unfathomable numeric complexity of some credit-card receipts, but does contain an inner logic and hierarchy. The titles and page numbers that relate to one another share a common size, weight, and colour, although the proximity of the column requires the reader to leap either forward or back across the page.

4 The simple double-page spread contents list designed by the author for *L.S. Lowry: A Biography* (2000) by Shelley Rohde uses a horizontal axis that relates to the position of the folios. The five parts of this two-colour book are identified with large Bembo doorstep-red numerals subdivided into chapters that use the same font in a smaller size. The folio number sits to the right of the chapter, and the chapter title to the right.

Part 3 Type and image

1   2

1 A chapter opener from *L.S. Lowry: A Biography* (2000) by Shelley Rohde uses the right-hand page. The chapter name and number are aligned with the folio numbers; this is helpful when moving from the contents to the chapter in a book that is likely to be used for academic purposes as well as reading for pleasure. The chapter parts are titled and numbered in a smaller type size and font that matches the running heads. Using a consistent hierarchy in terms of size and font throughout the book supports fluid reading.

2 The chapter dividers in *Colores digitales para Internet y otros medios de comunicación* by Carola Zwick, Burkard Schmitz and Kerstin Kuedhl (2003) uses a large dot-screen pattern for each of the double-page spreads.

'Magazines often make use of 'pull quotes,' enlarging a section of text to draw the reader into a particular article.'

Chapter openers

Chapters represent significant divisions within the editorial structure of a book. In many non-fiction books, each chapter is self-contained and may be read in an order determined by the reader. To make the start of a new chapter stand out, it is useful to give it visual significance. This may take the form of a double-page spread or a single right-hand page; left-hand pages generally work less well for this purpose, being hidden when flicking through a book.

Running heads

Running heads are usually placed at the head of the page, although they may also be found along the margins or at the foot of the page, as running feet.

Hierarchy of headings

Virtually all books make some use of headings, and reference and non-fiction books often include a hierarchy of headings. As part of the process of typeface selection, the designer should consider both the material's content and its form. Breaking a text down into sections signalled by headings aids readers in navigating their way through a book. Conventionally, headings are signalled by a new line, an increase in type size, or a change of typeface or weight.

Quotations

Quotations are a separate text element that can be signalled to the reader in a number of ways. Where the quote is relatively short, quotation marks can be used – conventionally single quote marks in Britain and double quote marks in the US, known as British style and American style, respectively.

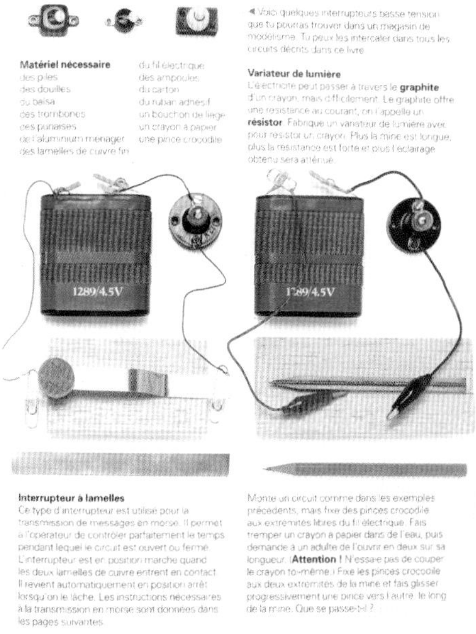

◀ Voici quelques interrupteurs basse tension que tu pourras trouver dans un magasin de modélisme. Tu peux les intercaler dans tous les circuits décrits dans ce livre.

Matériel nécessaire
des piles
des douilles
du balsa
des trombones
des punaises
de l'aluminium ménager
des lamelles de cuivre fin
du fil électrique
des ampoules
du carton
du ruban adhésif
un bouchon de liège
un crayon à papier
une pince crocodile

Variateur de lumière
L'électricité peut passer à travers le **graphite** d'un crayon, mais difficilement. Le graphite offre une résistance au courant, on l'appelle un **résistor**. Fabrique un variateur de lumière avec pour résistor un crayon. Plus la mine est longue, plus la résistance est forte et plus l'éclairage obtenu sera atténué.

1289/4.5V
1289/4.5V

Interrupteur à lamelles
Ce type d'interrupteur est utilisé pour la transmission de messages en morse. Il permet à l'opérateur de contrôler parfaitement le temps pendant lequel le circuit est ouvert ou fermé. L'interrupteur est en position marche quand les deux lamelles de cuivre entrent en contact. Il revient automatiquement en position arrêt lorsqu'on le lâche. Les instructions nécessaires à la transmission en morse sont données dans les pages suivantes.

Monte un circuit comme dans les exemples précédents, mais fixe des pinces crocodile aux extrémités libres du fil électrique. Fais tremper un crayon à papier dans de l'eau, puis demande à un adulte de l'ouvrir en deux sur sa longueur. (**Attention !** N'essaie pas de couper le crayon toi-même.) Fixe les pinces crocodile aux deux extrémités de la mine et fais glisser progressivement une pince vers l'autre, le long de la mine. Que se passe-t-il ?

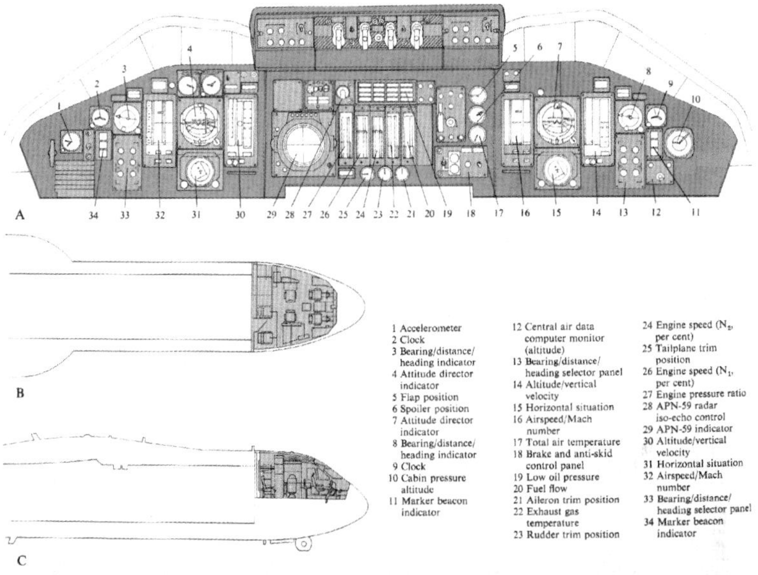
A
B
C
1 Accelerometer
2 Clock
3 Bearing/distance/ heading indicator
4 Attitude director indicator
5 Flap position
6 Spoiler position
7 Attitude director indicator
8 Bearing/distance/ heading indicator
9 Clock
10 Cabin pressure altitude
11 Marker beacon indicator
12 Central air data computer monitor (altitude)
13 Bearing/distance/ heading selector panel
14 Altitude/vertical velocity
15 Horizontal situation
16 Airspeed/Mach number
17 Total air temperature
18 Brake and anti-skid control panel
19 Low oil pressure
20 Fuel flow
21 Aileron trim position
22 Exhaust gas temperature
23 Rudder trim position
24 Engine speed (N_2, per cent)
25 Tailplane trim position
26 Engine speed (N_1, per cent)
27 Engine pressure ratio
28 APN-59 radar iso-echo control
29 APN-59 indicator
30 Altitude/vertical velocity
31 Horizontal situation
32 Airspeed/Mach number
33 Bearing/distance/ heading selector panel
34 Marker beacon indicator

3

4

Annotation

Most illustrations, photographs, diagrams, and maps within a book are likely to require some form of annotation such as a caption, label, or leader line. There are many editorial and design strategies to link text and image in this way. The following are some common approaches.

Plate and figure references

Older books in which the images are printed as separate sheets from the text do not use captions. The image is given a plate, figure number, or letter that is referred to in the text. Plate numbers are in decline, although some academic publications, art books, and exhibition catalogues that contain photographs printed as separate signatures make use of this system. If plate numbers are used, it is better to place the image after the text reference.

One image, one caption

The simplest captioning is to place the text description adjacent to the image using the baseline grid. It is not always necessary to use directionals (for example, 'above' or 'below'), as the text and image are grouped together.

Separating captions and image

The one-image, one-caption approach can also be used when the caption is divorced from the image. If a right-hand page image is full bleed, its caption on the left-hand page might begin with the directional 'opposite'. A double full-bleed spread can be captioned on the nearest possible page with a directional 'following page', 'preceding page', or 'overleaf'.

3 When creating the *Make it Work!* series of science books for children, it seemed most appropriate to adopt a one-image, one piece-of-supporting-text, or one-image, one-caption strategy. This page from *Make it Work! L'Electricité* (Sélection du Reader's Digest, 1995) uses a two-column grid with the image placed above its supporting text.

4 A detail from *The Lore of Flight* (BDD Promotional Books, 1990) shows how plate letters A, B, C, and label numbers 1–34 are used on the same page. The plate numbers are referred to in running text, indicating the appropriate image, while the numbers annotate a single illustration that would become cluttered by extended labels. Annotation strategies of this type require consistency of both alphabetic and numeric schemes. This caption has been written using a running scheme and the spread makes use of numeric as opposed to linguistic directors.

Linking text and image

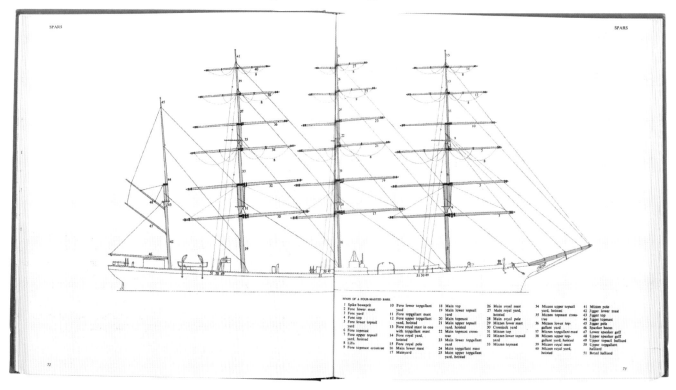

Above In this spread from *The Lore of Ships* (A.B.Nordbok, 1975), the labels on the diagram have been separated from the drawing and numbered. The drawing and the whole page is light and spacious. Thin leader lines would clearly have been in conflict with the fine line work of the rigging, and labels applied directly to the drawing would also have been disruptive. Reading the names requires the reader to refocus between the drawing and the label. Shortening the distance between the two elements while preserving the basic layout of a spread is always helpful.

The running caption

If the designer is looking to produce a very clean page that supports the reader's scrutiny of the images – perhaps for a monograph on paintings where extended captions beneath each image would clutter the layout – a single running caption column can be used. Directionals describe the position of the various images. Adopting the use of 'clockwise' and 'anti-clockwise', as favoured by some magazine editors, can be confusing; the use of numbers is far more succinct. The typographic detailing of a caption hierarchy is important; where there is space, each caption can start on a new line with a number. If the captions are to run on, emboldening or italicizing the numbers or directionals will conventionally denote the entry.

Captions over image

Captions can be run over or reversed out of an image – a system often used in magazines. There are several issues to consider when working in this way. In production terms, reversing type out of an image requires a separate set of plates for every new language. Therefore, if a book is designed with co-editions in mind, this will significantly raise the cost. Running black or a special colour over an image requires only a single plate change. Studying the image carefully is important, as text will be most readable on areas of the image that are consistent in both tone and colour. The tone of the type should be at least 30% different from that of the image it is reversed out of or printed on. Type reversed out of a colour should be relatively robust, with well-defined serifs and counters; this avoids letters being filled in by ink bleed.

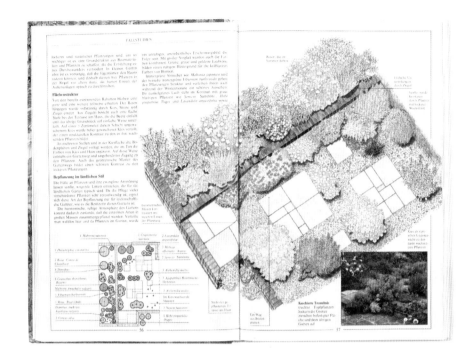

Left The German edition of John Brookes' *The Small Garden* (1989) includes bird's-eye illustrations of the planting schemes. A small schematic plan is used to identify the plant names. The reader is forced into a memory chain: look at the illustration, select a plant of interest, locate its position on the schematic plan, and follow the leader line to the plant name.

Caption lists

Some imagery requires a list of names to identify all the members of the group: for example, a school photograph may have a word list divided into sections: top row left, middle row left, seated, and so on. If the rows have several hundred people, however, this approach is impractical. Numbers can be added to the photograph, although this often detracts from the image; another approach is to make a small numbered line diagram linked to the caption.

Labels

Many diagrams, illustrations, or photographs will require labels to identify parts of the image. One approach is to add labels directly to the image, and this may work with a few labels and a simple diagram. If the word labels are too long and intrusive, numbers can be used as they occupy less space.

Leader lines can be used to point from the label to a specific element. These should generally be a different weight to the lines of the diagram and do not usually require arrow-heads. Generally the text and the line should have a consistent relationship: for example, the line should emanate from the type baseline, be centred on the cap height, and so on. The space between the label and the line should also be consistent.

Some designers have attempted to create labelling systems in which the leader lines move from the text labels at a common angle so that all the labels sit on the baseline grid; this apparently logical thinking often backfires, as the use of many leader lines forms a visual structure that then assumes greater prominence than the diagram itself. An alternative strategy in situations requiring hundreds of labels, such as anatomical or engineering diagrams, can be to use leader lines with numbers.

Foot-, shoulder-, source- and endnotes

Footnotes are placed at the bottom of the page and shoulder-notes[A] on the margins of the page. Source-notes cite the source of ideas that are referred to in the text but are not directly quoted. These can be placed at the base of the page, at the end of a chapter, or at the back of a book, where generic reference material is referred to as endnotes. Such references, commonly used in non-fiction and academic writing, require the addition of reference numbers in the text, and small numbers, letters, or symbols, printed in superscript, are used to identify the reference point throughout the main body of the text. If there are few reference points, standard characters can be used, such as an asterisk ★, a dagger †, and a double dagger ‡. Where numbers are used, they usually start afresh at the beginning of each chapter. Where footnotes and source-notes are to be used in combination, letters are adopted for one and numerals for the other. Careful crafting of the size in relation to the body text is required. Where these sources are extremely important, a bold number that produces a dark spot on the page will draw the reader's attention. This is sometimes used in academic papers where debate is focused around different intellectual ideas. Generally, the numerals can be secondary and, therefore, visually lighter than the body copy, as they really only have relevance for the reader at the end of a sentence. Some designers merely halve the point size and use numerals in the same font. Matching the space between the x-height and the cap height looks more considered, but is not always practical if the type is small and the x-height large.

   – Reference numeral half type size:[1] (here 5.5pts)
   – Reference numeral between cap and x-height:[2] (here 5pts relating to the ascender height)
   – If the font has short ascenders, a second colour could be used or the reference numeral enlarged to work between cap and x-height: [3]

Verse numbers

Bibles have used reference numbers for verses since Robert Estienne first printed a French Bible in Geneva in 1588. Verse numbers are helpful when identifying the beginning of a public reading, as they allow a congregation to find the passage. This approach to sequentially numbering the parts of a chapter is also used within some legal works and scientific reports. The verse numbers in some settings of the Bible stand outside the text in a separate column and are much more easily found than those integrated within the text. In most modern Bibles, the Psalms, which are often sung, have numbers separate from the text, which is set as verse rather than prose.

† Footnotes are placed at the bottom of the page.

Colophon

The colophon, which gives information about the author, publisher, and edition dates, is often found at the end of older books, but today may be printed at the front of the book before the half-title or at the end to form the final piece of endmatter.

Glossary

The glossary of technical terms found at the back of many non-fiction books is usually organized alphabetically, though some scientific books with an extensive glossary use alphabetical listings that group together words relevant to each chapter. As with any typographic listing, identifying the entry and separating it from the definition is important. This is often done by weight or the use of caps. Some books make use of a line break; others assign a line to the entry title in the manner of a heading.

Index

The indexing of a book cannot be completed until the pages have been laid out. The contents page at the beginning of a book gives the reader an overview of the structure, while the index allows the reader to hunt down specific text and image references. The indexer is briefed by the editor about the level of detail that is required for the title and then works through the layouts identifying key words and their folio numbers. Images are indexed by title. Many indexers and designers identify a page reference as an image by changing the typographic style of the folio numbers, thereby enabling the reader quickly to spot illustrations.

Above The verse numbers in this Italian Bible are ranged left rather than integrated within the text. As the passage in Psalms is poetry that is often sung, it is set line for line. The footnotes at the base of the page are cross-references to other books, chapters, and verses that are related.

Identification: using visual clues

1 A spread from *Fugle i Felten* (1999), showing birds of prey in flight, portrays the birds from the observer's viewpoint below. It shows the silhouettes and the plumage markings in juveniles and adults, all helpfully drawn to a common scale. Male and female birds are identified by a symbol adjacent to the drawing.

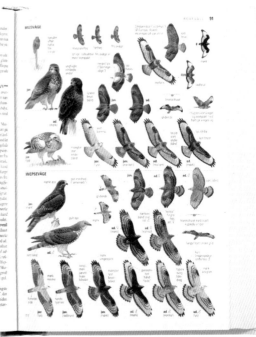

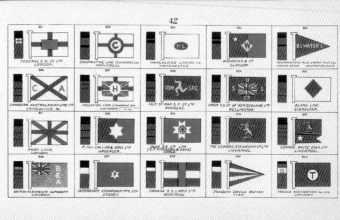

1

2

2 *Brown's Flags and Funnels* (1951) records the livery of merchant ships. The images are organized by the predominant colour of the funnel – on this page, red. This is key to the reader's successful identification; it allows all the red funnels to be compared quickly, which would not be possible if the images were arranged alphabetically. The book is arranged by what the sailor would observe when at sea. The book anticipates the chain of confirmation: 'I see a ship with a red funnel', find section with red funnel, 'The funnel has a black top and the flag is a red triangle'.

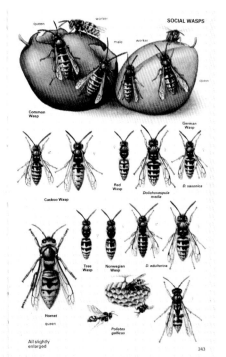

3 The *Collins Guide to Insects* (1991) by Michael Chinery shows the importance of reproducing accurate markings to aid identification in a spread titled 'Social Wasps'. The nine types of wasp are identified by minor variations in facial markings shown real size down the left-hand page. All the wasps are drawn to the same scale and reproduced actual size. Symbols are used to identify male and female.

4 This Japanese guide to Tokyo includes a series of schematic subway diagrams that are colour-coded to show which carriages are closest to the exit or where to alight when changing to another line. The stations are listed to the left of the diagrams. Passengers can thus improve the efficiency of their journeys.

Charts and graphs

Many non-fiction books contain numeric information that supports or illustrates the author's ideas. Charts and graphs make visual relationships that, when presented in tables, take time to decode. Readers are quickly able to identify patterns, order, and proportion within a chart. There are a number of conventions for presenting summative numeric information, numeric ranges, percentages, and special information, which this section will briefly examine.

Bar charts: comparing numeric quantities

Bar charts, or histograms, are used for comparing information of the same type. The numeric information is summative to specific data, though a set of bar charts can be used to show change. They can be arranged either vertically or horizontally and consist of a scale along one axis and categories along the other. The scale should consist of even increments and be continuous. Bar charts rarely require a frame and may not need a vertical rule.

Drawing bar charts

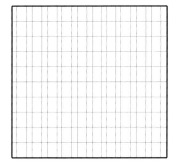

1 All bar charts are plotted on a grid structure that characteristically defines the numeric intervals up the vertical axis and classification listings along the horizontal axis. The grid increments should be defined in relation to the range of the anticipated data.

2 The increments on the vertical axis should be sufficiently large so that subtle differences in the height of the data bars is visible. If the comparable data is large *eg* 5–500, the increments may need to be reduced in size.

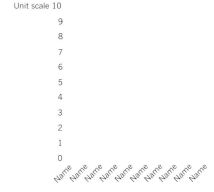

3 The arrangement of the chart's annotation should be subtle. The size of the type should not upstage the data, but needs to carefully aligned with the numeric increments up the vertical scale and the classification along the horizontal scale. Aligning the labels right at 45° links type to data.

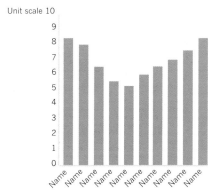

4 The bar chart can be visually refined by softening the tonal contrast between grid (here 20%), the data bar (here 50%), and the annotation (here 100%).

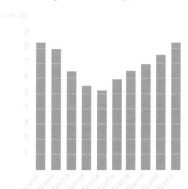

5 Further refinements can be made to the chart by removing the grid and vertical and horizontal axes and making the labels tints in order to improve visual clarity.

Box plots: identifying numeric range

A box plot, like a simple bar chart, presents data in a linear form plotted against an incremental axis, with a second axis used to identify the type of information. The plot can be represented vertically or horizontally. The box plot defines maximum and minimum values, quartile values, median values, and the inter-quartile range.

minimum   quartile   median   quartile   maximum

Pie charts: proportions of the whole

Pie charts visually present information as a slice of the whole. The 360° of the circle represents 100%; 180° represents half or 50%; 90° represents 25%; 36° represents 10%. Pie charts present summative information through a series of charts and can illustrate the passage of time. They are best represented as a circle, rather than inclined to form an ellipse, where the relative surface areas of the divisions become distorted. As with most forms of statistical presentation, identifying the slices of the pie using patterns is distracting. Subtle colours are generally more effective, though some statisticians argue that dominant colours attract the eye to a particular section and therefore influence the viewer's initial reading of the chart.

Drawing a pie chart

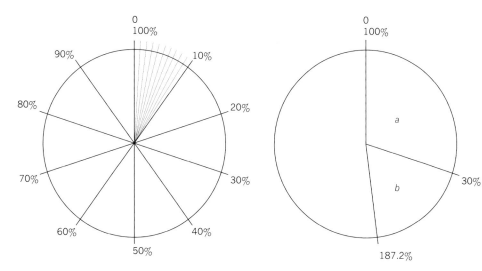

1 A simple pie chart grid divides a circle into percentages of the whole. As a circle can be divided into 360°, 1% is equal to 3.6°; therefore, 10% is equal to 36°.

2 The designer establishes the width of the 'pie sections' by multiplying the percentage by 3.6°. For example, 30% x 3.6° = 108° (a) and 22% x 3.6° = 79.2° (b). To establish the position of the next segment, 79.2° is added to 108° = 187.2°.

Line graphs: numeric quantities over time

Line graphs are used to show development over time. They can be oriented vertically or horizontally, though conventionally they run across the width of the page. In theory they can run on for ever. Unlike either bar or pie charts, they show both the present and a historical development. The link between present and past allows statisticians to extrapolate information and make forecasts about the future. Crudely, if an annual line graph measuring umbrella sales records a steep upturn from November to April and then declines gradually until the following November, and this is repeated over three years, creating a recognizable wave form, a similar pattern can be anticipated over the fourth year. Line graphs showing the development of a single information strand are very simple, but the same grid structure can be used to show several pieces of information relative to one another over time.

A simple line graph can also be used to record the positions of items or people relative to one another over time. A music chart could be drawn to trace the rise and fall of a number-one single. This could be repeated weekly for the top 100 and, over time, certain records would rise as others fell away to be replaced by new releases. Many machine plotters present information as a line graph and their outputs can be used immediately; examples include a heart monitor, a seismograph for measuring earthquakes, and a lie detector.

Right This diagram from the *AA Book of the Car* (1970) shows how tiredness can affect driving. Across the top of the page is a schematic drawing of a road. Below this are two line graphs. The upper one shows the driver's blood pressure up the left edge of the chart; the lower one shows the driver's heart rate. The vertical lines relate the two line graphs to the road situation. The paler brown line on the chart represents the driver's blood pressure and heart rate under normal conditions; the black line represents the stress of sitting in a traffic jam.

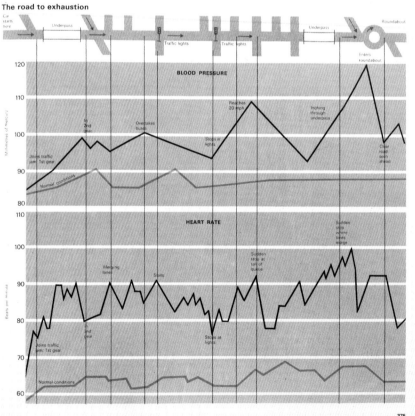

The road to exhaustion

375

Scatter plots: density and frequency

Scatter plots enable types of information to be compared. The grouping of information clusters indicates the type of correlation between two sets of data, such as the correlation between a rise in outside temperature and ice-cream sales. A positive correlation is indicated as the increase in one set of data matches the other. By contrast, the correlation between a rise in outside temperature and sales of hot drinks is a negative correlation, which is shown when two sets of data meet at a crossover point, one increasing as the other decreases. In contrast, there is no correlation between a rise in outside temperature and dog-food sales. The line of best fit represents the general direction of the plotted points on a scatter diagram.

Time lines: representing history

A simple time line shows a single sequence of events documenting order in relation to time. Time lines characteristically run across the page, but can work vertically. Scales can be drawn to represent different periods, from geological time to the speed of sound. Complex time lines allow the reader to compare the timing of events. They can contain systems of grouping: for example, a time line of twentieth-century art could list the artists in groups by movement or by nationality or even both with the use of a coding system. Many diagrams of this type are illustrated and it is important to align the illustration and the annotation consistently with each entry, or the visual impression of contemporary issues becomes distorted. A consistent scale on which the data are plotted ensures that all information is comparable. However, this is not always possible, as the number of data entries for each period may be inconsistent, meaning that part of the scale becomes overwhelmed while another is empty. Plotting information that has an annual cycle, such as crop planting, can be represented on a circular time line. This shape prevents easy comparison but is very succinct when referencing the phases of a single entry.

The graphic schedule: representing time and distance

Conventional railway timetables present typographic information as numerals within a matrix. An alternative form of timetable is the graphic schedule invented by Charles Ydry, a French engineer from Paris. Ydry's invention visualizes both time and distance. The graphic timetable shows the departure and arrival times and also provides a visual commentary of relative speed and the distance between stations. The approach was considered overly complex for use by the general public, but was adopted by railway companies throughout the world as a means of planning schedules.

Representing time visually

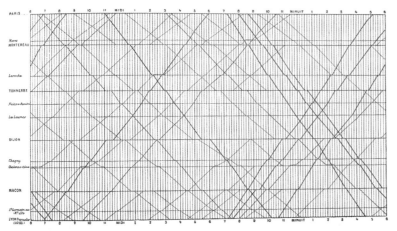

1

1 The Marey Schedule represents time across the top horizontal axis. The vertical axis records the relative distance between stations. Diagonal lines indicating a train's movements run from top left across the time/distance grid. The steeper and shorter the line between stations, the faster the train; the shallower and longer the diagonal, the slower the train. If a train stops at a station, the line is drawn horizontally, representing the passage of time but not distance. If two diagonal lines descending the page cross, the later train has overtaken an earlier train.

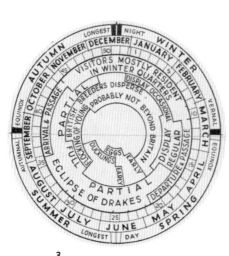

2

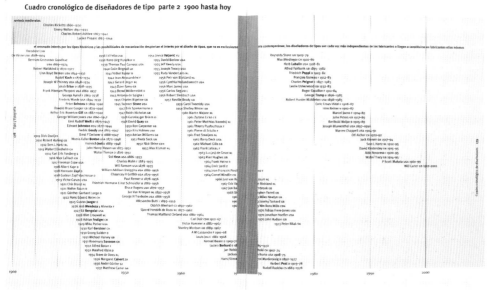

3

2 A 1951 Pelican publication, *Bird Recognition* by James Fisher, has a diagram representing a year as a circle.

3 (detail of 2) The circle is reproduced actual size (57mm wide); it has 69 words annotating the sections that represent discrete activities. The base grid for the diagram is 12 concentric circles divided into 52 weeks of the year. Starting from the outer circle: 1 represents the four seasons and is marked with the longest and shortest days; 2 represents the months; 3 the weeks; 4/5 plumage description for summer and winter; 6 migration arrival and departure dates; 7, 8, and 9 egg hatching and rearing young.

4 From the Spanish edition of *Type and Typography*, this timeline plots type designers' birthdays. The 50 years on the left-hand page (1900 to 1950) are drawn at one scale; the decades from 1950 onward are drawn against larger increments. The data are divided into two types: names of the deceased are plotted by date of death and aligned to the left of the plot. Names of the living are plotted by birth and aligned to the right. This strategy enables 148 names and dates to be compressed onto one spread while retaining visual clarity.

Geographical projections: representing area visually

Cartographers have attempted to solve the problem of how to represent a three-dimensional globe on a two-dimensional surface through a variety of different types of drawing known as 'projections'. The three-dimensional surface of a globe cannot be peeled away as a flat continuous sheet. Only by dividing the globe into flattened segments, or gores, can a map be drawn on a two-dimensional surface.

The word 'projection' relates to a light source, and the principle of projection drawings is to imagine the shadows made on a flat sheet of paper by a focused light source projected through the lines of longitude and latitude. Simply put, a range of projections is produced by placing the light source and the flat sheets in different positions in relation to the globe. For example, the tangent cylinder is drawn by placing the imaginary light source in the centre of the globe and wrapping the sheet of paper around the sphere so that it touches at the circumference, or equator. A secant cylinder is produced in the same way, although the cylinder penetrates the sphere.

All projections distort the presentation of the globe in some way. No projection preserves all the features of the globe: distances, bearings (directions expressed in degrees), and area. All projections retain only one of the three key qualities: equidistance, conformality (directions true to globe) or equivalence (area true to globe). Some projections have none of these qualities and are referred to as 'conventional', but it is more helpful to refer to them by their particular characteristics, for example, 'minimum error'. Cartographers, realizing the relative strengths and weaknesses of certain projections, have begun to combine projections, which are then referred to as 'hybrid projections'.

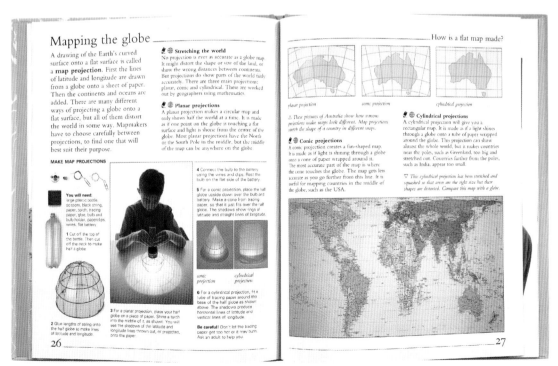

Left This spread from *Make it Work! Geography: Maps*, by the author and Barbara Taylor, shows the principles of geographic projections representing a three-dimensional world in two dimensions. Lines of longitude and latitude, shown by cotton threads, are glued to the outside of half a sphere, representing the globe; a torch projects light from the centre of the sphere, casting shadows to create a planar projection.

Below *The State of the World Atlas* (1981), written and designed by Michael Kidron, uses the world map as a basis to compare national assets: minerals, water, wealth, and so on. Kidron scaled up or down the area of a country to reflect the data and then simplified the geographic borders and coastlines to retain a schematic representation of the world map.

Using map projections

Selecting a map projection for a particular purpose or book must be undertaken carefully and most publishers seek advice from specialist cartographers. As the editor of the 1982 edition of the *Times Atlas* wrote, 'An atlas is a series of compromises in the choice of area, scale and projection of the maps included in it. Rigid uniformity in scales and projections, though desirable in theory, can provide undesirable results.'

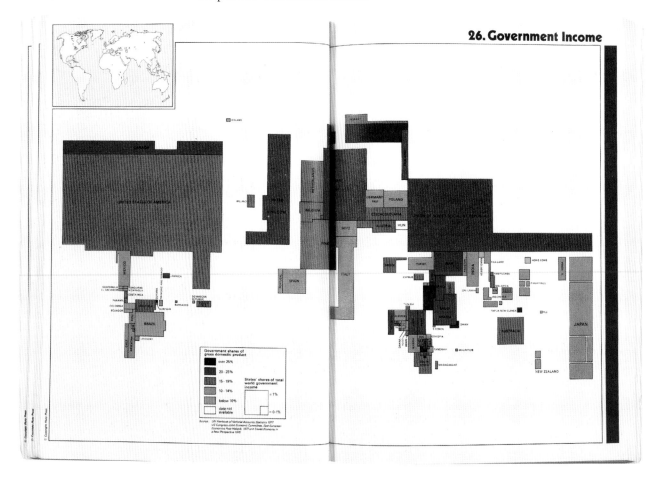

Types of projection

The Mercator projection is referred to as the navigators' projection. The longitudes and latitudes are arranged in a geometric grid at 90º. It is a conformal projection and its special characteristic is that bearings can be plotted as straight lines.

Gall's projection is neither conformal nor equal area and its special characteristic is that it reduces the distortion of northern latitudes when compared with Mercator's projection. The scale is true to globe at 45º north and south.

The Sinusoidal (Sanson-Flamsteed) projection is equivalent, showing the area occupied by land masses and oceans true to globe.

The Mollweide projection is equivalent, showing the area occupied by land masses and oceans true to globe, with the longitudinal meridians (circles of the circumference of the globe) drawn as ellipses.

The Hammer (Hammer-Aitoff) projection is equivalent, showing the area occupied by land masses and oceans true to globe. Unlike the Mollweide projection the lines of latitude are drawn as curves rather than straight, which produces less distortion at the outer edges of the drawing.

Bartholomew's Regional projection is an interrupted projection, dividing the globe into gores yet retaining a continuity within the land mass.

Bartholomew's 'The Times projection' presents the meridians of longitude as increasingly curved lines radiating from 0º longitude and the parallels as straight lines. It was drawn to minimize the distortions in area created by cylindrical projections while principally retaining the rectangular format.

The Dymaxion projection The mathematician and designer R. Buckminster Fuller developed a projection of the world based on a 20-sided triangular-faced polygon termed a 'dymaxion'. This representation of the globe could quickly be assembled from the flat net to a three-dimensional form and was one of many outcomes of Fuller's investigations into geodesic structures.

Mercator projection

This is the navigator's projection and the most renowned of all projections. It is conformal and its special merit is that lines of constant bearing (loxodromes) or compass bearings (rhumb lines) plot as straight lines. Since great circles other than meridians and the equator are curves in the Mercator projection a great circle route cannot be plotted directly but it can be transferred from a gnomonic projection and then divided into rhumb lines.

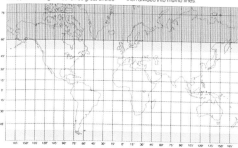

Gall's Stereographic projection

This projection is a stereographic projection from an antipodal point on the equator, on to a cylinder which cuts the Earth at 45°N and 45°S. It is easy to construct and has been widely used for world maps including those showing distribution data. The projection is neither conformal nor equal-area. Its principal merit it that it reduces greatly the distortion in northern latitudes of Mercator's projection, scale being true at 45° latitude N. & S.

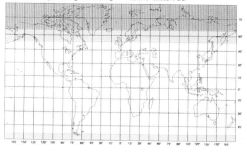

Sinusoidal (Sanson-Flamsteed) projection

This projection is equal-area and is a special case of the Bonne projection in which the standard parallel is the equator made true to scale. The central meridian is half the length of the equator and at right angles to it. Parallels are straight parallel lines, equally spaced and equally subdivided. Meridians are curves drawn through the subdivisions of the parallels.

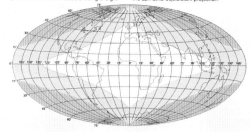

Mollweide projection

In this equal-area projection the central meridian is a straight line at right angles to the equator and all other parallels, all of which are straight lines subdivided equally. The spacing of the parallels is derived mathematically from the fact that the meridians 90° east and west of the central meridian form a circle equal in area to a hemisphere. Meridians are curves drawn through the subdivisions of the parallels. Except for the central meridian, they are all ellipses.

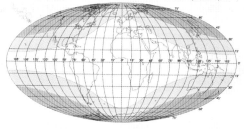

Hammer (Hammer-Aitoff) projection

This equal-area projection is developed from the Lambert azimuthal equal-area but with the equator doubled in length and with the central meridian remaining the same. Because the parallels are curved instead of being straight and parallel there is less distortion of shape at the outer limits of a world map than in the similar-looking Mollweide. This projection has been wrongly named Aitoff's. Aitoff is based on the azimuthal equidistant projection.

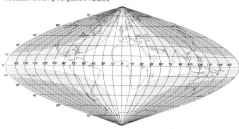

Bartholomew's Nordic projection

This projection is equal area. It is an oblique case of the Hammer projection which is a development of the Lambert azimuthal equal-area. The main axis of the Nordic projection is an oblique great circle passing through 45°N and 45°S. Its equal-area property makes it a particularly well suited to the depiction of such data in the temperate latitude zones and the circum polar areas.

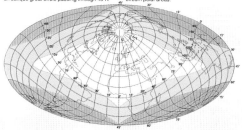

Bartholomew's Regional projection

An interrupted projection which aims to combine conformal properties with equal-area as far as possible. It emphasizes the north temperate zone, the main area of world development. From a cone cutting the globe along two selected parallels symmetrical gores complete the coverage of the Earth. In this modified example Pacific Ocean overlap usually included, has been eliminated to show land areas to the best advantage.

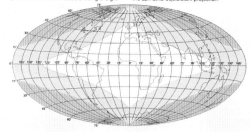

Bartholomew's 'The Times' projection

This projection was designed to reduce the distortions in area and shape which are inherent in cylindrical projections, whilst at the same time, achieving an approximately rectangular shape overall. It falls in the category of pseudo-conical. Parallels are projected stereographically as in Gall's projection. The meridians are less curved than the sine curves of the sinusoidal projection. Scale is preserved at latitudes 45°N and 45°S.

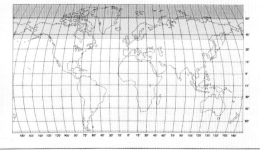

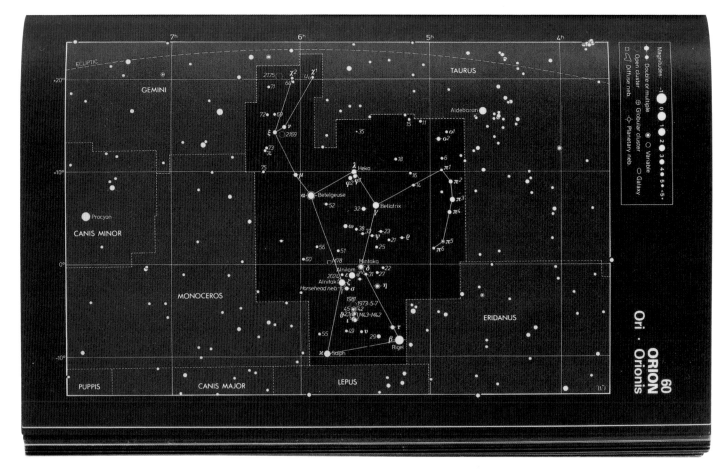

Above A map of the stars from *Collins' The Night Sky/Guide to Stars and Planets* (1984) shows the position of each of the stars relative to one another but cannot represent time or distance from the earth using this projection. The stars are represented by different-sized dots; these do not relate to the size of the stars but classify their brightness or magnitude – the larger the star, the brighter it appears in the night sky.

Mapping space

Astronomers face similar problems to landscape cartographers when attempting to represent the night sky. They have developed charts based on the premise that the night sky takes the form of a large ball containing a smaller ball, the Earth. For the reader, the star map appears to be plotted as points on the inner surface of the large ball viewed from the small ball. In reality, the sky is divided by astronomers into geometric shapes that reflect groups of stars, and these geometric shapes extend out into space infinitely. They are plotted on two circles, one for the stars viewed from the northern hemisphere, and one for the southern hemisphere. A strip referred to as the equatorial zone plots stars visible from the equator. Stars of differing magnitude (brightness) are indicated by the size of the dot, 0 being the brightest star and 5 the dullest. Some star maps use colours to indicate the temperature of stars.

Diagrams that represent relationships

Statisticians have developed and borrowed a range of diagrams that visually present the relationships among elements or groups of elements. These can be very useful to the reader providing they are familiar with the particular diagrammatic convention; they are useful to the author and designer as relationships between elements do not have to be numerically or linguistically described as their internal patterns can be visualized.

Venn diagrams

A Venn diagram shows the relationship between groups of elements. Circles are conventionally used to define the groups, though ellipses or other geometric shapes are occasionally incorporated. Each circle represents a single group of information, and the area where they overlap contains elements common to both groups. The number of groupings represented by circles can in theory be infinite, though the size of the diagram and need to identify the overlapping forms limits the number of groups.

Below The circles in a Venn diagram group common elements or ideas. The content of each circle is determined by a *rule*. Here, the first circle groups together circles by the simple rule 'circle'. In a similar way, the centre diagram adheres to the rule 'square'. The third diagram, in which the two previous circles overlap, illustrates the first two rules, and in the overlap a new rule, that of 'small shapes', containing small circles and small squares, is established.

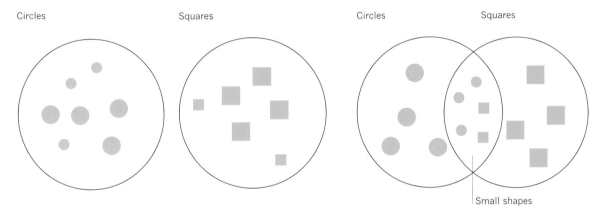

Circles   Squares   Circles   Squares

Small shapes

Mapping diagram

A mapping diagram, like a Venn diagram, presents relationships either as words or as numerical values. Mapping diagrams indicate the relationship between data using line. They are used to sort information mathematically into groups.

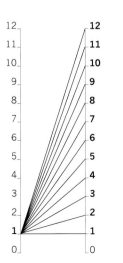
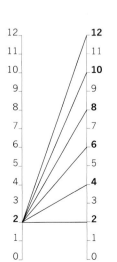
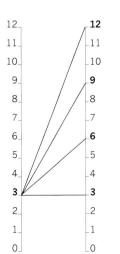
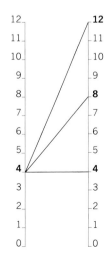

Left a series of mapping diagrams showing the factors of 12 (1, 2, 3, 4). By using bold type for the labels of connecting increments, the relationships are visually reinforced. This form of diagram can be used to show links between numbers or linguistic connections.

Right This tree diagram, printed as a gatefold from *Heraldry Sources, Symbols, and Meaning* by Ottfried Neubecker (1976), illustrates part of the French monarch's family tree. Successive generations are placed in rows, although only the line of male succession to the throne is followed.

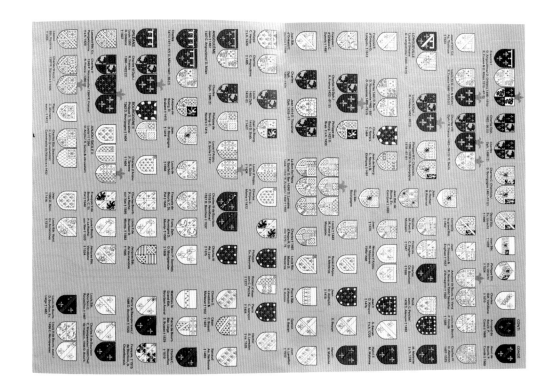

Right An inverted tree diagram can be used to analyze the components of an information field, successively breaking down the elements into its constituent structure. Unlike the family tree above, this information field, from the Spanish edition of *Type and Typography* (see p. 118), is self-contained. A single sentence is broken down into its grammatical parts, which are labelled to define function and class.

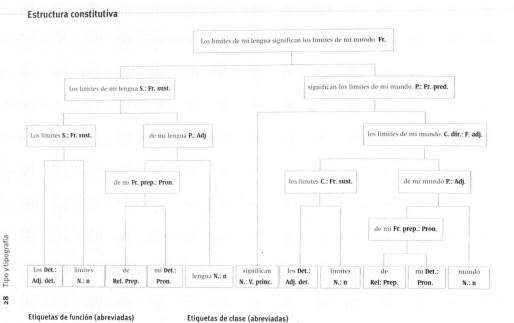

28   Tipo y tipografía

Estructura constitutiva

Tree diagrams

Tree diagrams lay out information by showing how objects, ideas, or people relate to or are derived from one another. A family tree is probably the most obvious example. The tree in this form is inverted, with the various branches growing out from the node points representing the union of parents. The tree diagram can be used to show relationships between styles of music or philosophy, artistic schools, and so on.

This type of diagram is illustrating additive information; each new generation adds to the diagram's complexity. Additive diagrams can grow with every generation and, depending on the width or height of the page, can be accommodated in books. The same diagram can represent reductive information, where the whole is broken down into its constituent parts from the top of the page. Diagrams of this type can be used to demonstrate analytical thinking that allows the reader to identify the constituent parts of information.

Linear diagrams

Linear diagrams are not maps, as they represent the relationship between points or nodes and not their geographical position. Colour-coding is frequently used as it allows the reader to follow the linear paths through the sequence of intersections. Electrical circuits, plumbing layouts, and subway and rail networks are presented in this way.

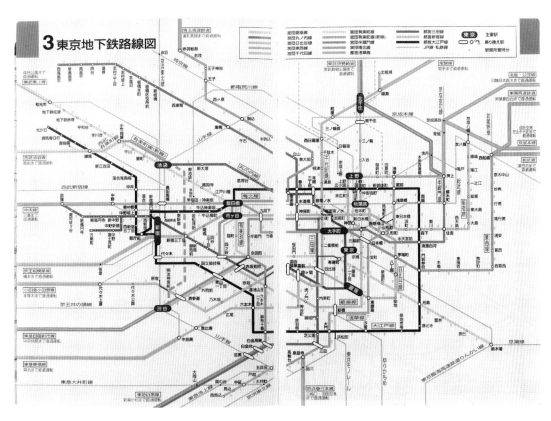

Left The Tokyo subway diagram shows the relationship between the order of each station on the line. Colour-coding is used to identify the lines. The diagram represents the relationship between the stations and is not a map, as it does not attempt to plot their geographic positions.

Representing three dimensions in two

Architects, engineers, and ship builders use drawing conventions that present complex three-dimensional relationships in two dimensions. These conventions have developed over time to record a scale version of the three-dimensional world in two dimensions. A basic understanding of the conventions is helpful to the book designer and art director, as technical illustration often relies on engineering drawing principles.

Orthographic drawing systems

Engineering drawing is a complete graphic language that describes three-dimensional objects in two dimensions, able to describe the exact position, size, and form of any three-dimensional object. Engineering drawings are often reproduced in books, but the influence of orthographic drawing systems in visualizing three-dimensional space extends far beyond engineering and architectural publications. Technical illustrators and designers have appropriated some of the descriptive geometry of orthographic drawing and used it to explain concepts and subjects far removed from engineering.

Most solid objects consist of surfaces that are defined by lines and corners. The corners can be viewed as points in space. Orthographic drawing defines the exact position of points and their connecting lines in space. This is achieved in two or more drawings that represent the same point in space. Two planes, vertical and horizontal, shown at right angles to each other, enable the exact point to be located.

Space can be divided into four quadrants by intersecting vertical and horizontal planes. These quadrants can be numbered first, second, third, and fourth angle. Orthographic drawings can be made in any of these quadrants, but convention makes use of only first- and third-angle projections. First- and third-angle affect the order of presentation of the three basic drawings: front elevation, side elevation, plan. Drawings of this type can be made at any scale, although they should use a common scale to represent true lengths. Auxiliary views of an object can be made to describe details. Accurate cross-sections of an object are possible recording true length drawn to scale.

Axonometric projections: viewing three sides

This is a form of engineering drawing that presents all three surfaces of an object in a single drawing, as opposed to orthographic drawing, which presents the three principal surfaces in three separate drawings. None of these drawings presents what we would see with our eyes, as they do not represent perspective, but they do present objects in a way that is easily understood. Axonometric drawings are often used to give an overview of a landscape space, building or object and can be combined with cross-sections or made into sequences to show change over time.

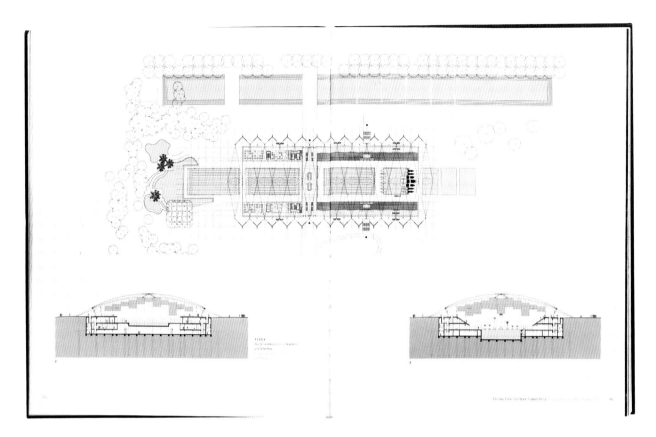

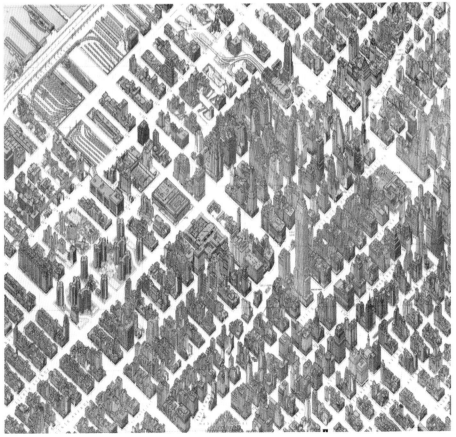

Above This spread from *Stadium und Arenen* (2006) shows a range of orthographic sections of sports stadiums. Conventionally, orthographic drawing presents an object square to the view-point in front elevation, side elevation, and plan.

Left Axonometric projections, like this isometric map of New York drawn by Hermann Bollmann, show an object with axes inclined at 45° to each other. This example is both beautiful and highly informative, as it shows the street layout and the height of Manhattan's buildings.

Right A Haynes car manual for the VW Passat 3 (1999) uses an exploded perspective drawing to explain how the components of the suspension connect to one another. It is interesting to note the annotation strategy of leader lines linked to numbers and then to a numeric list.
The sequence of the numbering relates to the order of assembly and does not merely run around the drawing sequentially.

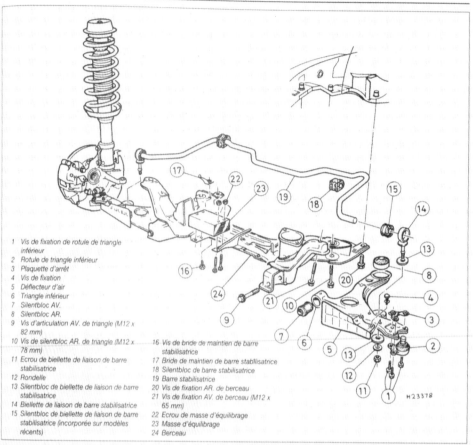

1 Vis de fixation de rotule de triangle inférieur
2 Rotule de triangle inférieur
3 Plaquette d'arrêt
4 Vis de fixation
5 Déflecteur d'air
6 Triangle inférieur
7 Silentbloc AV.
8 Silentbloc AR.
9 Vis d'articulation AV. de triangle (M12 x 82 mm)
10 Vis de silentbloc AR. de triangle (M12 x 78 mm)
11 Écrou de biellette de liaison de barre stabilisatrice
12 Rondelle
13 Silentbloc de biellette de liaison de barre stabilisatrice
14 Biellette de liaison de barre stabilisatrice
15 Silentbloc de biellette de liaison de barre stabilisatrice (incorporée sur modèles récents)
16 Vis de bride de maintien de barre stabilisatrice
17 Bride de maintien de barre stabilisatrice
18 Silentbloc de barre stabilisatrice
19 Barre stabilisatrice
20 Vis de fixation AR. de berceau
21 Vis de fixation AV. de berceau (M12 x 65 mm)
22 Écrou de masse d'équilibrage
23 Masse d'équilibrage
24 Berceau

H23378

6.4 Train avant et suspension

9 Dégager le triangle inférieur en le manœuvrant vers le bas tout d'abord à partir de son articulation avant puis vers le bas et l'intérieur depuis le pivot porte-moyeu et enfin vers l'avant depuis son silentbloc arrière. Si besoin est, abaisser légèrement le berceau pour pouvoir dégager le triangle au niveau de son silentbloc arrière. Utiliser un levier approprié pour libérer le triangle de ses silentblocs en veillant toutefois à ne pas endommager les pièces attenantes.

Démontage

10 Après l'avoir déposé, nettoyer le triangle inférieur.
11 Vérifier que sa rotule ne présente pas de signes d'usure exagérée et que les silentblocs d'articulation ne sont pas abîmés. S'assurer également que le triangle n'est pas endommagé ni déformé. Changer si nécessaire la rotule et les silentblocs.
12 Pour procéder au remplacement de la rotule, repérer sa position de montage exacte sur le triangle, ce qui est impératif compte tenu que la position respective du triangle et de sa rotule a été ajustée en usine et il y a lieu de respecter ce réglage lors du montage d'une rotule neuve. Desserrer ses vis de fixation et dégager la rotule avec la plaquette d'arrêt. Monter la rotule neuve en observant le repère de montage effectué à la dépose puis serrer les vis de fixation au couple prescrit. En cas de montage d'un triangle neuf, centrer la rotule par rapport aux trous oblongs.
13 Pour changer le silentbloc avant du triangle, l'extraire à l'aide d'un boulon long muni d'un tube métallique et de rondelles. Monter le silentbloc en utilisant la même méthode, en le trempant au préalable dans de l'eau savonneuse pour faciliter sa mise en place.
14 Le silentbloc arrière du triangle peut être extrait en faisant levier mais dans certains cas, il y aura lieu de couper ses parties en caoutchouc et métallique pour le chasser ensuite. Cette dernière solution n'est en principe nécessaire qu'en cas de difficulté à dégager le silentbloc du fait de la corrosion.

10

Exploded drawings: representing components

This type of drawing can have an axonometric or perspective basis and shows all the component parts of an object arranged as though it had been systematically dismantled. The basic premise for the drawing is that components that connect to one another are laid out along a single axis. All the components are drawn from the same view and characteristically arranged so that they do not obscure one another, though in very complex objects, such as car engines, overlaps may occur. This form of drawing is extremely helpful in naming all the components, providing an exact overview, visualizing how elements link, and describing the first stage in assembling an object. Car repair and DIY manuals make use of this form of presentation.

Perspective: representing the world from a fixed viewpoint

Perspective is a drawing system that represents a three-dimensional world from a single viewpoint. Unlike in orthographic drawing systems, the size and length of objects within the drawing are not true. The elements of the drawing relate to one another when viewed through one eye from a fixed position. Mathematical laws for perspective were worked out by the Florentine architect Filippo Brunelleschi (1377–1446) at the beginning of the Italian Renaissance.

We look at the world through two eyes, and our brain combines the two slightly different images. Perspective drawings are based on viewing the world from a single point: the viewpoint. Objects that are close to that viewpoint appear large, while others further away appear smaller. When we look out to sea from a beach we see the horizon, which appears to be a flat line running horizontally across our field of vision: the horizon line. If we were to stand in the middle of a straight section of railway track, the parallel rails would appear to converge at a single point on the horizon: the vanishing point. Perspective drawing takes the relationship between viewpoint, object, horizon line, and vanishing points and plots them on an invisible 'picture plane', as represented by a sheet of paper that stands between the viewpoint and the object.

Three-dimensional drawing programs

Digital three-dimensional drawing programs enable the illustrator to construct a virtual three-dimensional object or scene in wire frame. Unlike traditional methods, the viewpoint can be changed throughout the process of drawing. A virtual object can be viewed from many sides simultaneously. This split-screen multiple viewpoint is used in animation, motion graphics, and architectural presentation, but has yet to be fully exploited within book design.

Utilice este procedimiento para instalar el cartucho de impresión. Si el tóner cae en su ropa, límpielo con un paño seco y lave la ropa en agua fría. El agua caliente fija el tóner en el tejido.

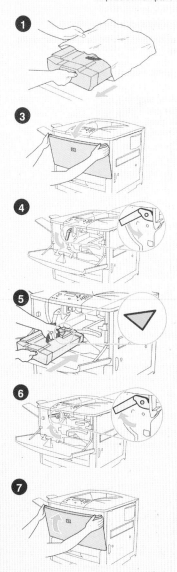

Para instalar el cartucho de impresión

1   Antes de quitar el cartucho de impresión de su embalaje, colóquelo en una superficie firme. Saque con cuidado el cartucho de impresión de su embalaje.

Para evitar que el cartucho de impresión se dañe, utilice las dos manos al manejarlo.
No exponga el cartucho de impresión a la luz más de unos minutos. Tape el cartucho de impresión cuando esté fuera de la impresora.

2   Mueva el cartucho de impresión con cuidado de delante hacia atrás para que el tóner se distribuya correctamente en su interior. Ésta es la única vez que deberá agitarlo.

3   Abra la puerta delantera de la impresora.

4   Gire la palanca verde hacia abajo hasta la posición de apertura.

5   Sujete el cartucho de manera que la flecha se encuentre en el lado izquierdo del mismo. Coloque el cartucho tal y como se muestra, con la flecha del lado izquierdo apuntando hacia la impresora y alineado con las guías de impresión. Introduzca el cartucho en la impresora tanto como pueda.

Nota
El cartucho de impresión tiene una lengüeta interna para tirar. La impresora quita automáticamente la lengüeta para tirar tras instalar el cartucho y encender la impresora. El cartucho de impresión hace mucho ruido durante varios segundos cuando la impresora quita la lengüeta. Este ruido sólo se produce con los cartuchos de impresión nuevos.

6   Pulse el botón de la palanca verde y gírela en el sentido de las agujas del reloj hasta la posición de cierre.

7   Cierre la puerta delantera.

Above From the Spanish section of a Hewlett Packard printer manual, a sequence of line perspective diagrams, supported by numbered text, uses flat colour to explain how to change an ink cartridge.

Diagrams in sequence: explaining a process

Sequential diagrams, or step-by-steps, have a long tradition in publishing. They can be drawn or photographic or can make use of models. Some diagrams are designed to work without words, and others work best with captions.

Diagrams of this type require careful planning and art direction. A compromise often has to be found between the optimum number of stages required for a satisfactory explanation and the number of columns within a book's grid. For example, visual explanations with seven or eleven stages may do justice to the process but are unlikely to fit into a six-column grid as easily as explanations provided in six or nine stages.

Simple flick books that allow the viewer to visualize a short sequence, almost like a film, are often used as novelties. However, the short animation of a flick book can provide a very quick explanation of a short process.

If carefully designed and thought out, diagrams can make explanations without supporting words. This can be useful in books that are intended for co-edition publication or in manuals accompanying objects that will be sold in many different countries, as it obviates the need for translation.

Above Sequential diagrams often communicate a step-by-step process more effectively than photographs, as the illustrator edits out the details appropriately. Here, a diagram of how to carve a ham from *How To* by Jennifer McKnight-Trontz (2004) uses a single colour but a variety of line weights. All four illustrations share a common viewpoint and work without text.

Diagrams in sequence: explaining a process

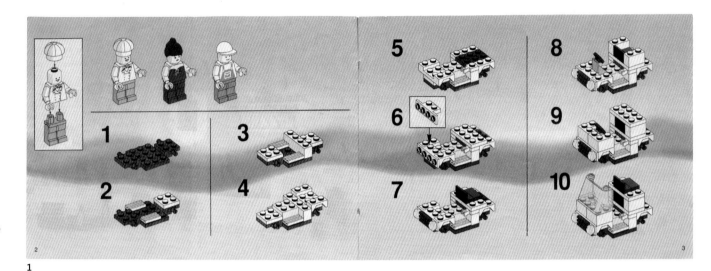

1

1 The famous construction diagrams for Lego models are designed to work without captions – vital for a company marketing a toy worldwide and aiming at children who may not be able to read. The diagrams use isometric drawings. Each diagram is broken down into a series of developmental stages. The drawings present the model from the same viewpoint, although details are indicated by an auxiliary drawing.

2

2 A spread from *Sci da manuale* (2001) by Markus Kobold uses numbered photographs running down the page, reflecting the way a skier moves down a slope. The figure gets larger as he moves down the page and appears to slalom from left to right. As both the page and the snow are white, the frames are probably unnecessary.

Points of sailing—close-hauling

The first thing we must remember about sailing is that a boat cannot sail directly into the wind. In the head-to-wind position the sail simply flaps and is unable to propel the craft forward. You might ask what happens when you wish to sail from point X to point Y when the wind is blowing from Y to X? The answer is that you must steer a zig-zag course first to one side of the wind direction and then to the other, keeping as *close* to the wind line as you can with the sail full and not flapping. If it starts to flap, the angle of travel must be increased until it fills again. Eventually, after a series of such manoeuvres you will reach your aiming point at Y.

Zig-zagging in the manner described is known as *beating to windward* or *tacking*. While sailing in this way the boat is said to be *close-hauled*, and this is one of the three main points of sailing. When the wind strikes the sail on the port side with the boom angled over to starboard we can say we are on the *port tack*; wind from starboard and boom to port is the *starboard tack*. Normally, an angle of at least forty-five degrees to the wind direction is as close as an average boat will sail.

14

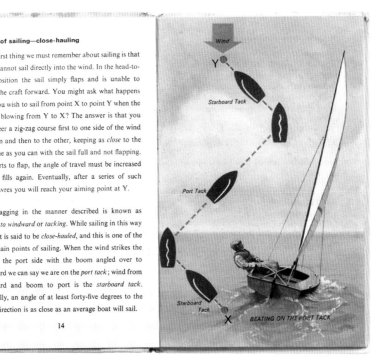

3 The *Ladybird Book of Sailing and Boating* (1972), designed for children but often much enjoyed by adults, separates the text description (on the left-hand page) from the image (on the right-hand page). The painted illustration shows a simple progressive diagram in plan. The diagram is annotated with X and Y points and the sequence moves up the page.

4 The *Handbook of Sailing* (1980) by Bob Bond, published by Dorling Kindersley, here shown in its German edition, uses introductory text, a small diagram, and two seven-stage step-by-steps on a spread with eight columns. The schematic diagram in the first column uses numbers that relate to the stages drawn across the page. The viewpoint of the drawings has been carefully selected to show the movements of the crew. In reality, the boat would appear to move away from the viewer and therefore get smaller, but the illustrator has drawn all seven images the same size.

3

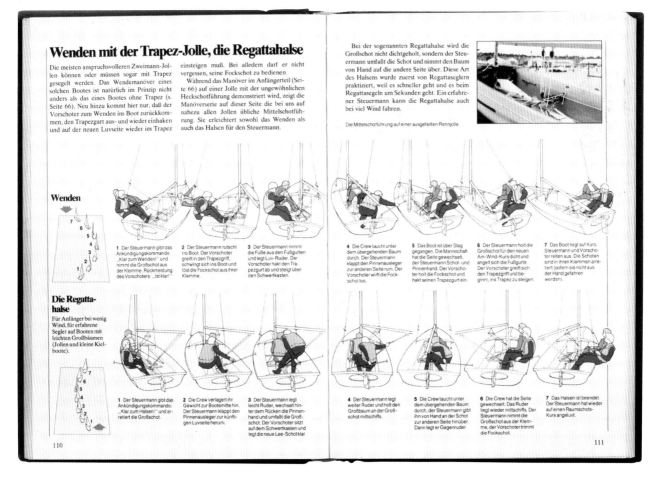

4

Drawings that reveal hidden details

Technical illustrators have developed a range of approaches to drawing based on orthographic and axonometric conventions, which present objects in ways in which they could not be photographed. Many of the drawings combine cross-sections, cutaways, and schematics in a single illustration. The technical illustrator needs a very clear brief concerning viewpoint, page format, and size, together with a list of the details that the editor and art director want labelled. The illustrator has to control line weight, tone, and colour in a way that provides great detail but retains clarity when printed on the page.

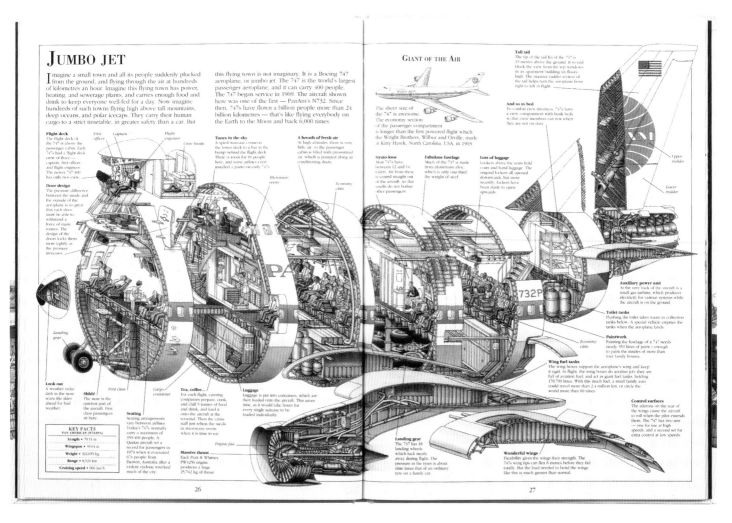

Above The illustrator Stephen Biesty developed an approach to visualizing objects that was particularly well suited to books. If the Jumbo Jet (see small drawing right-hand page) were drawn as a cutaway in the manner of the aircraft opposite, the internal details would have been very small. Biesty has sliced the aircraft into eight and drawn the interior in great detail. The aircraft is still recognizable, although its proportions appear to have been compressed.

Cross-sections

Cross-sectional drawings, essentially a drawing of a slice taken through a solid object or building, are often associated with architecture, engineering, or geology, where they form part of the design or documenting process. Beyond these professional uses this form of presentation is used widely in books to explain hidden details.

Cutaway drawings

These are drawings in which both the outside and the inside of a person, object or location are shown from a single viewpoint. Part of the skin, shell, or wall is removed and the inside is revealed. This approach is often helpful to the reader as it provides a visual overview of elements. Technical illustrations of this type may show a side elevation and a three-quarter view formalized in isometric or perspective. An object is drawn so that front, top surface, and side can be seen, and the skin is stripped away to reveal the inner workings.

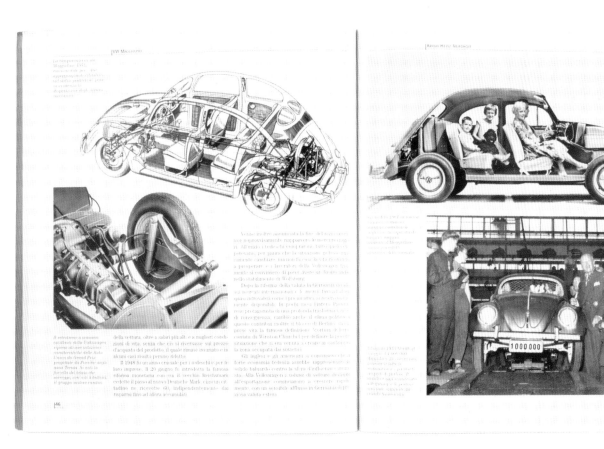

Schematic drawings

Schematic drawings, unlike cross-sections and cutaways, do not show the detail of all the individual elements but explain the broad principles. The drawings tend to be generic rather than based on a specific object. This is useful for editorial purposes, as the principles of how something works can be explained without the text having to refer to all of the items that might be expected to be labelled in a cross-section or cutaway drawing.

Above A spread from *Volkswagen Maggiolino* (2006) by Marco Batazzi and published by Giorgio Nada shows a cutaway drawing of the Beetle on the left-hand page. Through careful use of tone, the interior of the car is defined, while the outer shell makes use of line. The right-hand page shows a photograph used in some of the Beetle's advertising, where the cutaway has been taken literally: the engine, passengers, luggage, and spare wheel are all shown clearly in a car from which the side has been cut away. Neither illustration nor photograph uses labels.

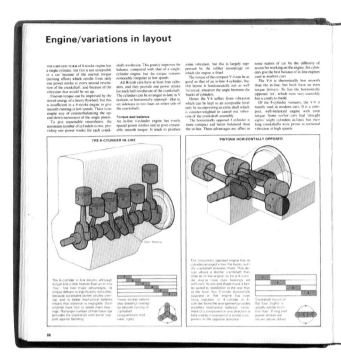

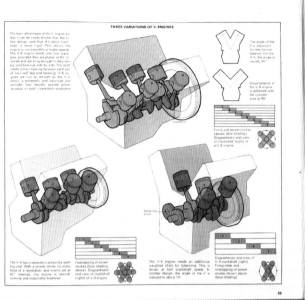

Above The *AA Book of the Car* (1970) explains variations in engine layout. None of the five diagrams on the page is based on a specific car engine; instead, they explain different arrangements used by a variety of manufacturers. The engine block is minimally represented in black line and tone, while the piston heads are more detailed. The cylinder heads are numbered in each of the main schematic drawings, linking the power strokes of each piston to the black and blue line drawings. The very small green auxiliary drawings show the rotation of the crankshaft.

Symbols: pictograms and ideograms

Symbols or images that represent meaning are often used in books on maps, charts, and diagrams. Sometimes symbols are used to replace words as they occupy less space. Symbols can explain an idea within multi-language publications where the onus is on the designer to ensure the greatest clarity through ease of recognition (although variations in cultural traditions can lead readers to interpret the meaning of symbols differently, so that the notion of symbols operating as a universal language is flawed). Pictograms represent people or objects, acting as visual nouns; ideograms represent actions and ideas, like visual verbs. Pictograms can be used in a table or bar chart to indicate quantity. By using symbols in this way to replace the bar, the need for labels can be reduced, the pictogram representing both quantity and meaning. A system named 'Isotype' (International System of Typographic Picture Education) was invented in 1936 for just this purpose by the Austrian philosopher and educator Otto Neurath (1882–1945). Neurath believed that complex quantitative information could be made accessible to readers independent of written language by simple pictorial presentation.

Pictograms can also be used in a sequence to convey a process. Each symbol is used to represent a specific object or idea and the viewer makes connections between the pictures. When translating the symbols literally, the viewer is made aware of the limitations of the picture language, as such words as 'the', 'of', 'it', and 'as', which are used in speech and writing to connect ideas, have no visual form of representation.

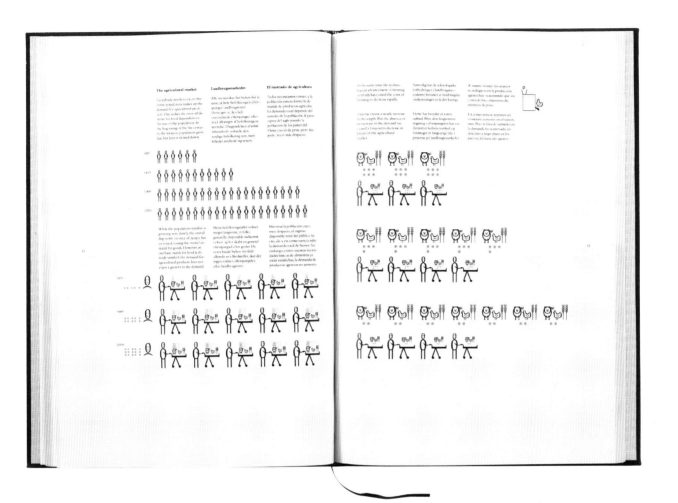

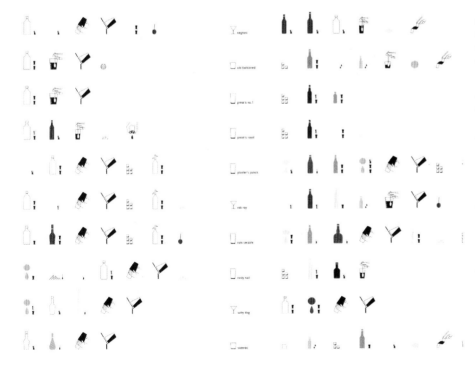

Above Annegeret Mølhave's *For Sale: an Explanation of the Market Economy* (2003) features text in English, Danish, and Spanish. This is illustrated with symbols made from the text font Bembo. The three languages always appear in the same order, and the illustration is placed after each text section. The symbols are annotated with numbers so the illustrations are not cluttered with labels in the three languages.

Left A detail from Werner Singer's book *Pic-a-Drink* (2004) shows a series of symbols that explain how to make a range of cocktails. The concept behind this work was to explain the recipes without words. The tiny symbols identify drink through bottle shape and colour and quantities through a measure. The pictograms are accompanied by a key (not shown) and read from left to right like type.

Tables and matrices

Data presented in a table may take many forms: numeric, alphabetic, or pictographic. The grid structure of the table enables the viewer to see the whole information field at once. The annotation on vertical and horizontal axes allows the reader to identify a specific item of data within the field. For example, a train timetable often has stations listed in sequence down the vertical axis and time represented across the horizontal axis.

Right The Japanese railway timetable lists all the destination stations in alphabetic order down the left edge. The train departure times are arranged in hourly columns across the table. The reader locates the destination station by running a finger down the alphabetic list, then reads along the line to identify the next available train – expressed as a number using the 24-hour clock.

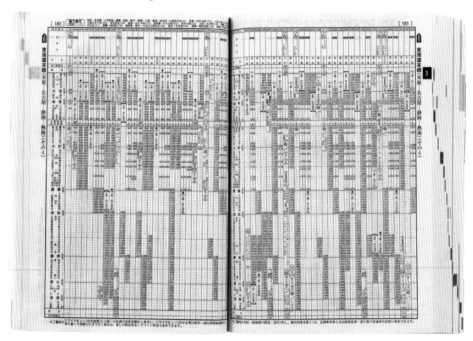

Right When laying out tables, the designer should consider how they can be read. Tables consist of two main elements: the data and the grid, which should support the data and aid its readability. If the two elements are given the same importance, there is often a loss of clarity. In tables with many lines, a tinted ground can be used to reinforce each line. In this example, ellipsis points are used for omitted figures, and two weights of type, roman and bold, emphasize the columns. This hierarchy could be helpful in timetables or in comparing financial information.

398	435	86	975	227	945	879	364	765
25	321	45	859	658	25	369	225	214
398	435	86	975	227	945	879	364	765

Data dominated by grid = confusion.

398	435	86	975	227	945	879	364	765
25	321	45	859	658	25	369	225	214
398	435	86	975	227	945	879	364	765

Data supported by grid = clarity. Here rules support reading across the row.

398	435	86	975	227	945	879	364	765
25	321	45	859	658	25	369	225	214
398	435	86	975	227	945	879	364	765

Vertical rules help the reading of columns.

12·00	...	13·00	...	...	...	15·00	16·00
12·13	13·20	...	...	13·56	14·00	...	...
12·36	...	...	...	...	14·22	15·28	...
13·05	13·40	...	...	14·39	14·55	16·05	...

Here a tint is used to identify the row while alignment and ellipses points reinforce the column.

Notational systems and the book

This chapter has briefly examined different approaches to the presentation of visual information. Books about a wide range of subjects make use of graphs, charts, diagrams, and tables, and some disciplines have devised specific notational codes, which can be reproduced in a book. Typography is the formal notational code for recording language; the notation of sound is recorded through musical scores; the notation of topography is found in atlases; mathematics and physics through algebra; chemistry through formulae; architecture through orthographic drawing. Notational systems symbolically represent a three-dimensional experience in two dimensions, and therefore books are the obvious medium for their reproduction. The book has become the container for the world's wisdom, preserved in many different notational codes. When we describe the activity of reviewing a book's codes we use a common word for all: we *read*, words, music, maps, and so on. All the notational systems have common features:

- They document an experience, object, or abstract relationship.

- They encode and miniaturize a three-dimensional experience by means of a two-dimensional symbolic code.

- They make permanent what may be ephemeral.

- They can be read and the original experience may be re-created.

- They can be used as a mechanism for planning or envisioning the future.

Below Designer and musician Maria Gandra in her book *Musical Notation* (2004) developed a series of symbols that reflect the historical period in which the featured music was written. The symbols are placed on a grid that reflects the musical scale and can therefore be read and performed by a musician.

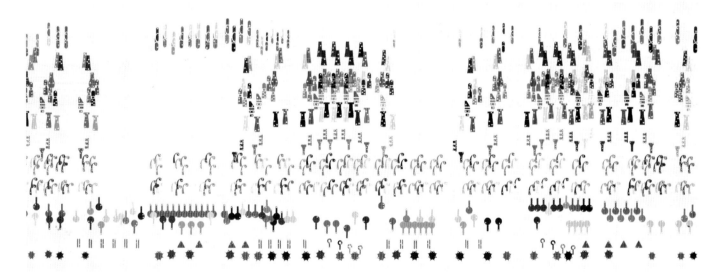

10

Layout

The laying out of a book involves designers making decisions about the exact positioning of all the elements on the page. This chapter will initially describe how flatplans and storyboards can help the designer gain an overview of the content of a book, and will go on to examine elements of composition and models of layout. The two poles of layout are the text, which is organized around the reading sequence, and the images, the arrangement of which is determined by compositional considerations derived from picture-making. It is the balance between these two principles that guides the descriptions of the various models of page layout.

When we browse in a bookshop, we 'pre-read' books, flicking through the pages and making instinctive judgments about content, quality, and overall appeal. Our first impression may be of space, colour, or arrangement. These communicate subliminally a set of values about the page and as a consequence about the text and by association the author. If the layout is scruffy, the print poor, and the space cramped, then the text, no matter how eloquent, is intrinsically devalued. If the first impressions of a spread fill the reader with confidence, a sense of order, purposeful construction, or even deliberate disjunction, the pre-reading of this semiotic code can elevate the value of the text.

Preparing the content for layout: text and image files

Organizing the content prior to laying out a book's pages is very important. Today it is likely that this will be done digitally on a computer in software programs such as QuarkXPress, InDesign, or PageMaker. The designer will have a hard copy of the manuscript, a digital file of all the text, and a well-organized file of illustrations, transparencies, and digital photographs. It is worth spending preparation time checking that the text is divided into the book's parts, sections, or chapters and that the editor has made the most extensive edit possible prior to the layout stage. It is helpful for the author, editor, or designer to mark the exact or approximate position of illustrations in the text and count the number of images per chapter before layout begins. Organizing the picture files in hard copy and digital form chronologically, numbering and labelling the images through the chapter, makes the design process run more smoothly. Often there are missing transparencies for which the picture editor has yet to get permission or photographs that are yet to be shot. I generally organize the hard-copy file with blank sleeves inserted in the correct order labelled and awaiting the arrival of the missing images; digital files can be arranged in the same way to accommodate the digital images.

Organizing layouts: flatplans showing text and image position

Many editors on non-fiction books will have worked with the author on a rough flatplan. The flatplan is a diagram of all the pages of the book drawn as spreads numbered sequentially, and may include signature breaks (showing the length of each signature) or colour distribution if the book is to be printed in two- and four-colour sections. The editor frequently marks out the approximate length of frontmatter, chapters, and endmatter.

If this process has not been undertaken by the editor, the designer can draw up a flatplan based either on the hard-copy manuscript or by importing the text into the templates and seeing how many pages it runs to. When formatted in the selected typeface and size and applied to the baseline grid, the text should occupy less space than the anticipated extent of the book. For example, if the text in a book with an anticipated extent of 256 pages runs out at 121 pages then the designer knows that just over 50% of the remaining space can be used for the imagery. This process can be further broken down by chapter. The first chapter of solid text may run to 14 pages. If the images are evenly distributed throughout the book at a text:image ratio of 1:1 then the chapter will be approximately 28 pages long. If the designer has calculated that the frontmatter will occupy ten pages and the design scheme is to open chapters on a right-hand page, then chapter one can be marked on the flatplan as starting at page 11 and running through 28 pages until page 39. This will be a right-hand page and should, therefore, be used as a chapter opener. The designer can therefore 'go long' on the flatplan and mark the chapter as finishing on page 40 with the new opener on page 41 or 'go short' and finish on page 38, opening chapter two on page 39.

Careful juggling of the flatplan in relation to the chapter content enables the designer to gain a clear overview of how the book fits the anticipated extent. If a section of the book does not include any illustrations or significantly deviates from the established text:image ratio, the designer can reflect the allocation of potential space on the flatplan. Continuing the example used above, chapter two may include no illustrations and occupy 18 pages and, therefore, can be marked on the flatplan as starting on page 39 and running to page 57. If it becomes apparent that the book will not fit into the predicted extent then the designer is able to discuss with the editor additional signatures or text or image edits. The flatplan can also be used by the designer during the layout process to mark off the page locations of the illustrations as they are positioned on the layouts.

Above The rough flatplan of this book provides an overview of the signatures and chapter breaks. Here, I have marked the part openers in green and the chapters with a left- or right-hand green corner flag. The numbers are colour-coded: black for folios, red for photographs, and blue for diagrams. These are numbered sequentially from the start of the book, but could be broken down into part or chapter sequences. A flatplan can also be used to show picture fall and colour distribution, and a change of stock.

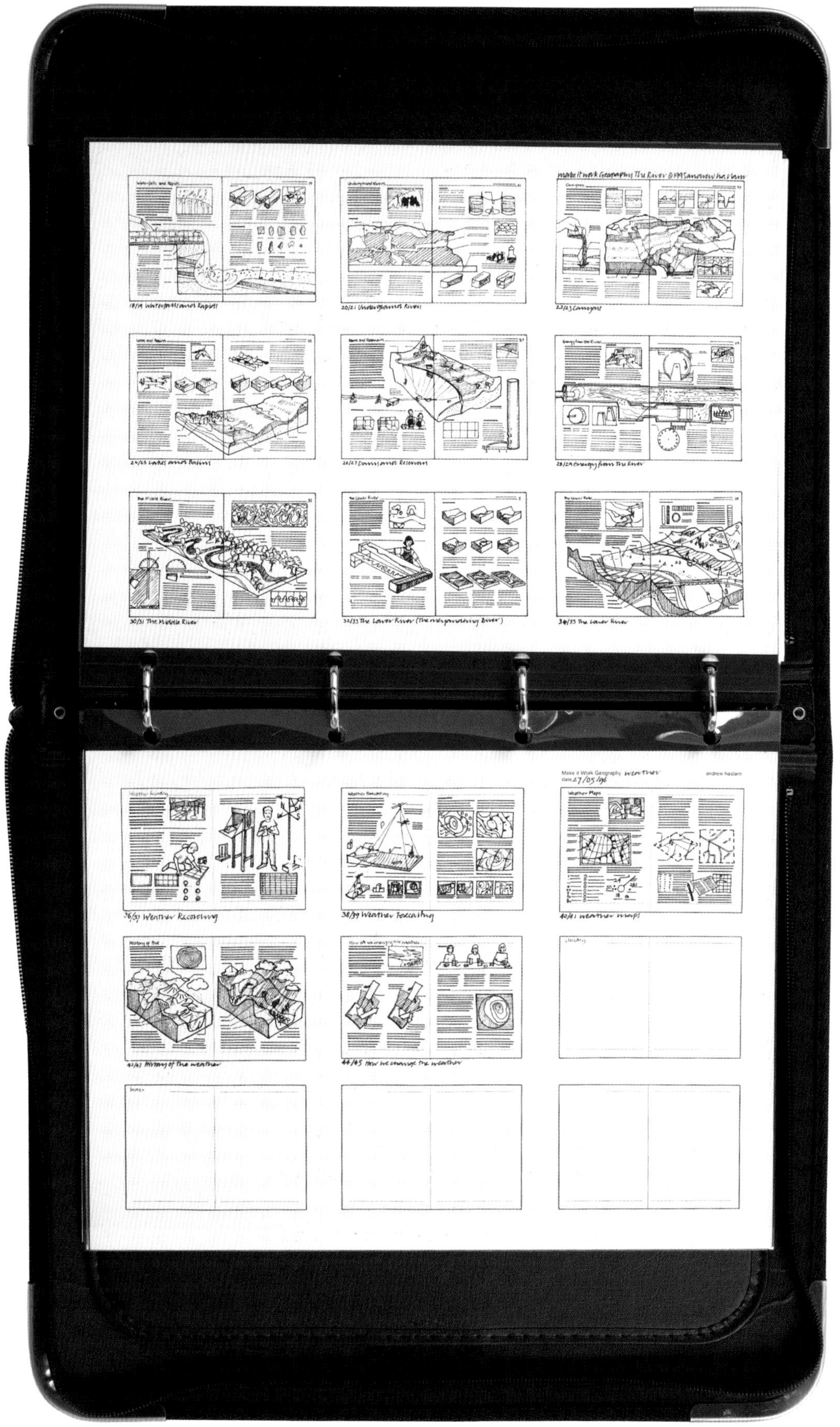
18/19 Waterfalls and Rapids
20/21 Underground Rivers
22/23 Canyons
24/25 Lakes and Basins
26/27 Dams and Reservoirs
28/29 Energy from the River
30/31 The Middle River
34/35 The Lower River
Make it Work Geography weather
andrew haslam
36/37 Weather Recording
38/39 Weather Forecasting
40/41 weather maps
42/43 History of the weather
44/45 How we change the weather

Storyboards: writing to fit and commissioning images

The flatplan described above is one that is prepared immediately before the book is laid out, when the designer has a completed text and virtually all the images. This usually relates to a traditional model of authorship in which the writer initiates content. However, a flatplan can also be useful if the content of a book is authored by a publisher, editor, or designer. When devising the *Make it Work!* series of books, I drew detailed provisional layouts on a flatplan for the entire book. These were referred to as 'storyboards' and served much the same purpose as the storyboards drawn prior to the shooting of a film. I had decided on the editorial content of the book, researched extensively each of the elements, and then drew detailed layouts that predicted the use of library photographs and models that I would subsequently make, showing the angle from which they would be photographed and the number of stages required in their construction. The storyboards, along with the detailed synopsis, formed the agenda for all editorial meetings. The storyboards also became a marketing tool: as the *Make it Work!* series ran to 26 books, co-publishers and sales representatives began to understand the link between the tiny drawings and the look of the final page.

Layouts based on the text

The functional aspects of page design are those that enable the reader to relate directly to the author's message. A functional approach to the layout of the page is determined by the nature of the content. Books that consist primarily of text are designed to be read. The German designer Eric Speakerman (b. 1947) notably talks of 'designing from the type down', implying that it is the message that is most important. The designer lays out the text in a way that is sympathetic to the content and guides the reader through the information. Considering the book's potential readership, the designer makes subtle decisions about the use of the typographic palette. This form of functional design for reading works most successfully when the designer's influence on the layout of the page goes almost unnoticed throughout the reading process. The designer's work is invisible, or at least transparent. The reader feels confident with the text arrangement and is able to concentrate on the author's message, moving smoothly through a sequence of pages. If the page becomes opaque, or if the reader is distracted or loses the sense of flow through a passage of text owing to the designer's clumsy layout, then the intimate relationship between writer and reader has been intruded upon.

These comments about the close relationship between function and convention might be viewed as advocating tradition, endorsing an unchanging approach to layout. Unfortunately, for some designers this has become the case, with the replication *ad infinitum* of successful layouts of eras past, justifying and defining the design as 'good for all time'. The real challenge for the designer is not merely to repeat the conventions of the past but to reinterpret the orthodoxies and conventions in relation to the present.

Opposite A section of the storyboard from *Make it Work! Weather.* The storyboards were drawn using a reduced series grid. Each of the line counts for the pages was accurate and could be used to commission the written elements. The proportions of the images were accurately represented on the storyboards. The models I made were designed to be photographed from the viewpoint and in the way indicated by the storyboard drawings and layout.

A range of approaches to layout: text-driven books

In this description of a range of approaches to layout, it is easiest to start with pages that have few elements, such as a single column of text, and gradually introduce more complex schemes. The guiding principle for examining layout through this discussion is the balance struck between the reading sequence of the text and the compositional considerations of picture-making that determine the page layout and the appearance of the spreads. Examining a series of characteristic layouts from different types of books provides an insight into some well-established publishing conventions, many of which are based on a functional premise that enables the reader to access information quickly.

Below This page and the three following illustrate schematically a range of approaches to page layout in relation to reading.

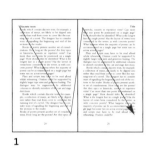

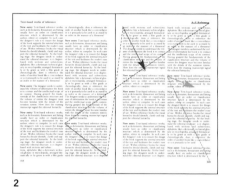

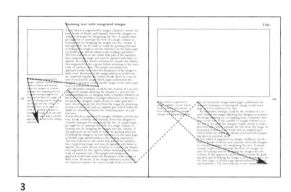

1

2

3

1 Layout using running text

A novel is clearly designed to be read, and the picture-compositional considerations are therefore minimized. Having decided on format, grid, and margins of the template, and the nature of the typographic elements in the style sheet, the designer imports the text into the grid. The text flows from one column to the next from top left to bottom right. The reading pattern across the page is smooth and consistent; the paragraphs containing common units of thought are clearly visible from an initial glance at the page.

Likewise, headings introducing new themes within the copy are signalled to the reader at the turn of each page. The symmetrical page shows text flowing from the left-hand page to the right with a line of symmetry falling along the gutter. The layout of the asymmetrical text page is similar, though any shoulder-notes are consistently positioned in relation to the text regardless of left- or right-hand page.

2 Text-based works of reference

Text-based reference works, such as dictionaries, thesauruses, and listings usually have an order or classification structure determined by the author, editor, or compiler. In such cases, the designer's role is to ensure that the design of the book supports the internal structure of the text and facilitates the reader's ease of use. Within reference books, the visual hierarchy should identify, clarify, and support the editorial hierarchy.

Here the text has been arranged in two columns. The magenta line indicates how a reader using an alphabetic reference book might typically locate an entry. Flicking through the book looking at the alphabetic running heads, the reader would locate the page, scan the headings from the top right of the right-hand page, find the required entry, and read through to the end of the passage.

The cyan line shows the way a reader might use a reference book that is not ordered alphabetically or where the reader is working from the contents page or index. A thesaurus is characteristically used by working from the index to the page and then to the entry. Some reference books that are alphabetically listed may be accessed in both ways illustrated here.

3 Text supported by images

A largely text-based book that incorporates limited supporting imagery, such as a biography or a history, is primarily designed around the reading sequence. The reader's need to link images with text references is key to his or her understanding. To support this link, the images can be dropped into the text column immediately after the reference. If the image is placed before the reference, the reader is given no context for its inclusion.

Simple layout variations might include: hanging or sitting the image at the head or the foot of the page; using the side margin to position the image next to the reference; or isolating the image on a single page or spread. This schematic page layout is based on an asymmetric grid, but could work equally well on a symmetrical grid.

The diagrams on this spread and the next are annotated with arrows: magenta for text passages, and cyan where a reference directs the reader from the main body copy to an image, side story, or caption. The solid lines indicate reading through a text; the dotted lines indicate the movement of the eye between elements. I have shown reading as a sequence from top left to bottom right, as this is the premise upon which most books are laid out. However, readers are at liberty to dip into any reading matter where the fancy takes them. Designers can organize the arrangement of the page using the 'premise' by reinforcing the reading order or, as with the schematic diagrams on the next spread, create focal points through the size and position of text and image.

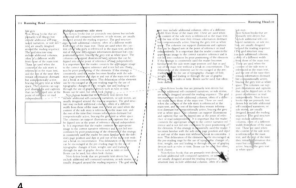

4

5

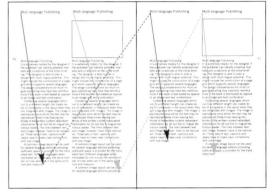

6

4 Multiple narratives: side story

Non-fiction books that are primarily text-driven but include additional self-contained narratives, or side stories, are usually designed around the reading sequence. The grid structure may include additional columns, often of a different width from those of the main text. These are used when the content of the side story is referenced in the main text, and the rest of the time they remain information-dormant but compositionally active, bracing the grey text as white space.

The columns can support illustrations and captions that can be dipped into at the point of reference or read independently. It is important that the reader connects the appropriate image to the correct narrative reference and is not led into confusion by poor positioning of the elements. If this strategy is used consistently, the reader becomes familiar with the side-story page position and dips in and out of the main text without a break in concentration. This delineation of the elements can be encouraged at the pre-reading stage by the use of typographic changes of font, weight, size, and leading, or through the use of graphic devices such as rules or tints. Boxes can be used, but often look clumsy.

5 Using images in columns or rows

In non-fiction, the explanation of information often includes illustrated step-by-step text. Depending on the content, some readers will deduce what is being explained from the illustrations, while others will concentrate on the text. The designer needs to decide how the elements work together. If the reading sequence is most important and space is tight, running text and image down the page (left-hand page, magenta) produces a repeat text–image sequence to each column at the expense of the picture sequence. The pre-reading impression of the composition will be one of disjunction, as none of the text or pictorial elements share a common alignment.

Alternatively, a natural sequence can be implied by aligning the pictures in a row across the page (right-hand page, cyan), reinforced by numbering the step-by-step text. The pre-reading impression of this page is one of order; the elements are unified through alignment and braced by white space. The information occupies more space but communicates content more efficiently. The layout for this spread is based on rows, as it allows the reader to compare the diagrams.

6 Multilingual publishing

There are several approaches to multilingual publishing that affect page layout. If a work is exclusively text-based, a publisher wishing to publish the book in a second language is likely to buy the rights and translate the text before designing the book from scratch. In such cases, the format, extent, cover, and layout of foreign editions is very different from the first-language edition.

Another approach to multi-language publishing, shown above, is to have both languages on the same page. The designer constructs a grid that accommodates one or more languages and consistently positions the body text in the same column. Books of this type may include images that can be positioned in relation to both languages and referred to by readers of either text. Often this type of book features minimal captioning, as translating and positioning two or more texts in narrow columns makes the page messy.

A third approach, which is used extensively in non-fiction illustrated books, is to design pages in which the CMYK photographs appear in the same position in all language editions and the text translations use only the black plate. This type of layout must be designed to support the text in other languages that occupy more or less space.

A range of approaches to layout: image-driven books

Image-driven books may have many elements. The complexity of the spread and the order in which it is read is determined far more by the designer's layout than with many text-based spreads. The designer tries to create visual focal points that lead the reader into the spread in much the same way as one views a painting. Principal focal points are supported by secondary images.

7.1

7.2

7.3

7.4

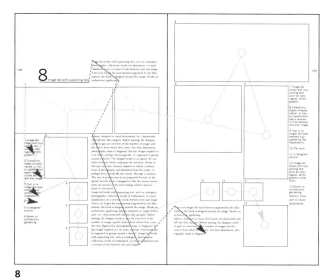

8

7 A modernist grid

The modernist grid (see p.56) is designed to support layouts that formalize the relationship between text and image but allow each page to be different, creating individuality within a coherent structure. The baseline is a division of the picture unit and therefore alignment between text and image is assured. Both the text and images are linked directly to the grid. The vertical gutters and the horizontal baselines have a common width, which determines that the thin intervals of white space that separate the elements are consistent across the page and throughout the book. Grid systems of this sort regulate the space but support hundreds of layout alternatives.

The four diagrams demonstrate a range of layouts. The principal and secondary alignments are marked in magenta. **7**.1 uses three sizes of square but the text and image areas on the right-hand page are half that of the left-hand page. **7**.2 uses a contrast of small and large shapes centrally positioned. **7**.3 uses four shapes but has two principal axes of alignment that are symmetrical in relation to the gutter, although the layout is asymmetrical. **7**.4 uses four shapes and an asymmetric layout. The circles indicate a hierarchy of focal points; some of these are in the centre of an image, others are formed between images.

8 Pictorial pages supported by text

In pictorial books, the viewer is initially attracted to the images, and the text has a subservient role. The most important visual relationship is that which exists between the images themselves. These can convey a narrative through the way they are ordered on the page, the viewer making connections between the pictures; or they can be used to form an impression of a single subject.

The order, size, and crop of each of the images affect the message and the visual dynamics of the page. For all the variables of the strictly modernist grid, it places restrictions on the image format and size, as all dimensions relate to the unit field. Simply by using alignment, the designer can impose order on the page and unify a group of entirely unrelated image formats and sizes. If the designer wishes to combine a group of photographs or artworks in different formats, the use of alignment and size ensures that all can be positioned on the page without cropping.

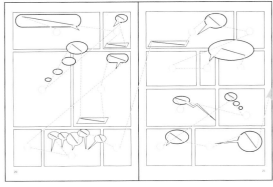

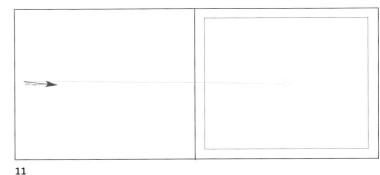

10

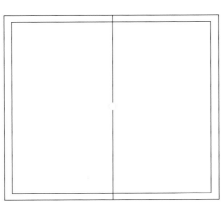

11

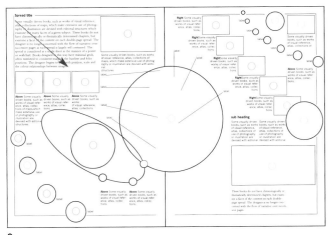

9

9 The spread as wall chart

There is no need to consider the flow of information from page to page when the spread is self-contained. Spreads designed in this way usually break with conventional top-left to bottom-right reading, which is why the diagram does not indicate a reading sequence. The gutter merely serves to fold in half what is essentially a wall chart. The reading sequence is determined by the reader rather than the designer. The captions and labels are positioned in relation to the images and often the alignment and position of the captions are inconsistent.

The layout of the page is composed to create a balanced picture, though the formal use of white space is little considered. Spreads designed in this way have minimal grids, often restricted to decisions about consistent margins, baseline, and folio position. The designer begins to play with position, scale, and the colour relationships between images. If the images are cut-outs rather than cropped square, the tessellation of shapes across the page has to be finessed. The spread is considered as a whole, with images, though rarely text, running across the gutter. Rectangular- and square-cropped photographs and images relate to the horizontal and vertical axes of a grid. When images are cut out to reflect the shape of the object, the irregular outline is usually a contrast to the regularity of the grid. The relative size of each of the pictorial elements and how they relate to the text need to be carefully considered.

10 Comic books and graphic novels

The layout of comic books or graphic novels is determined by the illustrator, who develops both the picture boxes for the spread and the drawings in relation to the narrative. The drawings' shape and the proportions of the boxes are considered in relation to the story. The speech bubbles may be contained within the picture frame or connect two or more elements of the story.

11 Passe-partout: the use of frames

This term refers to the card mount often used to surround a picture inside a frame. It has been appropriated within book design to refer to all framing devices within a layout. It is frequently used to offer a simple formal structure to photographic layouts.

12 Full-bleed pictures

Pictures that break the grid and reach to the edge of the page are referred to as 'bleeding'. If a picture occupies the whole of the page and bleeds off all the edges, it is referred to as 'full-bleed'. Images used in this way maximize visual impact and are often used as a contrast to pages that use a lot of white space.

12

Layouts based on the page as a picture

Text layouts are designed to be read as linear progression down the page from top left to bottom right, while image-based pages are designed to be 'viewed'. Arranging the elements on the page, the designer contemplates the relationships between the pictures and the text narrative. The text is also considered as a pictorial element forming a grey tone that works to counterbalance the image elements made up of photographs, paintings, or illustrations.

Right A spread from the Dutch publication *Een Huis Voor de Gemeenschap* (2003) by Jeanne van Heeswijk shows how a photographic image can be combined with a page that carries the text.

1.1

1.2

Above and right In *Mapping Sitting – On Portraiture and Photography*, group photographs, all reproduced to the same scale, are arranged across a series of spreads. The first spreads of the section, titled 'Group', feature full-bleed images (**1**.1) of groups sitting in rows, setting up a predictable rhythm in the viewer's mind. However, the second spread (**1**.2) features one group photo bleeding off to the right. This continues over the page (**1**.3), and for a further 21 spreads. The position of each image is determined by the fall of the previous image plus a 4mm gutter.

1.3

Extending the page

Throughout most publications, the page format remains the same, but additional impact can be given by surprising the reader with a change of proportion, unexpectedly making use of a short, long, or die-cut page. These irregular pages create new opportunities for the designer and change the pace of the book for the reader. Short pages force the designer to consider new relationships, as part of the larger page frames the smaller page, effectively a spread within a spread. The small page can be short in both length and height and therefore be framed by the larger page. Images or text can run from full page to short page and crop an image or visually edit a text by obscuring a section. Die-cuts on a right-hand page give a reader an insight into the future as the reader peeps through a window onto the subsequent page; when the page is turned, and the die-cut falls on the left-hand page, the past is reframed. Gatefolds or throwouts are pages that, as their name suggests, open up from the foredge of the book. They can work as single throwouts on left- and right-hand pages, adding an additional third page to a spread, or can be used in combination as a double gatefold, doubling the area of the spread. The gatefold page is fractionally smaller than the page, as it has to be free of the binding pinch to allow the reader to open it. More complex throwouts may involve a series of concertina pages unfolding from the foredge. The page can be extended from both foredge and head, producing a sheet nearly four times the page size with a vertical and horizontal crease running through the middle.

Right The book *Full Moon* (1999), produced and directed by Mark Holborn and Neil Bradford and designed by Michael Light, makes use of several double gatefold pages. It features photographs of the moon taken by Apollo astronauts on a 6 x 6 medium-format camera. The square format of the camera is used for the book, as most of the photographs are reproduced full-frame. However, when the gatefolds are opened, a full-colour panorama of seven photographs is revealed.

Integrating text and image: working to your own rules

Considering composition in relation to the page and grid has been the principle discussed throughout this chapter. The text and image elements are placed on the page in relation to the grid. Recently, some designers have begun to develop ideas about layout that are less to do with visual arrangement but are based on the systematic application of a set of internalized 'rules'. The designer establishes a set of rules or 'behaviours' for each of the elements and then applies them throughout the book. The page layout is no longer the product of decisions made primarily on visual criteria; it has a kind of internalized determinism. Careful selection of the internalized 'rules' in relation to the content and narrative is very important when this strategy is adopted.

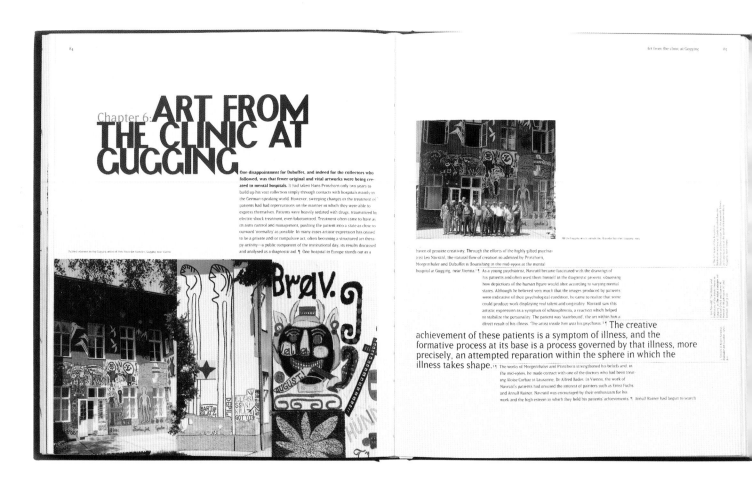

Above Phil Baines when designing *Raw Creation: Outsider Art and Beyond* (1996) worked in a systematic way. The page layout was determined by the application of a set of rules of his own devising. Each new paragraph was aligned with the end of the preceding paragraph; images were aligned directly with their text reference; captions were placed in the leading of the main text. This somewhat manic system was similar to the obsessional work of the featured artists.

The impression of depth: layers

Left Irma Boom's *Nederlands Postzegels* (1987) is printed on both sides of very thin Bible paper. The images printed wrong-reading on the reverse of the paper show through and are overprinted on the front face of the page. The placement of elements on front and reverse of the page forms sophisticated layers of print. In this concertina book, the number 87 is printed on the front of page 3, which has a blank reverse; 88 is printed on the reverse of page 4, which has a moth on the face; and page 5 has a square of text aligned at 90°. The pages combine to form the layers.

By carefully controlling the tonal values of the page, images and text can be overlaid. This collage of elements creates layers and conveys the impression of depth. This effect can be achieved with overprinting or show-through, where the paper stock is thin enough to allow an image printed on the reverse to be visible on the front face. If show-through is used, the paper stock must be sufficiently thin so that the image is visible through the page.

Books on visual culture

There is a growing market for books about visual culture: architecture, design fashion, furniture, and art. Some books are practical manuals, others collections of themed contemporary work accompanied by critical essays. There has also been a growth in the number of art and design monographs. Some of these publications are designed as a series; others are one-offs. It is here that designers have begun to give full rein to their creative ambitions, pushing the complexity of the production values to the limit.

1.1

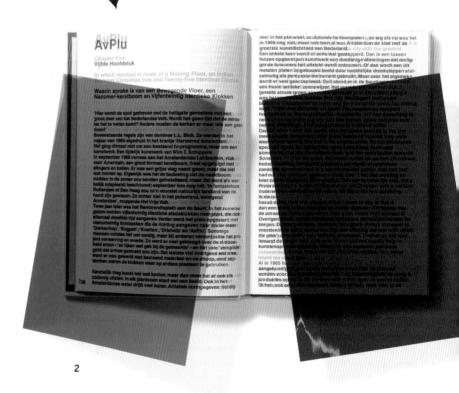

1.2

1 To celebrate the centenary of James Joyce's legendary novel *Ulysses,* Irish designer Orala O'Reilly proposed that quotes from the book be positioned around Dublin in the locations referenced in the text. The texts were sand-blasted into Dublin stone (**1**.1) and set full-size in a leather-bound landscape concertina book, *Dirty Dublin* (2004) (**1**.2). O'Reilly designed the unusual coloured ligatures, which reflect the way Joyce wrote in longhand, and assigned a colour to each chapter of the book.

2 *Het Beste Van* (1998) by Wim T. Schippens, is a Dutch book of essays that uses red and green type printed over one another and therefore occupying half as much space as conventional line-by-line setting. The text is read by placing a coloured acetate over the page. The green acetate hides the green text and makes the red text appear almost black, while the red acetate has the same effect on the green type.

2

The levels of exuberant indulgence are a joy to the designer and, it is hoped, a pleasure for the reader. Independent publishers have traditionally printed highly crafted limited-edition books that become collectors' items, and this tradition has been recognized by larger art and design publishers specializing in visual culture. They have established imprints that publish very expensive – £250 to £2000 – limited-edition copies of monographs. These are often signed by the author and may include original prints and pieces of ephemera relating to the artist. The buyer's perception is that of owning art by the artist, rather than merely buying a book about the artist.

3 The *Dries van Noten Book* (2005) celebrates 25 years of the Belgium fashion designer's work. It has a wraparound cover held in place by a tummy band. When broken, this reveals sumptuous photography, gilt-edged pages, and gold endpapers.

4 *'Ha, daar gaat er een van mij!'* (2003), written and designed by Jan Middendorp, is a beautifully illustrated history of graphic design in The Hague 1945–2000. The yellow and green of the cover are picked up in the book ribbons.

3

4

1 *A Dog's Life* by Sara Fanelli is an amusing illustrated book that combines drawn imagery with photographic montage. The text is set in an irreverent way and combined with some hand-drawn lettering. The front and back endpapers have fold-out elements so that the book becomes a dog.

2 The Italian children's book *Pollicino* by Charles Perrault is more conventionally illustrated by Lucia Salemi, with a painting on the right-hand page and a type-based left-hand page.

3 The Spanish children's book *Alfabeto Sobre La Literatura Infantil* by Bernardo Atxaga, with illustrations by Alejandra Hidalgo, uses handcut type and lino-cut illustrations set in a formal way but conveying a sense of childlike mischief.

Children's illustrated fiction

Children's fiction has vastly expanded in the past 20 years or so. Books for pre-school children are read aloud by an adult, while others are intended for young readers to read themselves. Children's books can open up a world of fantasy in which mythical characters and extrordinary powers exist and impossible feats are undertaken: the combination of words and pictures must capture the imagination of the young reader. Many young children's books work on the principle of repetition, allowing the child to anticipate events.

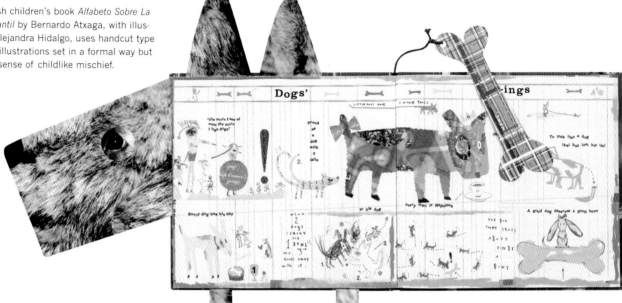

1

2

3

It is a feature of children's literature that animals take on human qualities such as speech and often have lives that parallel those of children. Traditionally, many children's stories are tales of moral guidance or are confidence-building or reassuring stories. Many publishers have begun to produce oversized copies of children's classics so that the nursery-school teacher can read and show the pictures to a group of chidren.

4 Alexander Calder's *Circus* features pages with model characters made of wire and wood, photographed and reproduced on a solid black ground. The type is reversed out of the ground and arranged in an expressive way to link the models and carry the narrative. All the elements of the page are considered as parts of a picture within the spread.

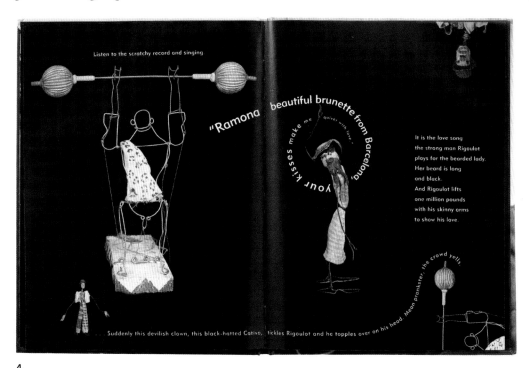

4

5

5 The cover of the children's story *Le Petit Prince,* by Antoine de Saint-Exupéry, is illustrated with simple watercolour illustrations that are integrated throughout the text. These images support the poignant writing and the book has become an enduring children's classic.

6 A spread from *Mr Lunch* by J. Otto Seibold and Vivian Walsh is drawn digitally but reproduced on soft paper and references the subtle colours of gravure printing of the 1950s. The drawings, which use line, flat colour, and some tints, have a childlike quality, as the perspective within the spread is irregular.

6

Photographic books

Photographic monographs rely on extremely high-quality printing to reproduce the carefully crafted prints of photographers. The designer will usually work closely with the photographer to order the photographs, also deciding how many should be reproduced per page and which should be paired on a spread. This has to be considered sensitively, as the pictures on a spread form a relationship with each other and may tell a story or offer contrast. The relationship between the photographic format and that of the book should be

1 *Tulipa*, a book featuring the work of Dutch photographer Leendert Blok (1895–1986) and designed by Willem van Zoetendaal, has a cover without type: the image is the title.

2 A gatefold page from a book featuring the American photographers Mike and Doug Starn shows three related images. The fracturing of the image is reflected by the creases of the fold.

1

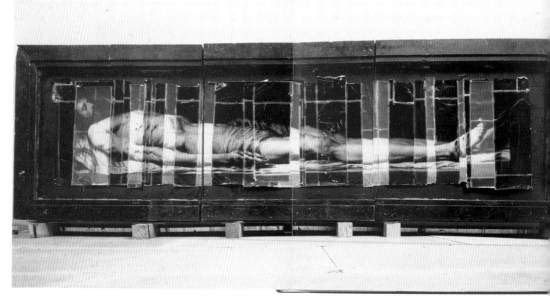

2

3

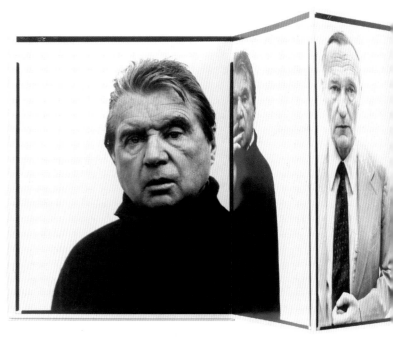

carefully considered, as portrait or landscape pictures will create different margins. The colour of the page is another consideration that, together with issues of crop and bleed, determines the way the photographs appear on the spread. Some photographs benefit from contrast and might be reversed out of a black page, while others work better on a neutral grey or white page. The positioning of the captions and style of type should complement the photographs and not create a distraction.

3 The book *Portraits* (2003) by American photographer Richard Avedon is made up from a concertina fold. It has no spine, only a cover and back-cover boards. One side of the book is images, and the reverse is a supporting essay.

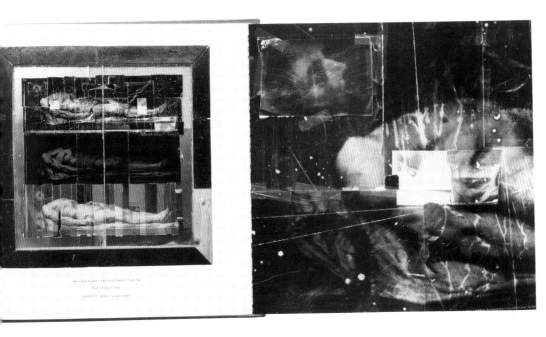

4 James Cotier's book *Nudes in Budapest* (1991) features photographs of elderly Hungarians. The photographs are printed on the right-hand page, and the format is the same as the image. The photographs are reproduced as duotones. A pale parchment tint has been printed on the left-hand page to mirror the position of the image. The tint emphasizes the woman's contemplations of a past that is fading from memory.

I GRÉTE DISZTL : *do ierres where now lives in America.*

11

Covers and jackets

The cover of a book serves two roles: to protect the pages, and to indicate the content. I will examine the first function in chapter 16 (Binding), and explore the second one here. The old adage about not judging a book by its cover is inherently critical of designers' and illustrators' abilities to communicate content within a miniature poster. A book cover is a promise made by a publisher on behalf of an author to a reader. It serves as an enticement to open the book, or to purchase a copy. This chapter will list the elements that are likely to be included on the front cover, back cover, and spine, then examine a range of approaches to cover design.

Working to a clear brief

Covers are frequently a cause for concern to authors, publishers, and designers. The author wants the cover to represent the content; the publisher must consider the views of both the in-house art director and the marketing manager; while the designer and illustrator take a brief from a commissioning editor. A clear brief is crucial and the designer should attempt to present the work directly to those who are to make the decision. Cover designs are often required for promotion purposes, often before the writing is completed. The brief should include a list of all the typographic elements and a summary of the issues to be considered in relation to the imagery and any additional information pertinent to a series, co-editions, or the publisher's vision for the book.

Cover formats: boxes or wraps

When we enter a bookshop, we expect to be confronted with illustrated covers for virtually every subject on the shelves. Communicating the contents of the book through both type and image is a strategy that has been adopted by the vast majority of publishers. However, if we could travel back in time to a bookshop in 1900, virtually all the covers would be typographic, with lettering embossed into leather or cloth bindings. From the 1950s to the 1980s, most illustrated book covers placed the illustration on the front cover only, with the spine and back cover often having very different treatments. Some more traditional publishers continue with this approach. A standard text format was often used for spines, blurbs, and dust-jackets. The inside back flap on a dust-jacket was used to give a brief biography of the author, frequently accompanied by a flattering photograph; the inside front flap was characteristically used for review quotes from critics.

Today, the front cover, back cover, and spine work together to sell the book. Once purchased and stored on a shelf at home, the spine's title serves as a data tag, but it is surprising how we search for books on our shelves by visually recalling the spine colour and design. The range of approach to covers is ever-broadening, as all publishers view the cover as a marketing device. In recent years, designers and illustrators have begun to consider the front cover, spine, and back cover as a single item rather than as the separate sides of a box. Viewing the cover as a wrap around the book block provides the art director with a greater sense of freedom and a larger canvas.

Front- and back-cover hierarchy

Irrespective of the format treatment of the cover – wrap, or the more conventional front cover, spine, and back – the designer generally needs to use imagery and type in a way that reinforces the status of the front cover. The front cover usually has a greater visual impact than the back cover: the front cover proclaims, the back cover reminds; the front says 'hello', the back 'goodbye'. These functions relate to both the imagery and the hierarchy within the text. Although the blurb on the back of a book is drawing the potential reader into a purchase, visually it plays a secondary role to the impact of the title.

The cover, spine, and back-cover elements

It is unlikely that every one of the elements listed below will be included on every cover, though it is important that the designer's brief for the cover identifies all the required elements before the design is begun.

Cover elements
- image
- author name in full
- book title, plus subtitle where required
- additional cover text
- format and size (may be larger than page size), spine depth, flap lengths, and surfaces available for print
- print requirements, for example, one-colour, two-colour, four-colour, special embossing

Spine elements
- author name in full
- book title, plus subtitle where required
- publisher's logo

Back cover elements
- ISBN/barcode
- registered retail price
- blurb or book description
- bullet-point breakdown of issues covered
- reviewers' quotes
- author biography
- list of previous publications

Flaps
- registered retail price
- book description
- bullet-point breakdown of issues covered
- reviewers' quotes
- author biography
- list of previous publications

Below The ISBN number is linked to a barcode that is usually printed on the back cover of a book and that is read electronically when the book is purchased.

ISBN 1-85669-437-2

The ISBN
This number is reproduced on the the back of a book as a barcode and used throughout retail packaging as a set of reproduction requirements.

Barcodes
- must be visible on the back of the book and not hidden on flaps or inside covers
- must be reproduced at a size between 85% and 120% of their original size
- must be printed in dark solid colour on white, or have a colour-free frame 2mm from the edge of the code

Above Publishers' marks, logos, or imprints are characteristically printed on the spine of the book. The position varies, but the spine symbol effectively reinforces the brand in the minds of the book-buying public.

Spines

The type on a spine on most European books runs from top to bottom, the baseline being adjacent to the back cover, although some American publishers run the title from bottom to top. Larger books with broad spines occasionally have their titles printed horizontally, though this generally means the type size has to be reduced and may cause some difficult word breaks. For the designer, it is important to know which way the title runs, what the relative importance between title and author's name is, and where the publisher's logo or name should be positioned.

Endpapers

Endpapers are pasted to the back of the cover boards on hardback books and are generally of a thicker stock than the book leaves. They may be plain or decorative. In older books, the decoration might be marbling or might feature a specially designed pattern relating to the book's content. Today the endpapers are often four-colour and make use of photography or illustration.

Cover and title sequence

The relationship between front cover, spine, back cover, and the preliminary pages of a book forms the initial reading experience. It should be carefully crafted by the designer to form a coherent whole in much the same way as the title sequence of a film combines credits and imagery and sets the tone for the subsequent narrative.

Types of cover

For a designer, it is worth spending some time in a bookshop looking not only at the books and their various designs but also at the way people browse and buy books. Cover styles for different types of book reflect their readership. The business section of a bookshop will feature very different covers from the classical literature or poetry sections. On looking at the browsing public, it is likely that there will be noticeable differences in their age, gender, and dress code, which, without falling into stereotypes, the designer should be aware of. Different types of books even in an age of multilingual publishing do not rely on the same cover genres worldwide. This makes browsing bookshops abroad exciting, as one realizes that book design and covers can reflect national and local culture as well as the global vision of multinational publishing groups. It is worth examining a number of approaches to covers. First, we consider covers that work to reinforce the brand as well as promote the individual title, and then turn to the application of some approaches that were discussed in chapter 3: documentation, concept, and expression.

Above The spines of the books opposite arranged in chronological order from left to right. Three key elements are common to all: the author's name, the title, and the Penguin logo. The hierarchy, type orientation, and size and style of the penguin have changed over time.

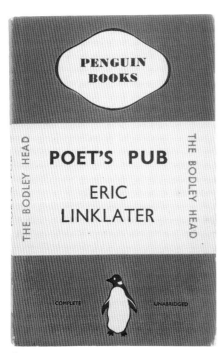

1

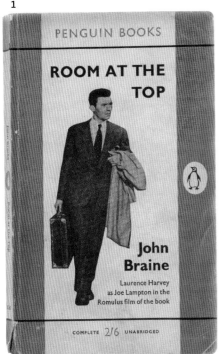

2

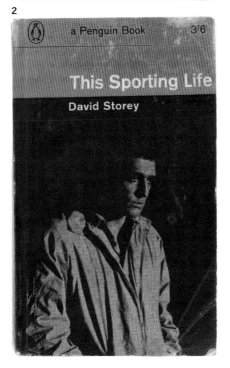

3

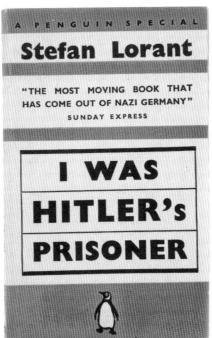

4

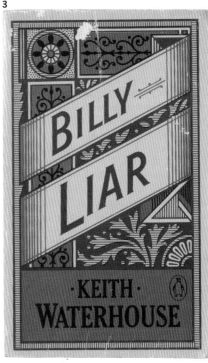

5

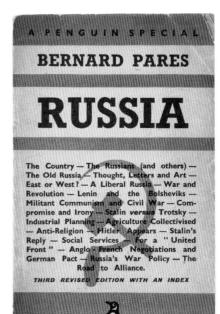

6

Above Early Penguin books, with orange covers and a white band, had their titles and authors set in the same font; the series brand was very strong, but the content of the individual title was largely disguised. Later editions had illustrated or photographic covers that were reproduced in black line or halftone, and these worked in combination with the orange identity and title.

1–3
1936 *Poet's Pub* by Eric Linklater
1939 *I was Hitler's Prisoner* by Stefan Lorant
1942 *A Penguin Special: Russia* by Bernard Pares
4–6
1959 *Room at the Top* by John Braine
1962 *This Sporting Life* by David Storey
1974 *Billy Liar* by Keith Waterhouse

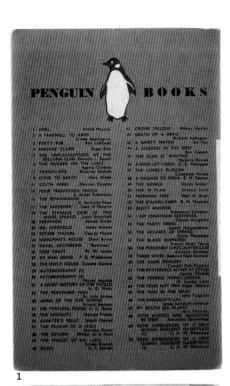

1

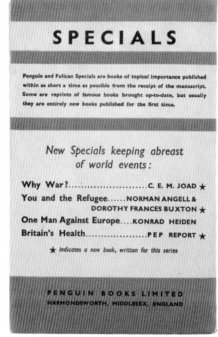

2

3

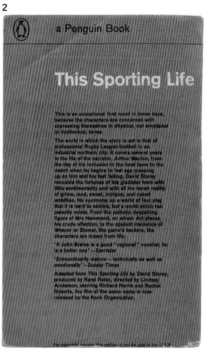

4

5

6

Above

The back covers of the books shown on the previous page reveal how a series style developed over nearly 40 years. The earliest book, from 1936 **1** uses the back cover to list all the other Penguin paperbacks in print. The back of the 1942 book **3** has been used to advertise a shaving stick – a product entirely unrelated to the title, *Russia*. The more recent books **4–6** have the blurb placed on the back cover, though the alignment of the text is varied: justified **4**; ranged right **5**; and centred **6**. These developments in the use of the back of the Penguin paperback series show how the characteristic conventions of paperback novels today were developed. Note the use of the author's portrait and the development of the Penguin logo, which faces both left and right.

Covers that promote the brand

Covers that work in series serve a double purpose: that of promoting the individual title, and that of alerting the reader to the range of books in the whole series. Books in a series begin to have a greater shelf presence if they are displayed as a group.

Some older bookshops with traditionally organized stock remain true to the idea of ordering their shelves by subject and author, whereas others, aware of brand status, are prepared to group a series together independently of title. This marketing strategy has huge benefits for the publisher, as it promotes instinctive sales and collectables.

Documentation: visualizing the content

Covers designed from a documentary position seek, simply, to record what a book contains. This might take the form of a typographic title or a selection of representative images from the pages; an approach based on 'what you see is what you get'. The relationship between a book's cover and the design of the interior is an issue the designer must be aware of: the composition of the cover can pick up on the layout of the spreads.

Conceptual covers

Covers that are based on conceptual thinking attempt to represent a book's content through visual allegory, pun, paradox, or cliché in an amusing fusion of image and title. The potential reader browsing the spines may pull a title off the shelf and, viewing the cover, experience a frisson of pleasure, a moment of euphoria – what has been called 'a smile in the mind', a term used as the title of a book about conceptual design. The browser turns buyer, his or her purchase affirmed by the cover, with reasoning along the lines of: 'This book has a witty cover: I recognized its wit because I'm intelligent.' As we all erect scaffolding to support our own prejudices, it is likely that the buyer will repeat-purchase other books using a similar approach.

Expressive covers

An expressive approach to cover design is often used in relation to novels and short stories. The aim is not to make a summative visual in a conceptual way but to evoke content, to hint at what is within and entice the prospective reader. Covers of this kind often make use of drawings, illustrations, photography, and appropriate images from fine art. The art director or illustrator tries to make an arresting image that, in combination with the book title, intrigues the reader and alludes to an element of the story or attempts to visualize the emotional heart of the text. The potential reader is drawn in by the image and title in combination. Drawing, mark-making, and symbolism are often used, creating a poetic ambiguity and inviting the reader to reflect. This approach views content as a starting point from which an interpretation is to be made. A tension exists between honouring the author's original text and visualizing the designer's individual ideas.

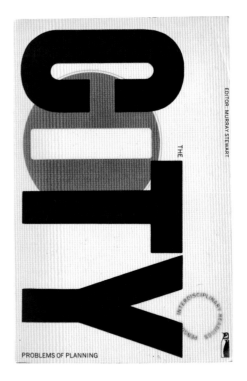

Above Designer Derek Birdsall applied a conceptual approach to the Penguin Education covers. The breadth of the series content was held together by two elements: the use of a single typeface (Railroad Gothic), and a cover arrangement that reflected the content of individual volumes. The range of spine widths and title lengths within the series was accommodated by common alignment. Here, the title *The City: Problems of Planning* is illustrated with the 'no access' road sign.

Covers: using documentary photography

Knaur

Gernot Gricksch

Die Herren
Hansen erobern
die Welt

Roman

1

Роберт Валзер

JAKOB ФОН ГУНТЕН

ТЕМПЛУМ

2

dtv

Heinrich Böll
Wanderer, kommst
du nach Spa...
Erzähllungen

Sandra Lüpkes
Die Sand-
dornkönigin
Inselkrimi

3

4

Above Four covers that make use of reportage or documentary photography. **1** The angled crop at the bottom of this photograph echoes the comic quiffs and contrasts with the formal centred type. **2** Perspective plays an important part in the composition of this image. The black band crops the figure's feet oddly, but is the same distance from the base of the page as the horizon is from the top of the page. **3** This apparently everyday scene is made poignant as the man on crutches has only one leg. The type and the road taper to a common vanishing point. **4** The image of the boat is locked into the rectangle of the cover on the right by cropping and on the left by the mooring line coming from the boat.

Covers: an expressive approach

1

FRANZ KAFKA
Der Proceß
Roman
Originalfassung
Fischer

PABLO NERUDA
Fulgor y muerte de Joaquín Murieta
EDICIÓN Y NOTAS DE HERNÁN LOYOLA
PRÓLOGO DE LUIS CHITARRONI
CONTEMPORÁNEA

DeBOLSILLO

2

MEMORIA DE MIS
PUTAS TRISTES

GABRIEL GARCÍA MÁRQUEZ

LITERATURA MONDADORI

3

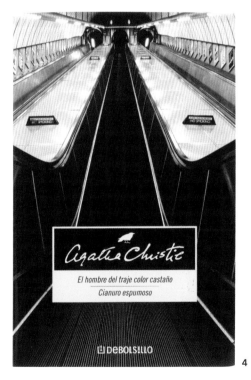

Agatha Christie
El hombre del traje color castaño
Cianuro espumoso

DeBOLSILLO

4

Above A set of covers where the photographic images have been manipulated to evoke the nature of the content. The images are all designed as miniature posters. The text on all four is centred; in **1** the type is reversed out of a block, and on **2**, **3**, and **4** the text appears in a panel over the image.

Covers: expressing ideas through illustration

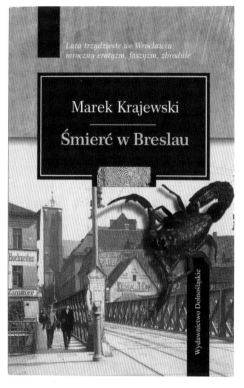

1

2

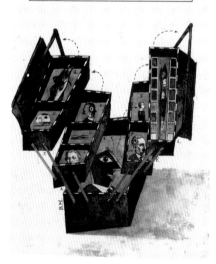

3

4

Covers: using pattern

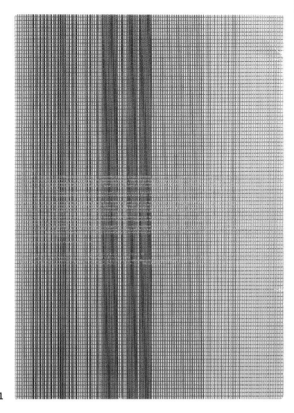

1

2

Opposite Four covers that make use of illustration as an approach. **1** The illustration of this Polish novel is a montage of photography, painting, and a three-dimensional found object. **2** This illustration by Lorenzo Mattotti is a painting that forms a graphic red band of blood reminiscent of a flag. **3** The conceptual illustration by Bruno Mallart used on this cover visualizes elements of the book's content in an artist's toolbox. **4** Again, the illustration has a conceptual basis: the small red symbol of a male figure is trapped somewhat helplessly between the female's legs.

Above and right This page shows three wraparound covers that make use of pattern. All three are for books about design. **1** The back cover of a book about the design group Faydherbe/De Vringer, *Grafisch Theatre*, uses a fine linear grid. **2** The London College of Printing catalogue from 1998 uses overlapping numbers arranged in such close proximity that they become a pattern. **3** The wraparound cover of this graphics book, *Printed Matter\Drukwerk*, features Dutch design and is decorated with overprinted circles.

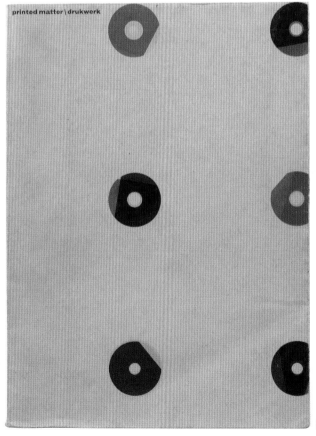

3

Typographic covers

1

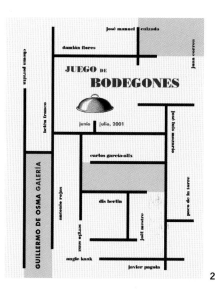

2

3

4

Above Typographic covers that do not incorporate imagery are widely used for a variety of subject-matter. The title and author name are played with experimentally and can be combined with striking colours to produce covers with considerable impact. **1** Laurie Rosenwald's *New York Notebook* uses type in irregular sizes and overprints the cloth binding of the spine with the first letter of each word in the title. Perfect alignment of these two elements would be difficult; irregular positioning of the letters on the cover disguises any inconsistency and perfectly reflects the content. **2** The cover of this catalogue for Guillermo de Osma's Galeria is made up of blocks and type labels that surround the central title like a maze. **3** The title of the cover of Emil Ruder's book *Typographie* reads easily in reverse. It reflects perfectly type before it is printed and emphasizes the modular nature of type and how as a consequence it forms a grid structure. **4** In contrast, the cover of Wolfgang Weingart's *My Way to Typography* reflects his experimental approach to the subject, cropping the text yet retaining the readability and making use of very strong contrasting colours.

Manufacture IV

Manufacture

The manufacturing process of a book includes all the elements of production that are undertaken once the writing and design have been completed. The process includes pre-production, printing, and binding, each of which is addressed in a separate chapter. I have also included chapters on paper, without which no book would ever be printed, and on paper engineering.

A designer's involvement with the production process may vary with different publishers and different books. Sometimes the designer may visit a book on press or at the binders; at other times the involvement may be by telephone, fax, or email, or consist of marking up proofs for correction. Independently of the level of involvement in the process, a book designer must have a knowledge of how a book is produced in order to work creatively and effectively, liaising with writer, publisher, editor, printer, and binder. Knowledge of the production process affects the way we design books, providing both constraints and opportunities. For example, the style of binding affects how a book opens and if it will lie flat when open. For a photographic book, this may be important, but is not really necessary for a paperback novel.

Pre-production

'Pre-production' is the term used by printers to cover a variety of processes that prepare the spreads laid out by the designer for printing. 'Reproduction' is often used generally to describe the same process but, until the wide-scale adoption of digital software, had a more specific print definition – repro was the process of assembling film in preparation for making plates. All designers should aim to have a broad overview of this process, since understanding how images and text are handled in print is important in realizing the required finish in a book. Designers anticipate and plan for print reproduction qualities that cannot be visualized on screen and often cannot be reproduced through studio-based laser or inkjet printers. By working with a printer, viewing and responding to proofs, the full range of print finishes can be realized. The pre-production processes examined in this chapter for line and colour can be reproduced using the four principal forms of printing which I will examine in chapter 14: relief, intaglio, planographic, and stencil.

Line and tone

For a printer, line work is any form of print reproduced in a single flat colour that is consistent across the surface of the print with no variation in tone or density. Line work is used for text or image and can be made up of solid areas, dots or, as the name implies, lines. Line printing is used to reproduce type, line drawings, etchings, woodcuts, linocuts, and engravings. Illustrators and designers have developed ways of fooling the eye into seeing tone, by making use of cross-hatched lines or dots. By clustering together many dark marks in specific areas of the illustration and using fewer marks in other parts, the viewer is made to see different tones. However, when the illustration is examined through a loupe, or magnifying glass, it is clear that all the marks are printed in the same density and it is merely their relative size and proximity that are

jsem věděl, že je to marné. Nic nenajdu, všechno je-
nom ještě víc popletu, lampa mi vypadne z rukou, je
tak těžká, tak mučivě těžká a já budu dál tápat a hledat a bloudit místností, po celý svůj ubohý život.

Švagr se na mne díval, úzkostlivě a poněkud káravě.
Vidí, jak se mě zmocňuje šílenství, napadlo mě a ho-
nem jsem zase lampu zdvihl. Přistoupila ke mně sestra,
tiše, s prosebnýma očima, plná strachu a lásky, až mi
srdce pukalo. Nedokázal jsem nic říci, mohl jsem jen
natáhnout ruku a pokynout, odmítavě pokynout a v du-
chu jsem si říkal: Nechte mě přece! Nechte mě přece!
Cožpak můžete vědět, jak mi je, jak trpím, jak strašlivě
trpím! A opět: Nechte mě přece! Nechte mě přece!

Narudlé světlo lampy slabě protékalo velkou místností, venku sténaly stromy ve větru. Na okamžik se
mi zdálo, že vidím a cítím noc venku jakoby ve svém
nejhlubším nitru: vítr a mokro, podzim, hořký pach
listí, rozletující se listy jilmu, podzim, podzim! A opět
na okamžik jsem já nebyl já sám, nýbrž jsem se na se-
be díval jako na obraz: Byl jsem bledý, vychrtlý hudeb-
ník s roztěkanýma planoucíma očima, jenž se jmeno-
val Hugo Wolf a tohoto večera se propadal do šílenství.

Mezitím jsem musel znovu hledat, beznadějně hledat
a přenášet těžkou lampu, na kulatý stůl, na křeslo, na
hraničku knih. A prosebnými gesty jsem se musel brá-
nit, když se na mne sestra znovu smutně a opatrně díva-
la, když mne chtěla těšit, být u mne blízko a pomoci mi.
Smutek ve mně rostl a vyplňoval mě k prasknutí, obrazy
kolem mne nabyly podmanivě výmluvné zřetelnosti, by-
ly daleko zřetelnější, než jaká kdy bývá skutečnost; ve

(106)

variable. Artwork for line reproduction is often prepared larger than it is to be
reproduced, so that by reducing the size of the final print, the image is tight-
ened up, imperfections in the original drawing are lost, and an impression of
tone is created.

If the designer wants to retain common line widths in line illustrations, it is
important that the illustrator is briefed appropriately at the commissioning
stage. The illustrator is then in a position to draw all the required illustrations
at the same scale, which can then be reduced by the same percentage. This
requirement often forces the designer to have a fairly tight preparatory layout
or confirmed column widths within a book before commissioning. Today, software such as Freehand, Illustrator, and InDesign enables line weights to be
corrected at the layout stage, but this is time-consuming, and rescaling can be
minimized by forward planning and clear briefing.

Above The left-hand page of this novel by
Hermann Hesse, *Pohadky,* is printed in a single
colour, while the right-hand page illustration is
printed lithographically in two colours.

Screens

Screens are used to reproduce tone in images or text. The American inventor Frederick Ives (1856–1937) patented the glass screening process in the 1880s. Screening an image literally involved placing a glass screen covered in tiny dots between the lens and the photographic paper. The resultant image was made up of a grid of tiny line dots of different sizes. This process is still in use today, but is being superseded by digital screening, which breaks down the image to be reproduced into thousands of dots.

Halftone screens

A halftone is an element of print that contains tones other than black or white. Tone is the amount of black found within an image: the darker the tone, the more ink is used for its reproduction. Continuous-tone images contain a range of tones that merge into one another. The original image may be a painting, a drawing, a photograph, or type. To reproduce a continuous-tone image, a screen is used to convert tone into line, a grid pattern of dots all the same colour. Where the original image contains dark tones, the dots are large; where the original is made up of light tones, the dots are smaller. The principles of the process remain the same when using digital screening. At 50% tone, each square of black ink lies adjacent to a no-ink or white square. Elliptical dots produce kite shapes in the midtones, which produce very smooth tonal graduation. When dots become so large that they begin to join up, this is referred to as 'dot gain' and it can create dark areas within an image and breaks the smooth, graduated tones: elliptical dots minimize dot gain more effectively than circular dots.

Halftone screens are calibrated according to the number of lines per inch (lpi) or centimetre. The greater the number of lines, the finer the screen and the better the reproduction; fewer lines indicates a coarser screen. Printing images with very fine screens will produce smooth graduation throughout the tonal range, provided the paper is of sufficient quality to hold the ink crisply. Halftone screens for newspapers and letterpress reproduction at 55lpi are coarser than those for offset lithography at 120lpi or fine bookwork at 170lpi. Screens are arranged at 45° to the horizontal so that the reader's eye is made least aware of the dot grid.

Types of screen

Screens in which the dots are arranged in a consistent grid pattern of rows and columns but change in size, like the early glass versions, are called 'amplitude modulated' (AM) screens. Screens in which the dots are the same size but are not positioned on a grid are referred to as 'frequency modulated' (FM).

Today, using digital technology, the designer can control how screens are used and specify different approaches to the use of halftone screen images. Much of this pre-press work can be done by the designer in software such as Photoshop, Freehand, and Illustrator. Designers can make use of special screens using lines or concentric circles or even make customized screens, changing the shape of the dots as well as the number per inch.

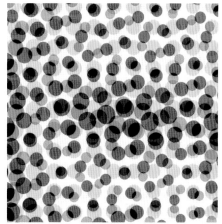

Below A detail from the cover shown left reveals how the light areas are defined by small dots, while the dark areas are made up of large dots.

Moiré patterns

If two halftone screens are laid over one another, slightly out of alignment, a moiré pattern is likely to be produced. This optical effect occurs when the overlapping and intersecting dots on both screens combine to create a new pattern. The effect can be used creatively and makes the reader aware of the print process, but it can also be detrimental to an image requiring crisp reproduction. Moiré patterns can also be caused by patterns that exist within the original image. For example, a very fine black-and-white dogtooth check in a piece of clothing when passed through a halftone screen may create an unwanted moiré pattern.

Moiré patterns may also be created when existing printed material, having passed through a halftone screen, is scanned again. The two dot screens clash and the resultant moiré pattern detracts from the image. Where the original material is a photographic print, transparency, or digital photograph, this does not present a problem. To reproduce existing print material – such as printing a postcard in a book – printers use 'dot-for-dot' reproduction, in which the new screen is shot in line that matches the original. Through modern digital scanning techniques, manipulation in Photoshop, and the use of frequency modulated screens, moiré patterns can be avoided.

Colour

The extensive use of colour in books has a lengthy tradition, extending right back to early medieval times in Western Europe, when calligraphic books were copied by hand. Illuminated decorative letters were drawn in many colours. Gutenberg's first printed Bible of 1455 included red capital letters and headings, known as rubrics, although these were filled in by hand. Today, presses can print up to six colours consecutively.

Single colour

Single-colour work, as the name implies, uses only one colour, although line and screens can be combined to reproduce text and halftone images. Printers can match colours with samples of paint or natural materials as the designer requires. This can be done through mixing inks in different proportions by eye, until both the designer and the printer are satisfied that the required colour has been achieved or by making use of a range of existing inks. Printing in a single colour is often referred to by a number of terms: matched, selected, flat, or spot colour.

Pantone Matching System

The most widely available, and the industry-standard, colour system is the Pantone Matching System (PMS). Other systems such as True Match, Focoltone, and Hexachrome offer similar colour ranges. The Pantone system offers the designer more than 1,000 basic colours in a swatch book. These can be used on their own in single-colour work, or in combinations in two-colour work. The chosen colours can also be matched to the process colours (colours made up of percentages of CMYK). The system also offers the designer pastel colours that are true colours rather than tints, and metallics and varnishes.

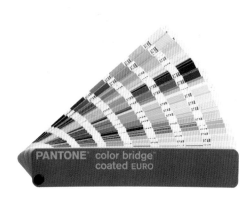

1 The Pantone colour bridge system links spot colours with process colours made up of percentages of CMYK. Some colours will be a better match than others. This is a very useful aid for the book designer as it enables a special colour, perhaps used on a five-colour cover (CMYK plus a special) to be matched to a process colour used for chapter openers.

2 Pantone metallic and pastel swatch books are used for specifying single colours or specials where they can be used in combination with CMYK as an overprint. The metallic ink can be sealed with a varnish that minimizes the effect of fingerprints but slightly affects the colour.

3 Pantone pastels are very subtle colour solids that are mixed with extenders so that the colour is very soft. They can be used in book design but are not made from the CMYK palette and therefore require an extra plate to print. Like metallics, these are termed 'specials'.

Quien no conoce nada, no ama nada. Quien no puede hacer nada, no comprende nada. Quien nada comprende, nada vale. Pero quien comprende también ama, observa, ve... Cuanto mayor es el conocimiento inherente a una cosa, más grande es el amor... Quien cree que todas las frutas maduran al mismo tiempo que las frutillas nada sabe acerca de las uvas. Paracelso

Left This spread from Erich Fromm's *El arte de amar* shows a two-colour text running across the gutter. The red and black solid colours are printed from separate plates that must be in perfect registration, as any misalignment would be clearly visible within the text.

Two-colour work

Modern printing presses are designed for single, two-colour, four-colour, or six-colour working. Two-colour work forces the printer to ensure that the colours are positioned in the correct place relative to each other. This process is known as registration. Two-colour work enables the designer to make use of the second colour as part of the organization within the text or to enhance the quality of the illustration. Much two-colour book work takes the form of black and a second, spot colour, although any two colours may be used.

Selected colour, multiple plates

Selected-colour line work is used for reproducing maps, as it allows the very fine line detail to be reproduced. It would not be possible to register accurately the four plates of the CMYK process colours to reproduce elements such as very fine contour lines.

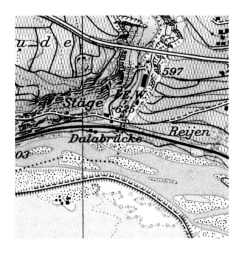

Above This detail from a beautifully printed Swiss map of the Alps is reproduced actual size. Each colour is printed on a separate plate. The fine line work in many colours would be very difficult to reproduce through a four-colour process. Each colour on a map sheet or atlas plate is printed in perfect registration over the previous one. Some maps may have as many as 15 separate plates.

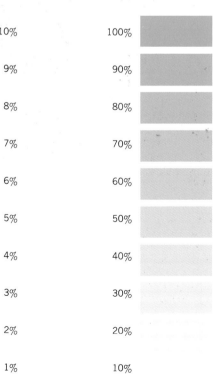

Solid colour (here 100% cyan)

Printing on (here 20% cyan)

Superprint (20% cyan ground
100% cyan numeral)

Reversed out (20% cyan
ground numeral not inked)

Overprint (20% cyan ground
numeral printed 100%)

10%	100%
9%	90%
8%	80%
7%	70%
6%	60%
5%	50%
4%	40%
3%	30%
2%	20%
1%	10%

Printing effects

When two or more colours are printed in registration they may overlap, butt up to one another, or stand alone. These effects work in different ways depending on how light or dark the colours are.

Printing on

'Printing on' is a term that is used to describe line or halftone printing onto a sheet of paper. It is the simplest form of print: one colour printed onto paper without overprinting or reversal.

Superprint

Flat colour printed solid 100% produces a flat, even ink on the page. By reducing the percentage of solid colour, a tint is produced. Tints of a colour are now created digitally by the designer on-screen. When two or more different tints are printed, this is referred to as 'superprint'. Tints have to be used carefully when working with type: if there is not sufficient tonal difference between the type and the ground, the type will not be readable. A rough guideline is that the type should be at least 30% stronger than the ground. However, for very dark or light colours, a greater differential may be required.

Reversed out

If the type or image appears white, or in a tint that is lighter than the ground it sits on, it is termed 'reversed out'. If type with fine serifs or illustrations that make use of very fine lines are reversed out in small sizes there is a danger of filling in. This is because the large area of ink bleeds out into the fine lines and they become lost. This effect will become worse the finer the line, the larger the area of flat ground, and the more absorbent the paper.

Overprint

Overprint is a term that refers to one colour being printed over the top of another. In this process two or more plates are used. A simple overprint might involve printing black type over a coloured ground. The type will be readable provided there is at least 30% difference between the tone of each colour. The designer can specify the order the plates are printed in as this will affect the presentation of the print. Unless instructed otherwise, the printer will order the plates so as to produce the greatest degree of contrast. Generally, lighter colours are printed first and darker colours second. For example, a blue (dark colour) printed over a yellow (light colour) will produce a clean green. If the lighter colour is printed over a darker colour, a third, midtone colour is created. For example, if a yellow (light colour) is printed over a blue (dark colour), a green will be created, but it will be subdued or even muddy. Complex overprinting may involve many colours in a variety of tints being laid over one another. In such cases, careful planning, experience, close consultation, and an extensive set of proofs will be required if the designer is to achieve the desired effect. Selected colours can be used in as many workings as are required, although the cost of each plate should be considered.

Overprinting CMYK colour solids

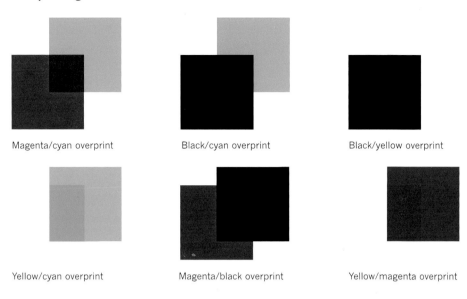

Magenta/cyan overprint

Black/cyan overprint

Black/yellow overprint

Yellow/cyan overprint

Magenta/black overprint

Yellow/magenta overprint

Overprinting specials

Overprinting four-colour print (CMYK) with a selected colour is referred to as a 'special' and this process is usually undertaken on a six-colour press (which prints up to six colours in one working). Specials might include a selected colour, a metallic colour, or a spot varnish or sealing varnish, all of which are overprinted.

Trapping

Often designers want to butt two flat colours up to one another. This requires perfect registration, otherwise a thin white line of unprinted paper will be visible between the two colours. To allow the printer greater tolerance with registration, designers can specify the trapping. This is the amount of overlap added to the lighter colour. The lighter colour is given a stroke width, usually specified in millimetres or inches, around the area to be trapped. When the darker colour is overprinted, the light and dark colours appear to butt. If neither of the colours is very dark in tone, a small halo where the two colours overprint may be visible.

Mixing colour and tone

A variety of print effects can be achieved by overprinting colour tones over solid or halftones. These effects are referred to as flat-tint halftones or duotones, tritones, and quadtones.

Flat-tint halftone

A halftone printed over a flat tint is referred to as a flat-tint halftone. The lighter colour, or tint, is printed first and the darker colour halftone is printed over it. This has the effect of evenly colouring the image and reducing the tonal range. This effect should not be confused with a duotone, where the aim is to increase the tonal range.

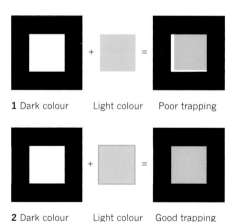

1 Dark colour   Light colour   Poor trapping

2 Dark colour   Light colour   Good trapping

Above 1 the black square has been overprinted by the smaller cyan square but without trapping. As a consequence, a tiny ugly white gap has appeared between the two print elements.
2 The cyan square has been framed with a stroke of the same colour, making the square slightly larger and providing a margin of error for the registration of the overprint.

Duotones, tritones, and quadtones

Halftone images reproduced in a single colour cannot carry the full tonal range of a black-and-white photographic print and there tends to be a loss of contrast. Duotone printing makes use of two plates of the same image that are superimposed on one another. The lighter colour, printed first, holds the highlights (very light tonal areas) and midtones, and the black holds the darker tones. When the two are superimposed, the image has a greater tonal range than a one-colour halftone. This is often referred to by printers as 'punch'. The second colour used in a duotone may be a grey or a colour that tints the image, and can be specified as a percentage to produce a softer image. Metallic colours and tinted varnishes can be superimposed as duotones.

Tritones and quadtones take this principle even further. As their respective names suggest, tritones have three plates dividing up the tonal range into three workings, and quadtones four plates. As each colour requires a new plate these can be very expensive to reproduce and tend to be used in very high-quality, lavish black-and-white photographic books where it is important to preserve the essence of the original photographic print.

Right top Nick Clark has produced a very useful book for designers: *Duotones, Tritones, and Quadtones* (1996). He illustrates the effect of changing the percentage of each colour. The large photo of Venice (left-hand page) is reproduced 100% brick-red halftone and 100% black halftone. The image on the right-hand page bottom left is a much subtler halftone but is significantly warmer, reproduced 25% brick-red halftone and 100% black halftone. The black is usually printed over the colour. Metallic or even fluorescent inks can be used effectively in duotones and tritones.

Right bottom A second spread from the same book illustrates how the CMYK process can be played with to create different effects. Each of the plates carries a halftone image of the original photograph, but the percentages vary, *eg* left-hand page 65% yellow, 30% cyan, 65% magenta, 100% black. The richness of an image printed in this way is very attractive, though expensive, and usually requires considerable proofing.

Full-colour reproduction

While it is possible to print books using any number of special flat colours, the cost escalates with each new plate. It becomes more economical to make a range of colours by mixing them from combinations of the three primary colours. Full-colour reproduction recreates the tonal and colour ranges recorded in a colour transparency or digital photograph. There are two sorts of primary colours: the light primaries and the pigment primaries.

Light primary: RGB additive colour

When white light is split through a prism, it is broken into the colours of the rainbow: red, orange, yellow, green, blue, indigo, and violet. White light is produced from mixing red, green, and blue (RGB) light together, and these are known as the light primary colours. White light is paler in tone than the primaries from which it is created and is referred to as additive colour. The light secondary colours are yellow, magenta, and cyan. These colours are created from combinations of two of the light primaries. Additive or RGB colour is used in film projections, television, and computer monitors.

Pigment primary: CMYK subtractive colour

The pigment primaries are red, yellow, and blue. When they are combined they theoretically produce black (though in practice the colour is a dark khaki-brown). Black is darker in tone than the primaries from which it is created and is a subtractive colour. As the basic pigment primaries do not produce a true black, printers use four different colours in combination to produce full-colour reproduction: cyan, magenta, yellow, and black (CMYK; a printer's term for black is *key,* and the abbreviation for this is used rather than B).

The relationship between the light and pigment primaries

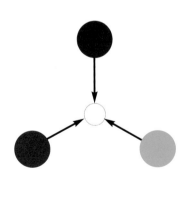

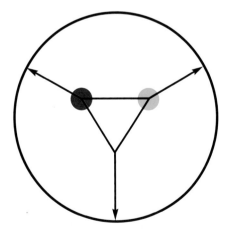

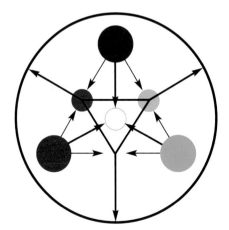

1 The light primary or additive colours are: red, green, and blue/violet. They combine to make white light.

2 The pigment or subtractive secondary colours are: cyan, magenta, and yellow. They combine to make black – shown here as the large outer circle.

3 When the two diagrams are combined, the relationship between light and pigment primaries can be illustrated. Light primaries are combined in pairs to make the pigment primaries:
blue/violet + green = cyan
blue/violet + red = magenta
red + green = yellow.

Stages of colour separation

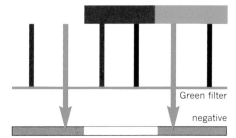 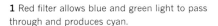 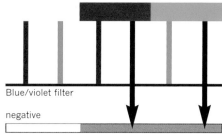

1 Red filter allows blue and green light to pass through and produces cyan.

2 Green filter allows red and blue light to pass through and produces magenta.

3 Blue/violet filter allows red and green light to pass through and produces yellow.

Colour separation

Colour separation was first achieved using coloured filters in 1860. The additive light primaries red, green, and blue/violet were used to produce the separation negative. The red filter allows blue and green light to pass through and produces the cyan film separation; the green filter allows red and blue light to pass through and produces the magenta; the blue/violet filter allows red and green light to pass through and produces the yellow. Black is added as a separate halftone to give images greater tonal ranges and to ensure a solid true black when required. Before the advent of digital separations, printers and reproduction houses used a process camera to make continuous-tone film, which was subsequently turned into screen halftones.

Colour gamut

The range of colours a process can produce is referred to as a colour gamut. Our eyes can see approximately ten million colours, though this is far more than any colour separation device can achieve or printing process can reproduce. The RGB colour gamut is far larger than the CMYK gamut. Pantone Matching Systems, realizing the limitations of the CMYK gamut, introduced two additional colours to the CMYK system, a strong orange and a green, and called the new system Hexachrome. This system, found in QuarkXPress and InDesign publishing programs, extends the basic CMYK gamut significantly.

Scanning

Digital scanning has now largely replaced the use of separations produced by process cameras. Scanners come in many forms, including the simple flatbed scanner used by designers to digitize transparencies or artworks so that they can be positioned within a book, and the much more sophisticated drum scanners used by printers for reproduction. While it is possible to produce scanning suitable for book production on a studio flatbed scanner, a better alternative is to send the original transparencies and artwork to the reproduction house. A scanner converts a full-colour image into the four-colour process CMYK. The image is scanned in a series of lines, or rasters. A laser is used to burn the screen dots directly onto the film as either positives or negatives. Illustrations and artwork for high-resolution drum-scanning should be mounted on flexible paper rather than stiff board, as board cannot be wrapped around the drum for scanning. If the surface of the illustration is not smooth, this will affect the quality of the scan. Illustrations that contain lumps of paint or collage elements are better reproduced through scanning a large- or medium-format photographic transparency or by taking a high-resolution digital photograph from which separations can be made.

Screen angles

The screens of the four-colour process are arranged at 30° angles to one another so as to avoid dot clash and the consequent moiré effect. The screen angles are: cyan 105°, magenta 75°, yellow 90°, and black 45°.

Grey replacement

Grey replacement is used by printers with reference to converting into black some of the grey colour produced by the combination of cyan, magenta, and yellow plates. The grey and neutral tones are removed from the coloured plates and replaced with black. This process is beneficial as it reduces the ink density (amount of ink printed onto the paper overall), minimizes the possibility of dot gain, speeds drying times, allows greater control on press, and saves money particularly on long runs as black ink is significantly cheaper than the other three process colours.

Colour sequence

The order in which the colour plates are printed is called the colour sequence, or the order of the lay. This order may vary, but many printers set up their presses to print black, cyan, magenta, and yellow respectively. If a book has a great deal of black in the images the black may be moved to the end of the sequence. The standard order of printing is in part determined by the qualities of the ink, and also enables the printer to make minor adjustments to the running of the press on a consistent basis. Black ink, for example, is slightly more tacky (adheres to the paper better) than the other process colours, which are ordered by their relative stickiness.

Dot gain

Dot gain is a term printers use to describe the unwanted increase in size of screen dots that can happen when printing on paper. This can cause the printed image to look muddy and impair the tonal qualities. It occurs when dots bleed into one another if the ink is not sufficiently tacky or there is too much ink on the plate. Some dot gain is inevitable as not all the CMYK colours have the same degree of tackiness. The more viscous the ink, the better it sticks to the paper, the less it bleeds, and the more it retains the crisp dot. Black is the tackiest ink; yellow is the least tacky. Coated papers reduce the effect of dot gain as they absorb less ink. For this reason coated papers are combined with very high screen values (175–200dpi, or dots per inch) to improve definition and clarity. The problems of dot gain are exacerbated when printing on uncoated or soft papers, as the unsealed fibres act as capillaries,

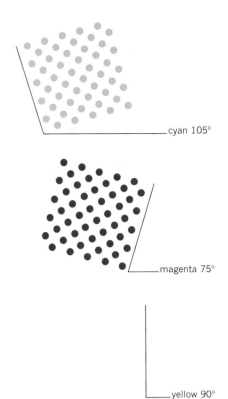

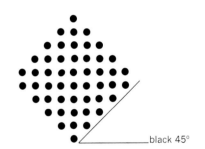

Above Each of the screens in the CMYK process is positioned at a different angle: cyan at 105°, magenta at 75°, yellow at 90°, and black at 45°.

Below Proof marks are used on proofs by the designer and production department to advise the printer how to refine the book before it goes into production.

Instruction	Margin mark
Passed for press	✓
Reproof	△2
Reduce contrast	□
Increase contrast	■
Improve detail or modelling	◨
Too hard, make softer	U
Too soft, make sharper	∧
Sort uneven tint	◕
Repair type rule or tint	X
Improve registration	⧉

Process colour	Increase	Decrease
Cyan	C+	C–
Magenta	M+	M–
Yellow	Y+	Y–
Black	K+	K–

Wet proofs

Wet proofs use the four CMYK plates on a proofing press and are in effect a short run prior to production. Wet proofs are the most accurate way of reproducing spreads. The four colours can be printed individually on separate sheets, which enables the printer and designer to review the ink coverage of each colour. When the colour sequence is printed onto a single sheet, the printer supplies the designer with 'progressives'. These are the progressive combinations of colours: black, black plus cyan, black plus cyan plus magenta, black plus cyan plus magenta plus yellow; if there are any specials or varnishes, these can be printed as an additional progressive.

Proofing marks

Proofing marks are used by designers to communicate to the printer the proof corrections needed. This set of common marks is accompanied by written instructions. The marks and instructions can be drawn directly onto the proofs or on a top sheet of tracing paper attached to the proof.

Scatter proofs and blads

Scatter proofs is a term printers use to refer to pages or spreads not proofed in imposition order but ganged up together so that colour throughout the book across a range of text, illustration, photographic halftone, and tint can be checked for consistency. Scatter proofs are sometimes used for promotional purposes by a publisher's marketing department. If a range of scatter proofs is produced as single-sided double-page spreads, they can be distributed by the marketing department at book trade fairs to encourage sales, distribution deals, and co-edition rights. Some publishers have two-sided scatter proofs printed and made up into little wire-stitched books called blads. These are trimmed to the correct size, printed on the chosen stock, and feature non-sequential spreads of the various sections of the book. They are usually no longer than 16 pages. Potential buyers and distributors in this way are given a taster of the book's content, written style, design layout, and production qualities.

Colour bar

The colour bar is printed along one edge of the sheet and provides the printer with a guide to the print qualities. Some printers and publishers devise particular types of colour bar for specific jobs, while others make use of certain standard colour bar arrangements. The Graphic Arts Technical Foundation (GAF) produces a commonly used colour bar layout. A colour bar will usually include tone scales, star targets, line resolution targets, vignettes, grey balance values, percentage screen patches, pixel line patterns, slur gauge, halftone scale, and registration.

- Star targets are printed in each of the four process colours. The higher the resolution of the print, the smaller the single white point at the centre of the star will appear.

- Vignettes for each process colour show the progress from highlight to shadow. This should be smooth and consistent across all four colours.

- The grey balance values is an overprinting of 50% cyan, 40% magenta, and 40% yellow, which should produce a neutral grey.
- The halftone scale reveals the dot gain for each of the four process colours. The scale is arranged with a series of coarse, medium, and fine dot screens. These often have numbers reversed out of the dots. When these are viewed through a loupe, the printer can compare the relative increase in dot size for each screen and all four colours.
- Registration marks at the centres of the sheet and on the colour bar demonstrate how accurately the four plates are registered across the printed area of the sheet.

Organizing the pages

A book is made up of a sequence of pages arranged as sequential spreads in the designer's digital file. The pages are printed on large sheets of paper. Each sheet has several pages on either side. The sheets are folded and guillotined down to the correct page dimensions. Each of the pages on the large sheets must have the correct page printed on the reverse. Ensuring that the pages back up correctly is determined by the way the large printed sheet is folded into a signature and by the imposition, or arrangement, of the pages.

Signatures

The origin of the term 'signature' comes from the capital letter or numeral assigned to each of the printed sections of a book prior to binding. The capital was usually positioned by the compositor in the tail margin on the first page of each section so that when the sections were collated for binding they were ordered by letter rather than folio number. In modern printing, this is removed when the page is trimmed, but in many early books the letter remains in the bound book. In older print shops, the original 23-letter Latin alphabet is used and the modern letters J, U, and W are omitted from the sequence – a tradition derived from the early manuscripts. Today the word 'signature' refers to a section of sheets of paper printed with several pages on either side, which when folded run in consecutive order. Unless a book is loose-leaf, where each of the pages is printed separately, it will be made up of signatures.

Signatures are usually multiples of four, as this is the product of folding sheets in half and half again. Signatures may therefore be four, eight, 16, 32, or 64 pages long. Larger signatures of 128 pages are possible, but require large sheet sizes and small page dimensions. Publishers and printers generally try to use multiples of the same signature length within a book. For example, a 96-page book might be made up of six 16-page signatures. If a designer or publisher realizes that the content cannot fit with a multiple of the selected signature length then a smaller signature may be added, usually at the end. For example, an eight-page signature might be added to a 96-page book to accommodate the endmatter (glossary, index, and acknowledgments), making the book 104 pages in total. Some printers occasionally vary the length of signatures in a book to accommodate a change in paper stock.

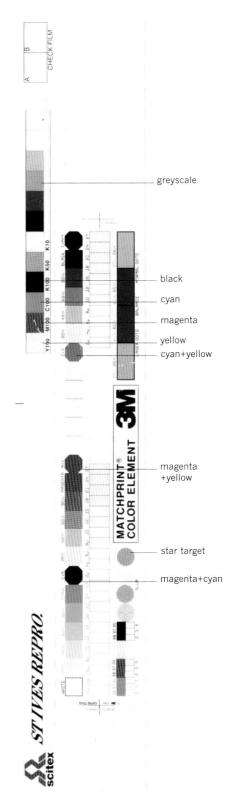

Below The colour bar runs along the side or bottom of the printed sheet and enables both printer and designer to review all the elements of the CMYK colours.

greyscale

black

cyan

magenta

yellow

cyan+yellow

magenta+yellow

star target

magenta+cyan

Imposition

Imposition is the ordered arrangement of pages on a plate so that when the sheets are folded the pages run consecutively. This arrangement is determined by the length of each signature. In an eight-page signature, the adjacent pages on the plate will fall at 1 and 8, 2 and 7, 3 and 6, and 4 and 5. The illustration shows a range of imposition schemes. The simplest way to check imposition and folio numbers is to fold up a sheet into the required number of pages, write the numbers on each page and then unfold the sheet. This shows the orientation of each page, which pages are adjacent or on the reverse.

Below The spine of *OMTE Stelen,* a Dutch book with an alphabetically organized series of poems and verses about art published in 1998, shows letters on each signature.

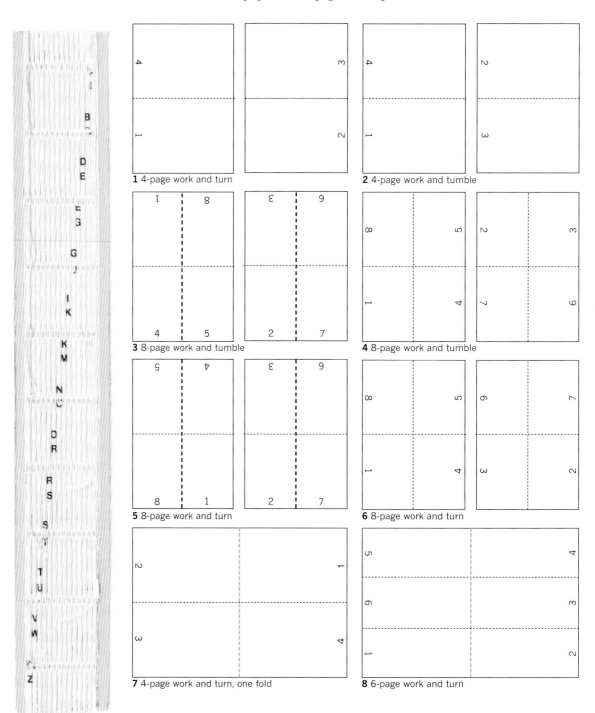

1 4-page work and turn

2 4-page work and tumble

3 8-page work and tumble

4 8-page work and tumble

5 8-page work and turn

6 8-page work and turn

7 4-page work and turn, one fold

8 6-page work and turn

Many non-fiction books, like this one, are printed four-colour throughout, meaning that every signature and every page can make use of four-colour imagery. It is useful for the designer to know the size and number of the signatures in a book. By using a flatplan, described earlier in the section on layout (chapter 10), the designer can mark the signatures. The pages that make up the double-page spread at the centre of each signature are printed as a pair and enable the designer to run large type across the gutter. The flatplan can also be used to plot the distribution of colour throughout a book.

Below A page from *Printers' Imposition* by F. C. Avis produced for apprentice letterpress compositors in 1957. The book contains well over 100 imposition diagrams that the apprentice was expected to learn.

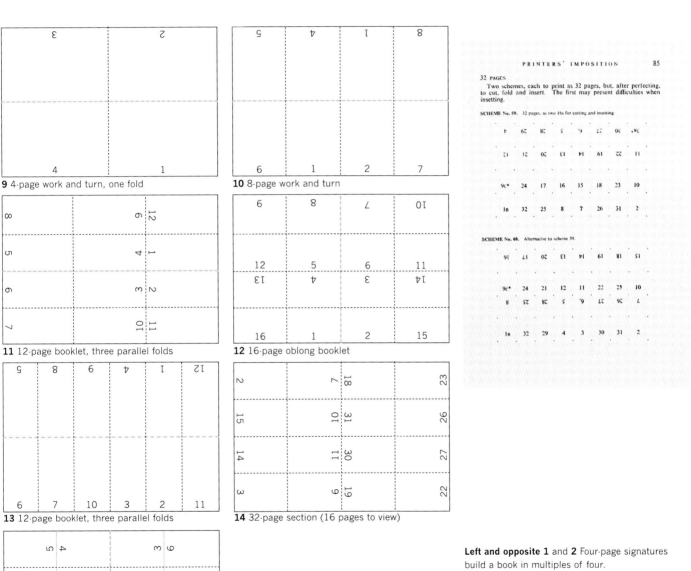

9 4-page work and turn, one fold

10 8-page work and turn

11 12-page booklet, three parallel folds

12 16-page oblong booklet

13 12-page booklet, three parallel folds

14 32-page section (16 pages to view)

15 16-page booklet

Left and opposite 1 and **2** Four-page signatures build a book in multiples of four.
3–6 Eight-page signatures (portrait 3 and 5; landscape 4 and 6).
7 Four-page work and turn imposition.
8 Portrait six-page work and turn imposition.
9 Landscape four-page work and turn, one fold.
10 Portrait eight-page work and turn imposition.
11–15 Five different 32-page impositions; all but 12 are portrait-format.

Above Two spreads from *Aftermath: Kuwait 1991*, a photographic book showing the remnants abandoned in the desert, alternates black-and-white images with full-colour photographs.

Below The colour distribution of a book that alternates spreads of single-colour (shown white) and four-colour (shown in green).

When books are printed using a mixture of four-colour and two-colour, knowledge of the relationship between signature length, imposition, and colour distribution is vitally important to the designer. For example, a 192-page book made up of 32-page signatures might be 50% four-colour and 50% two-colour, with three 32-page signatures of each. Pages 1 to 32 will be four-colour, pages 33 to 64 two-colour, and so on. This simple division of colour works well in production terms, but may be entirely inappropriate for the editorial presentation of the content. The designer and editor may wish to integrate the colour throughout the book. This can be achieved by looking carefully at the signatures and imposition. Six sheets printed both sides are required to print the six 32-page signatures in our example. Each sheet has 16 pages on one side and sixteen on the reverse, referred to by a printer as '16 to view'. One side of the sheet can be printed four-colour and the reverse two-colour: this is referred to by the printer as 'four back two'. Because of the imposition layout for a 32-page signature, the four-colour and two-colour pages will be integrated throughout the signature. This provides the editor and the designer with a far more flexible approach to the use of colour within a signature. By carefully planning the use of two- and four-colour throughout the book, the designer can position the colour for illustrations and photographs appropriately. A range of colour signatures can be combined in a book while retaining the 50% four-colour and 50% two-colour scheme. The six signatures could be arranged: two-colour (two back two), four-colour (four back four), (four back two), (four back four), (four back two), and finally (two back two) for the endmatter.

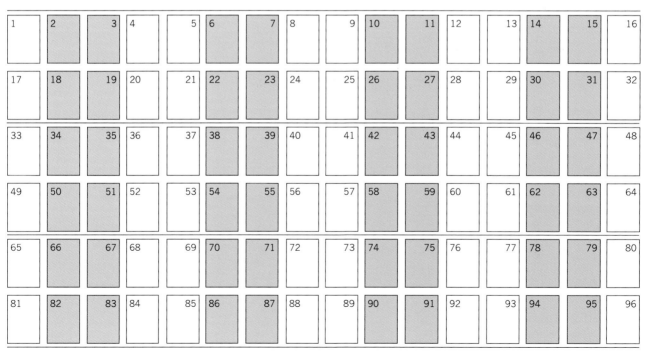

Paper

Books owe their form to the remarkable qualities of paper. Paper makes up the physical block of a book, the printed surface and the pages, and it is therefore important that book designers take an interest in its physical properties and are aware of the many different types that are available. This chapter will briefly examine the physical properties of paper, grain, weights, standard sizes, and the selection of appropriate stock.

Paper characteristics

Paper has seven key characteristics: size, weight, bulk, grain, opacity, finish, and colour. All of these must be considered, together with cost and availability, when deciding on an appropriate paper for book printing and binding. Other features of paper that the designer may wish to consider are its absorbency, its pH value, and its percentage of recycled waste content.

Paper sizes

When handmade paper was first produced, there was no set of standard sheet sizes: each mill made up deckles (the trays in which paper was produced) in proportions and lengths at its own convenience. With the coming of mechanized printing in the nineteenth century, it was necessary to standardize paper sizes so that they could be matched to printing presses. In North America and throughout the British Empire, the imperial inch was adopted to specify paper sizes, while in Continental Europe the metric millimetre became the standard length for specifying the DIN (Deutsches Institut für Normung) or ISO (International Organization for Standardization) paper sizes. Today, ISO papers are predominantly used in Europe; Britain has a mixed economy, with papers being produced in both traditional imperial sizes and metric A sizes, while in the United States, the majority of book and stationery papers are based on the inch – A sizes are available but are less popular. Papers and boards for book production are slightly larger than those made for pages, as this allows for turnover, the paper wrapping round the square of a hardback book, and being pasted down on the inside of the cover boards.

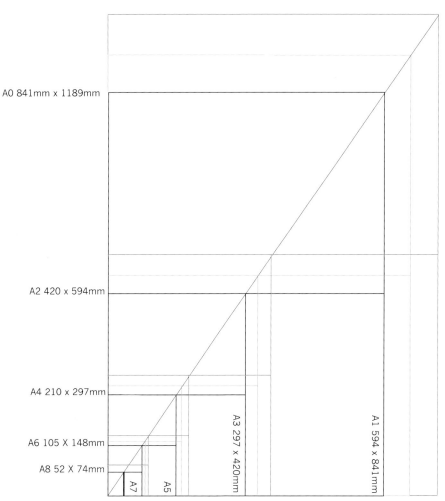

A0 841mm x 1189mm

A2 420 x 594mm

A4 210 x 297mm

A6 105 X 148mm

A8 52 X 74mm

A7

A5

A3 297 x 420mm

A1 594 x 841mm

Black: A-series papers drawn to 1 to 10 scale
A0 841 x 1189mm
A1 594 x 841mm
A2 420 x 594mm
A3 297 x 420mm
A4 210 x 297mm
A5 148 x 210mm
A6 105 x 148mm
A7 74 x 105mm
A8 52 x 74mm

Magenta: B-series papers drawn to 1 to 10 scale
B0 1000 x 1414mm
B1 707 x 1000mm
B2 500 x 707mm
B3 353 x 500mm
B4 250 x 353mm
B5 176 x 250mm
B6 125 x 176mm
B7 88 x 125mm
B8 62 x 88mm

Cyan: C-series papers drawn to 1 to 10 scale
C0 917 x 1297mm
C1 648 x 917mm
C2 458 x 648mm
C3 324 x 458mm
C4 229 X 324mm
C5 162 X 229mm
C6 144 X 162mm
C7 81 X 114mm
C8 57 x 81mm

Above The A, B, and C sizes have been drawn at
1:10 scale. A sizes are shown in black, B in
magenta, and C in cyan.

ISO paper sizes

A-series paper is based on the A0 sheet, which has an area of a square metre.
A-size sheets are all the same format, being divisions of the previous sheet size;
for example, A1 is half A0, A2 is half A1, and so on. The preface R or SR is
added to A sizes made with slightly larger margins to support full-bleed printing. The RA and SRA sheets allow machine grip and registration marks to be
printed and the sheet to be guillotined down to an A size. B-size sheets are
designed to fall between the A sizes, sharing the same proportions and the
principle of each successive sheet in the range being half of the larger parent
sheet. C-size sheets are designed primarily for stationery purposes and share a
common format with A and B sizes.

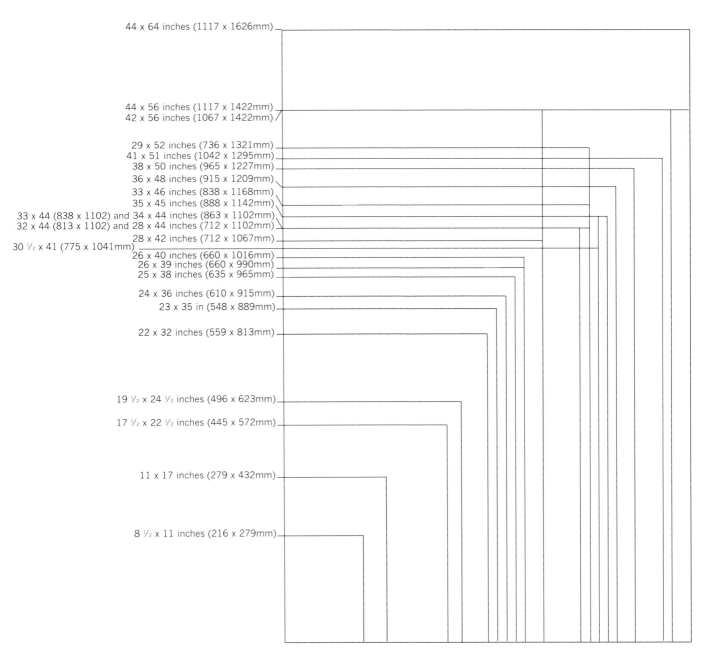

44 x 64 inches (1117 x 1626mm)

44 x 56 inches (1117 x 1422mm)
42 x 56 inches (1067 x 1422mm)

29 x 52 inches (736 x 1321mm)
41 x 51 inches (1042 x 1295mm)
38 x 50 inches (965 x 1227mm)
36 x 48 inches (915 x 1209mm)
33 x 46 inches (838 x 1168mm)
35 x 45 inches (888 x 1142mm)
33 x 44 (838 x 1102) and 34 x 44 inches (863 x 1102mm)
32 x 44 (813 x 1102) and 28 x 44 inches (712 x 1102mm)
28 x 42 inches (712 x 1067mm)
30 1/2 x 41 (775 x 1041mm)
26 x 40 inches (660 x 1016mm)
26 x 39 inches (660 x 990mm)
25 x 38 inches (635 x 965mm)

24 x 36 inches (610 x 915mm)
23 x 35 in (548 x 889mm)

22 x 32 inches (559 x 813mm)

19 1/2 x 24 1/2 inches (496 x 623mm)

17 1/2 x 22 1/2 inches (445 x 572mm)

11 x 17 inches (279 x 432mm)

8 1/2 x 11 inches (216 x 279mm)

North American paper sizes

In North America, paper sizes are measured in inches: stationery papers are based on multiples of 8 1/2 x 11 inches, while others are book paper sheets. Unlike the ISO range, the sheets do not have a common format; the paper sizes are derived from the traditional deckle sizes of North American paper mills. Individual mills do not usually produce all of their paper range in all of the sizes but select from the full range. This may mean that more unusual book formats do not work easily in the sheet sizes available, but can be accommodated within large sheets – albeit at the cost of significant waste, as a large proportion of the sheet is guillotined off unused.

Above North American sheet sizes on this page are drawn at 1:10. The sizes do not relate to one another in the same way as the A sizes opposite.

Foolscap

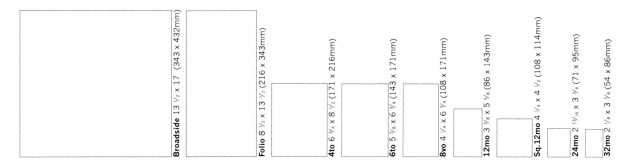

Broadside 13 ½ x 17 (343 x 432mm)

Folio 8 ½ x 13 ½ (216 x 343mm)

4to 6 ¾ x 8 ½ (171 x 216mm)

6to 5 ⅝ x 6 ¾ (143 x 171mm)

8vo 4 ¼ x 6 ¾ (108 x 171mm)

12mo 3 ⅜ x 5 ⅝ (86 x 143mm)

Sq.12mo 4 ¼ x 4 ½ (108 x 114mm)

24mo 2 ¹³/₁₆ x 3 ¾ (71 x 95mm)

32mo 2 ⅛ x 3 ⅜ (54 x 86mm)

Crown

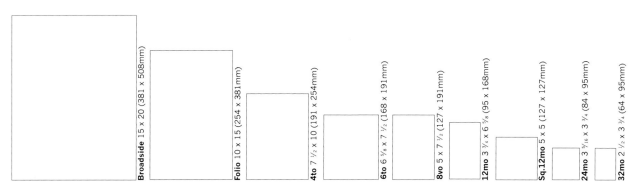

Broadside 15 x 20 (381 x 508mm)

Folio 10 x 15 (254 x 381mm)

4to 7 ½ x 10 (191 x 254mm)

6to 6 ⅝ x 7 ½ (168 x 191mm)

8vo 5 x 7 ½ (127 x 191mm)

12mo 3 ¾ x 6 ⅝ (95 x 168mm)

Sq.12mo 5 x 5 (127 x 127mm)

24mo 3 ⁵/₁₆ x 3 ¾ (84 x 95mm)

32mo 2 ½ x 3 ¾ (64 x 95mm)

Large post

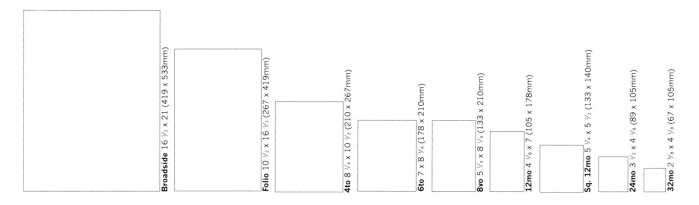

Broadside 16 ½ x 21 (419 x 533mm)

Folio 10 ½ x 16 ½ (267 x 419mm)

4to 8 ¼ x 10 ½ (210 x 267mm)

6to 7 x 8 ¼ (178 x 210mm)

8vo 5 ¼ x 8 ¼ (133 x 210mm)

12mo 4 ⅛ x 7 (105 x 178mm)

Sq. 12mo 5 ¼ x 5 ½ (133 x 140mm)

24mo 3 ½ x 4 ⅛ (89 x 105mm)

32mo 2 ⅝ x 4 ⅛ (67 x 105mm)

Above and opposite Here, the parent sheet sizes do not relate to one another, but the sheets are subdivided in the same way, *ie* Broadside, Folio, etc. These names are derived from the Latin terms used to describe the first Roman books, *eg* Octavo, meaning eight pages. The sheets on these pages have been drawn to the same scale (1 to 10) as those on the previous spread to convey an impression of the relative sizes.

British paper sizes

Originally, British paper sizes were specified in inches, but the sizes and proportions of the sheets differed from those in North America. In 1937, the British Standards Institution drew up standard paper sizes for Great Britain and the Dominions. These sizes had no systematic inner logic in the way that the A sizes are a division of a metre square, but many of the rectangles are related to golden-section proportions. The names of many paper sizes, such as

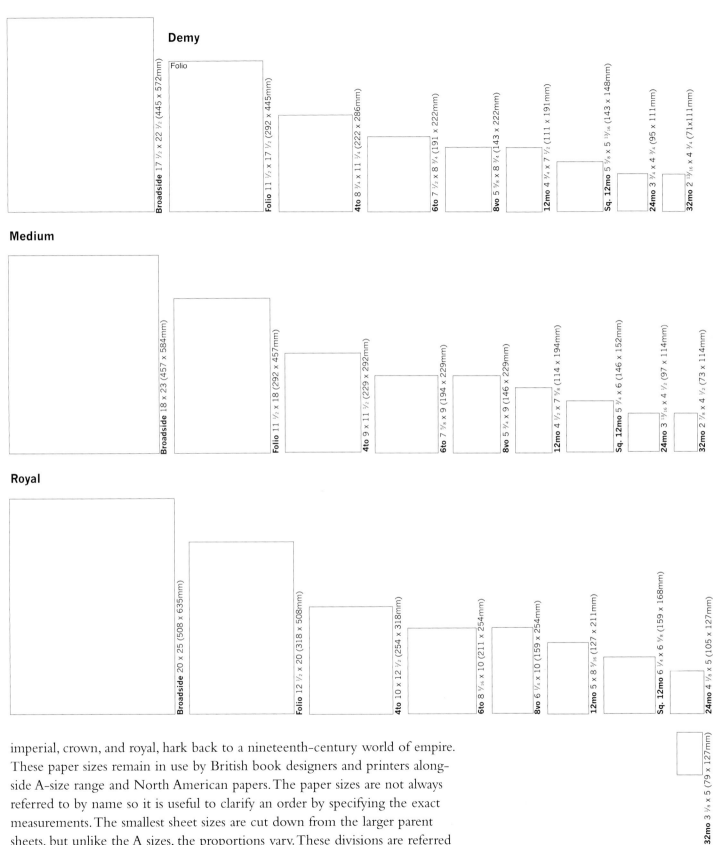

Demy

Broadside 17 ½ x 22 ½ (445 x 572mm)
Folio 11 ½ x 17 ½ (292 x 445mm)
4to 8 ¾ x 11 ¼ (222 x 286mm)
6to 7 ½ x 8 ¾ (191 x 222mm)
8vo 5 ⅝ x 8 ¾ (143 x 222mm)
12mo 4 ¾ x 7 ½ (111 x 191mm)
Sq. 12mo 5 ⅝ x 5 ¹³/₁₆ (143 x 148mm)
24mo 3 ¾ x 4 ¾ (95 x 111mm)
32mo 2 ¹³/₁₆ x 4 ¾ (71x111mm)

Medium

Broadside 18 x 23 (457 x 584mm)
Folio 11 ½ x 18 (292 x 457mm)
4to 9 x 11 ½ (229 x 292mm)
6to 7 ⅝ x 9 (194 x 229mm)
8vo 5 ¾ x 9 (146 x 229mm)
12mo 4 ½ x 7 ⅝ (114 x 194mm)
Sq. 12mo 5 ¾ x 6 (146 x 152mm)
24mo 3 ¹³/₁₆ x 4 ½ (97 x 114mm)
32mo 2 ⅞ x 4 ½ (73 x 114mm)

Royal

Broadside 20 x 25 (508 x 635mm)
Folio 12 ½ x 20 (318 x 508mm)
4to 10 x 12 ½ (254 x 318mm)
6to 8 ⁵/₁₆ x 10 (211 x 254mm)
8vo 6 ¼ x 10 (159 x 254mm)
12mo 5 x 8 ⁵/₁₆ (127 x 211mm)
Sq. 12mo 6 ¼ x 6 ⅝ (159 x 168mm)
24mo 4 ⅛ x 5 (105 x 127mm)
32mo 3 ⅛ x 5 (79 x 127mm)

imperial, crown, and royal, hark back to a nineteenth-century world of empire. These paper sizes remain in use by British book designers and printers alongside A-size range and North American papers. The paper sizes are not always referred to by name so it is useful to clarify an order by specifying the exact measurements. The smallest sheet sizes are cut down from the larger parent sheets, but unlike the A sizes, the proportions vary. These divisions are referred to as ordinary subdivisions, long subdivisions, and irregular subdivisions.

Paper weight

Paper weight is measured in two ways. In North America, paper is measured and specified in pounds per ream (500 sheets), per sheet size. This is often referred to as basis weight or ream weight. When using the American system to compare paper weights, the sheet size must be the same for each of the papers; if this is not the case then the designer should make use of a manufacturer's conversion table.

In the rest of the world, paper is measured in grams per square metre (gsm). The metric system measures the weight based on 500 sheets to a ream and a sheet as having an area of 1 square metre (A0). It is easier to compare paper weights in grams regardless of sheet size, as all of the papers are measured on a single scale, so that, for example, 50gsm is always a very light paper, whereas 240gsm is far heavier. Paper weight in Britain is now specified in gsm for both imperial and A-size papers.

Bulk

Paper weight and paper bulk are related, but it would be wrong to assume that a heavy paper is by nature bulky, as paper density varies. Blotting paper is not very dense, having loosely bonded fibres, yet is relatively bulky, whereas some pressed millboards are very dense and heavy, yet relatively thin. Paper bulk is referred to as calliper and is measured in thousands of an inch or millimetre. An imperial paper calliper unit is one-thousandth of an inch and called a point (though the paper point has no relationship with the typographic point, $\frac{1}{72}$ inch). The instrument used to measure bulk is called a micrometer. Four sheets of paper are measured and the figure divided by four to establish the paper stock's calliper, for example 12 or 15 point.

As paper calliper varies, so the height of a stack of paper varies. For the book designer it is therefore important to know the bulk of a paper, as this determines the depth of the spine. For this reason, paper bulk is not only specified by paper points but by the number of pages per inch, or PPI. Papers with a high PPI are thin, whereas those with a low PPI are relatively thick. In Europe, this figure may be given as pages per centimetre, or PPC. If a book is to be made up of two stocks, the designer must establish the number of signatures and pages in each paper, divide the respective PPI by the number of pages, and then add the two depths together to establish the spine width. Most major publishers ask binders to make up a dummy book bound to the correct size and in the same way as the production edition and using the correct stock. This is very useful for designer and publisher as it gives a feel of the anticipated publication and allows the spine depth to be checked and any minor modifications to the specification to be requested.

Grain

Paper grain is determined by the direction in which the fibres settle within the sheet during the manufacturing process. Machine-made paper has grain; handmade paper does not. Paper is produced in rectangular sheets: if the fibres are aligned lengthways along the sheet, it is called long grain; if the fibres run across the sheet, it is called short grain. Paper will tear straight and easily with the grain but raggedly across the grain. Folding down the grain is both easier and neater than folding across the grain. In the vast majority of books, the paper grain runs down the page parallel to the gutter, as this ensures that the pages are easily turned and the signatures are not bulky at the fold.

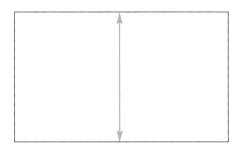

Above Short grain running across the paper.

Above Long grain running the length of the paper.

Opacity

Opacity is a measure of how much light will pass through a sheet of paper. This is determined by the thickness of the paper, the density of the fibres, and the type of surface finish. No paper is completely opaque, allowing no light to pass through it (though of course boards are 100% opaque). Paper opacity is important for the book designer as it determines the amount of show-through between pages. Highly opaque paper minimizes the amount of show-through, whereas a thin, low-opacity paper allows text and image to be seen from the reverse side. Show-through can be used creatively as a compositional element to form layers, but text showing through from the previous page can disrupt the reading experience. A simple opacity gauge shown here can be used to judge the relative show-through of different stocks.

Finish

The surface finish of a sheet of paper determines its capacity to hold ink and its suitability for different types of printing. Because of the way the different papers are made, the finish of a woven paper (produced on a consistently woven mesh) is even, while a laid paper (produced on a mesh with dominant stripes) has a recognizable pattern of lines running down or across the surface of the sheet. The lengthy calendering (pressing) process affects the smoothness of a paper's surface: the more rollers it passes between, the smoother the surface. Papers can have a different finish applied to each side; for example, poster papers are coated on one side only to receive the printed image, while the reverse is uncoated for pasting up on a hoarding. Special surface finishes such as pitting, pebbling, or pearl can be applied by running a textured roller over the paper during the calendering process. Many manufacturers produce ranges in which a single type of paper of a given weight, bulk, and opacity is made with several finishes. This offers the designer the possibility of making subtle changes between two finishes – perhaps a gloss for a picture signature and a coloured matt for a type section.

Above An opacity gauge: by placing different sheets of paper over the opacity gauge, the designer can make a judgment by eye of one paper's show-through as compared with another's.

Surface

The surface finish of a paper also affects the amount of show-through when it is printed, although unfortunately this cannot be measured by the opacity gauge. Uncoated papers are more absorbent than coated stocks and the printing ink is drawn into the paper surface, which makes it more visible from the reverse than the same type of paper with a coated surface. The initial opacity of the paper shown on the opacity gauge will inevitably be compromised. The ink absorbency of a paper is referred to as strike-through. Many paper manufacturers make paper-sample books that reproduce a CMYK image and black type on each of the sample sheets. This is extremely helpful for the designer, production department, and printer as it enables both the amount of show-through or print opacity to be judged as well as the relative quality of the dot-screen printing on different stocks.

Colour

Colour is generally added to a paper at the pulp stage. Some manufacturers produce a consistently coloured paper, but others, particularly with heavily recycled paper, will state that colour may vary between batches as the pulp is always from a different source. Some papers are dyed as sheets after the pulping process, while others have a coloured surface printed on one side only. The range of whites available is huge. Subtle differences in the whiteness of a paper stock have a significant effect on the colour of the imagery reproduced. Whites range from creams with a tendency towards yellow; parchments with a tendency towards brown; and arctic veering towards the blue. Carefully considering how the colour of type and image will sit on a particular stock is important. A gardening book with heavy colour-saturated, predominantly green photographs may look very clean on a cool, crisp, and modern white silk or matt finish, or slightly of the past on a parchment colour.

Selecting the appropriate stock

It is not always possible for the designer to select a paper for a specific book as books in series are generally produced on a common stock to retain the series feel and allow the publisher to work to a fixed cost. However, when the opportunity arises, the designer should carefully consider the seven characteristics of paper in relation to the physical feel, the subject and the readership of the book, and the printing and binding process. The publisher and production department will have a keen interest in the price of the paper stock and may be able to suggest competitive alternatives to well-known mills that produce an equally good stock. Paper manufacturers are constantly innovating to produce smoother, whiter, thinner papers with new finishes, so checking out websites and sending for new samples are useful. Building up a library of paper and board samples helps build knowledge and experience. Checking in the colophon of books you admire to see what stock has been used is useful; otherwise, a knowledgeable printer or member of a production department may be able to match the book to a sample.

Above Building up a collection of paper and
board samples is very helpful when the designer
has the opportunity to choose stock. Reviewing
the paper's characteristics – size, weight, bulk,
grain, opacity, finish, and colour – in relation to
the book's feel, subject, and readership and the
printing and binding process will steer the
designer towards an appropriate selection.

Paper engineering

Pop-up books are a specialist area of publishing, and any designer wishing to work in this field must become familiar with some rudimentary principles of paper engineering. Pop-ups can be used to illustrate fiction or non-fiction titles. When designing a fiction pop-up, the designer works with an author and illustrator to realize a three-dimensional narrative. Paper engineers often become visual authors, developing a book concept, devising the paper pop-ups, and commissioning an illustrator and a writer. Devising the pop-ups themselves is a time-consuming process of trial and error, involving cutting and folding many paper dummies to arrive at a successful prototype. Through experience, the paper engineer gains an understanding of different folds and becomes familiar with nets (flatplans for three-dimensional shapes). 'Fabrication' is the term used to describe the process of joining three-dimensional forms to each other. Pop-ups harness the kinetic energy of page-turning to create the three-dimensional models that rise from the flat spread. The paper engineer must balance complex pop-ups with the reality of production. The greater the number of components and glue points, the more time-consuming and expensive the construction of each page becomes for the specialist print finishers, who have extraordinary dexterity. This chapter will explain a selection of paper-engineering terms before examining some of the basic principles that were used to create the examples in this section.

Table of paper-engineering terms

angle: number of degrees between two lines emanating from a point. An acute angle is less than 90°; a non-acute angle is more than 90°.

arc: section of a circle.

base page: page to which the pop-up is glued.

circumference: outer edge of a circle.

die-cut: paper cut into a particular shape and illustrated on nets as a solid line.

dummy: pop-up page or book made by hand prior to production.

fold: line along which the paper is creased and bent.

glue knock-out: for two sheets of paper to be glued effectively to one another, the glue must not stick to a printed area: the knock-out is the unprinted glue space.

glue point: point at which sheets of paper are glued.

lift-up: sheet of paper that is glued on one side only and loose on the other, with a fold in the middle that allows it to be lifted up to reveal another element or image below.

out of page: part of the pop-up that is cut and raised from the base page.

page position: place where the pop-up attaches to the base page.

pull-tab: movable tab that the reader pulls to raise a pop-up.

score: line of indentation applied to the paper by a blunt die blade that enables the paper to be folded.

slot: section cut from one sheet of paper into which another piece of paper fits.

tab: strip of paper attached to the edge of a net that is either glued or fits into a slot. Wing tabs have wings that are unfolded once the tab has been inserted into a slot so as to lock a piece in place and pull up a structure.

tip-in: sheet of paper slipped into a slot.

tip-on: one sheet glued to another.

travel: amount of movement in a pop-up between the flat and erect state.

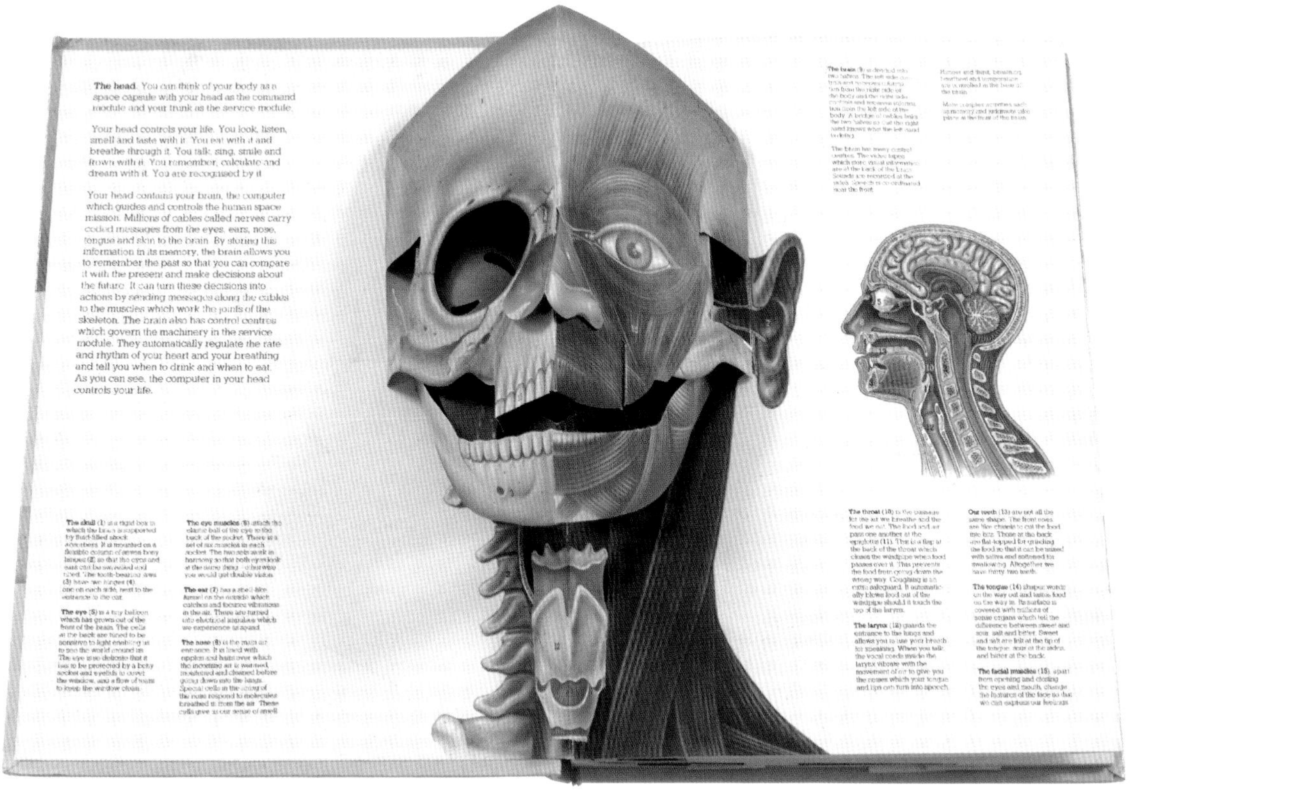
The head. You can think of your body as a space capsule with your head as the command module and your trunk as the service module.
Your head controls your life. You look, listen, smell and taste with it. You eat with it and breathe through it. You talk, sing, smile and frown with it. You remember, calculate and dream with it. You are recognised by it.
Your head contains your brain, the computer which guides and controls the human space mission. Millions of cables called nerves carry coded messages from the eyes, ears, nose, tongue and skin to the brain. By storing this information in its memory, the brain allows you to remember the past so that you can compare it with the present and make decisions about the future. It can turn these decisions into actions by sending messages along the cables to the muscles which work the joints of the skeleton. The brain also has control centres which govern the machinery in the service module. They automatically regulate the rate and rhythm of your heart and your breathing and tell you when to drink and when to eat. As you can see, the computer in your head controls your life.

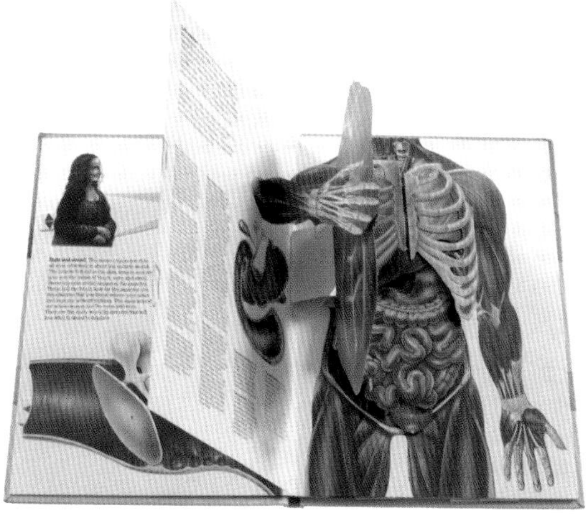

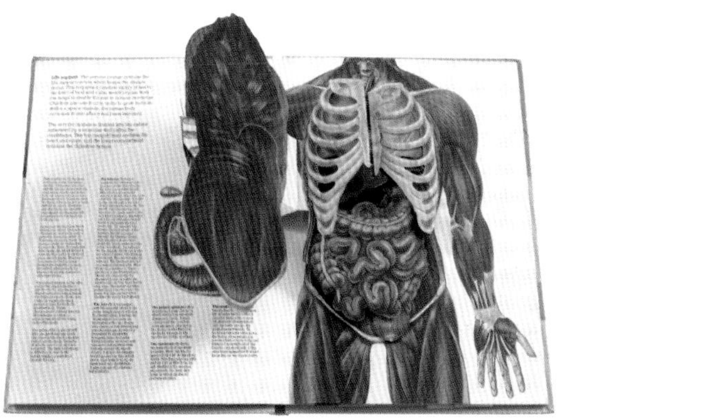

The pop-ups shown on page 202 have been drawn as flat nets and then photographed to show how they erect. Edges on the nets that must be cut are indicated with a solid line, while those that are to be scored and folded are indicated with a dotted line. Glue points are marked with a dot. The models have been made up at the same size as the nets shown, though the mechanism can be reproduced at a variety of sizes. Size is less important than the relative proportion of the lengths and folds: for this reason, the nets are numbered; folds or edges that have the same length or angles are marked =, and where one is greater than the other > is used. Pop-ups can be broken down into four basic classes: those that are erect at 90°; those that are erect at 180°; pull-tabs that create movement on the face of the page; and rotations of the page surface.

Top *The Human Body* by David Pelham and Dr Jonathan Miller makes use of pop-up and paper-engineering techniques to create three-dimensional models. The lifesize cutaway model of the head shows the skull on the left and the muscles of the face on the right. The pop-up and smaller longitudinal cross-section are labelled with numbers leading to extended captions.

Above In a spread from the same book, the three-dimensional figure opens up his torso to reveal the internal organs. The detailed medical illustrations have been developed to work with the layers of paper and are printed both front and reverse before being die-cut and hand-assembled.

Folds developed from the base page: 90° structures

These are probably the simplest pop-ups, as the folds and cuts are made directly into the base page and do not need to be glued. The flat sheet is cut so that a structure is created when the pop-up is at 90°.

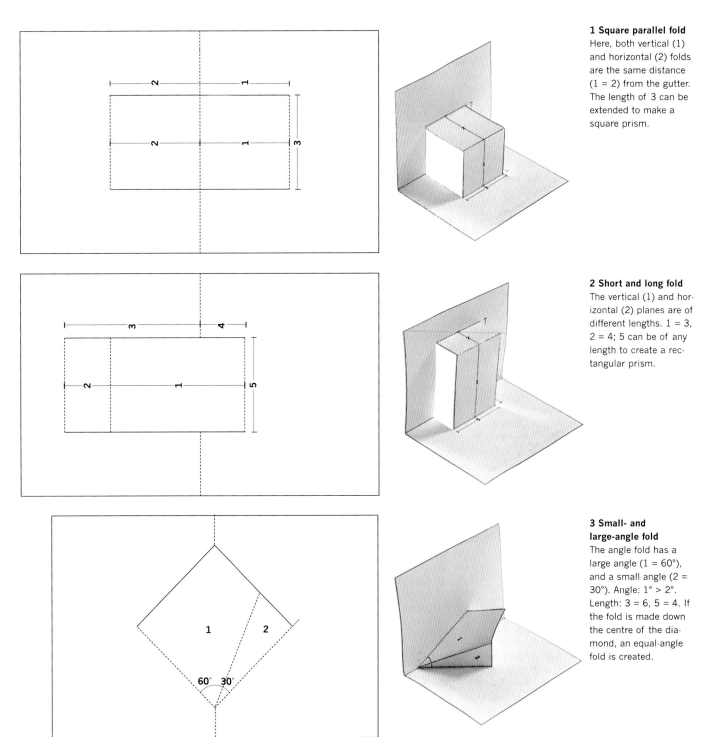

1 Square parallel fold
Here, both vertical (1) and horizontal (2) folds are the same distance (1 = 2) from the gutter. The length of 3 can be extended to make a square prism.

2 Short and long fold
The vertical (1) and horizontal (2) planes are of different lengths. 1 = 3, 2 = 4; 5 can be of any length to create a rectangular prism.

3 Small- and large-angle fold
The angle fold has a large angle (1 = 60°), and a small angle (2 = 30°). Angle: 1° > 2°. Length: 3 = 6, 5 = 4. If the fold is made down the centre of the diamond, an equal-angle fold is created.

Folds developed with tip-ons

All these folds are made by sticking pieces to the base page at glue points and are erect at 180° when the page is flat. All pop-ups of this type rely on the tip-on being attached to each page and the pop-up straddling the gutter.

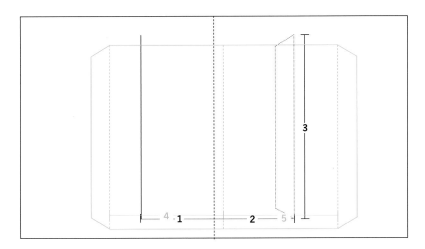

5 Pillar and buttress fold

The central pillar, in this case made from a double fold of card, is positioned on the gutter fold while the two buttresses are glued to the pages either side of the gutter. 1, 2, 3, and 4 are of equal length. 5 and 6, are of equal length. The length of the buttress + 1 should not exceed the width of the page or the pop-up will extend beyond the foredge when the book is closed. The pillar and buttress forms a very stable base for a horizontal platform. The various tabs A–D indicate the glue points, with the shaded letters indicating that the tab is passed through the slot and glued on the reverse.

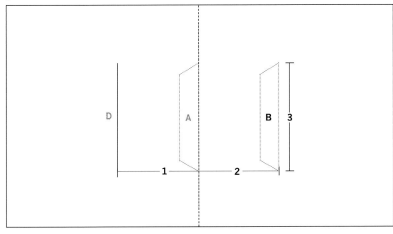

4 Triangular prism or symmetrical ridge

The triangular prism (net shown in cyan) is lifted above the page parallel to the gutter. Lengths 1 = 2, 3 = 4, 3 = 1; 3 > 2 and 3 > 4. By decreasing the relative lengths of 1 and 2 in relation to 3 and 4, an isosceles triangle with a taller apex is created. The pop-up can be glued to the front face of the base page or the tabs slipped through slots and glued to the reverse of the base page. Putting at least one of the tabs through a slot will increase the strength of the pop-up.

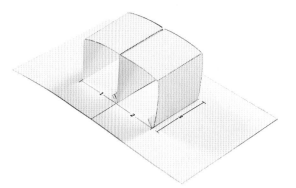

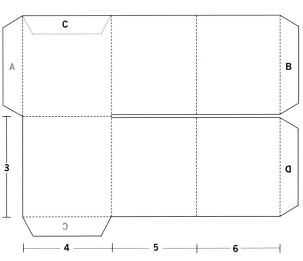

Right A pop-up sundial (1987) designed by the author makes use of a pillar-and-buttress fold to support the face of the dial. The gnomon (that is, the arc of the circle raised above the surface of the dial) casts a shadow that aligns with the numbers on the outer edge of the dial when the book is orientated toward the north by means of the tiny compass.

Cubes and cylinders using a 180° fold

Geometric shapes can be made to rise from the page using a 180° fold. All these forms require fabrication from separate die-cut sheets and gluing directly onto the surface or are passed through a slot in the page and glued to the reverse. The forms can be enclosed with tops and sides or open-ended or sided. Die cuts can be made in the sides to create windows or views of the interiors of models though this involves printing the sheets front and reverse.

6 Cube

The cube straddles the gutter fold and is a very useful form and can be adapted to make many objects. The folds in the top and sides are all of equal length. Lengths 1 and 2 are equal. Length 3 determines the dimensions of the cube and must be equal for A, B, C, D, and E.

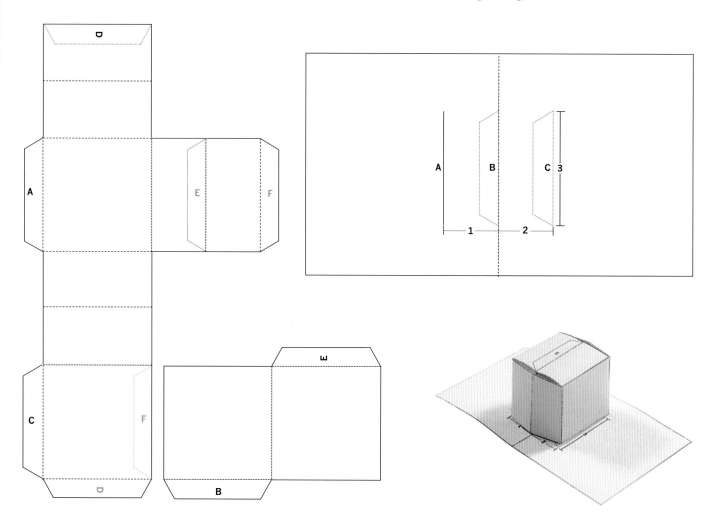

7 Cylinder

Pop-up cylinders, like perfect spheres, are difficult to realize as the paper engineer is reliant on bending the tube around a circle that for practical reasons must have a flat sides tab. C determines the height of the cylinder. Tab C is glued to the opposite end of the strip to form the cylinder. Tabs A and B attach the cylinder to the base cord.

8 Semicircular bridge or arch

The arch is created by tensioning the two edges of the paper. The base page has three slots, one on the right-hand page, which the glue tab passes through, and two on the left-hand page which the paper strip passes through. The span and height of the arch can be varied by changing the height and width of rectangle. A gothic arch can be made by putting a fold into the centre of the arch running parallel with the gutter. The letters indicate glue points, while shaded letters indicate that the tab is passed through the slot and glued on the reverse.

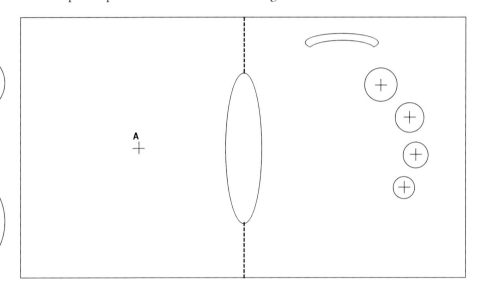

Wheels and rotation on the surface of the page

Rotating elements on the page enable new information to be revealed through die-cut holes in the surface of the page. Wheels attached to the front or reverse of the base page are a way of creating the rotation. The printed graphics, illustration, or text on the surface of the page and those revealed by the rotational movement need to be carefully considered when the artwork is made so that both elements align appropriately during the rotation. Cams can be attached to wheels to create additional movement or allow pistons to rise and fall. The length of the cam and the distance from the centre of the gear determine the height and fall of the beam, while the width of the slot through which a piston protrudes determines the range of movement.

9 Wheel mounted on reverse of page

Most paper engineers use a circular winged tab, the reverse of which is glued to the back of the page to form an axle for the wheel. The centre of the wheel has a hole that allows two wing tabs (A) to be slipped through and glued to the reverse of the base page, while the other two wings hold the wheel in place. The wheel-and-pivot mechanism is hidden within the concertina fold of the pop-up book. If the circumference of the wheel that protrudes through the foredge slot is notched, it is easier to turn than a smooth edge.

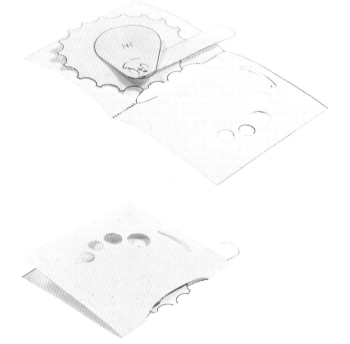

10 Wheel with rotating arm or cam

By attaching a cam and then an axle point to the wheel, a lever can be made to rotate on the surface of the page. The behaviour of the arm's movement is determined by how far the cam is from the centre of the rotating wheel. The wings of lever B passes through the hole in the cam B holding it in place.

Pull-tabs

Pull-tabs are generally used on a single page, as a tab will not work effectively if it straddles the gutter. The tab is often set in the foredge of the concertina page and used to create movements on the surface of the page. Pull-tabs are used as levers to turn planes over, reveal hidden pictures, or rotate objects.

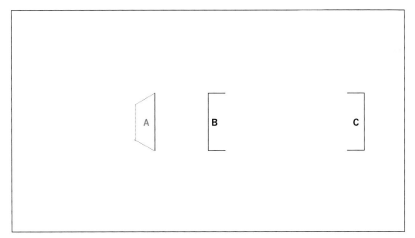

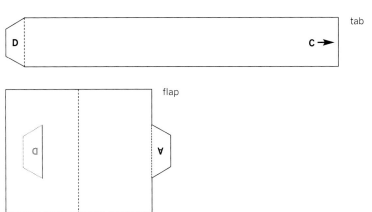

11 Pull-tab flipping wing

The flap is folded in half and glued to the long strip that forms the pull-tab. The long strip is passed through slot B to the reverse of the page and then passed out through slot C. Tab A on the flap is glued to the base page. When the tab is pulled at the end (C), the flap rotates through 180°. When the tab is pushed back in, the flap flips over the other way. Tab D on the long strip is glued to the reverse of the flap at the glue point.

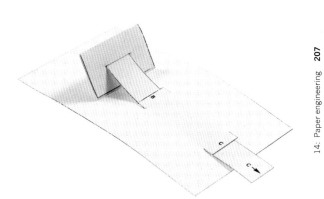

Combining pop-up principles

These basic pop-up principles can be adapted and combined to make endless three-dimensional models. Most of the mechanisms and glue tabs in a pop-up book are hidden within the concertina fold. By carefully opening up a book with a scalpel, the secrets of its construction are revealed. This surgical approach is the way most paper engineers work – when confronted with a new problem, they borrow and adapt existing models. I often feel that pop-up books look their best in the white card dummy form, when the models take on a pure sculptural quality. The colour on many realistic pop-ups is too bright and destroys the quality of the model. It is a sensitive balance between text, image, and pop-up that the writer, illustrator, paper engineer, designer, and art director must achieve if all the elements of the page are to work in harmony.

Pop-up books

1

2

3

1 *Blago*, a pop-up book of nonsense poetry, was designed and screenprinted by Gordon Davey.

2 This spread from *Alice in Super Pop-up Dimensional Wonderland* is a pop-up adaptation of Lewis Carroll's original tale by Robert Sabuda with illustrations by John Tenniel. This shows how complex pop-ups can become; the page resembles a model stage set.

3 Liza Law's concertina pop-up alphabet uses a 90° fold to elevate the specifically designed pop-up font from the surface of the page. The book makes use of a broken spine binding with flaps that allow the concertina to be unfolded.

4

15 Printing

Printing processes can be divided into four types: relief, in which the ink sits on the raised surface of the plate or type; planographic, where the ink sits on the surface of plate; intaglio, where the ink is held in grooves below the surface of the plate; and stencil, where the ink is forced through a mesh mask. This chapter will examine the four principal types of printing used to produce books in roughly the historical order in which they were invented.

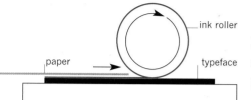

Relief printing. The ink (magenta) passes from the roller to the raised surface of the plate before the paper is pressed onto the type or image and an impression made.

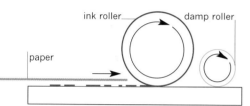

Planographic printing. The ink sits on the dry surface of the plate but not on the wet areas, which are moistened by the damp roller. The paper is pressed onto the surface and the impression is made.

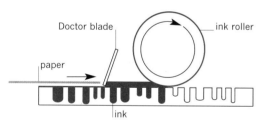

Intaglio printing. The ink sits below the surface of the plate, the doctor blade is scraped across its surface leaving the ink in tiny cells, and when the paper is pressed onto the plate the ink is drawn out of the cells onto the paper.

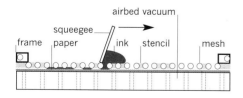

Screen printing. The ink is squeezed through a stencil supported by a fabric mesh on to the paper, where it sits proud of the surface.

Relief printing: the origins of letterpress

Relief printing includes woodcuts, linocuts, and letterpress printing. The ink sits on the surface of the reversed image or letter and is transferred to the paper laid on top of it through the press applying pressure.

As we have seen in chapter 1, the invention of movable metal type in Europe is attributed to Johannes Gutenberg, who first printed his 42-line Bible (so called as the column depth was 42 lines) in about 1455. Movable type revolutionized book production and led to the establishment of printer-publishing houses throughout Europe. Movable type enabled a single printer, having set a text, to reproduce multiples of that text, and thus the production of language was industrialized. Printing multiples was faster than copying by hand and, as a consequence, words became relatively cheap and the number of books in circulation increased. By 1600, two printers working on a single press at Christopher Plantin's publishing house in Antwerp, Belgium, were capable of printing 1,250 sheets per day, both sides. Type replaced individual hand-rendering and books were manufactured with modular and identical mechanized letterforms.

Hand-composing and letterpress printing

For more than 400 years, from 1455 to 1885, hand composition and letterpress printing were the means of producing printed books throughout the Western world. This has now been replaced by offset lithography. A resurgence of interest in small-batch production among younger designers, combined with the experience of older printers and devotees of letterpress, has ensured that letterpress printing has survived as a craft. Private presses may produce limited editions using letterpress.

Planographic printing: the origins of offset lithography

Planographic printing refers to any printing process that involves the ink sitting on the surface of the plate. Offset lithographic printing is the most common form of printing used to produce books today. The term 'lithography' is derived from the Greek *lithos*, meaning stone, and *graphien*, to write: writing on stone. The process was invented by the Bavarian dramatist Aloys Senefelder in 1798. Senefelder recorded his invention in *Vollständiges Lehrbuch der Steindruckerei* (1818), published in English as *A Complete Course of Lithography*. Lithography transfers the ink directly from the surface of the stone or plate to the surface of the paper. It is based on the simple principle that grease and water do not mix. Thin aluminium or zinc plates with a finely grained surface

are prepared, with a greasy substance being applied to the image areas of the plate and a fine film of water being retained on the non-print surface. Ink adheres to the greasy image areas, but is rejected by the wet non-print areas. The inked image is transferred to the surface of the paper while the clean damp areas of the plate leave no mark.

Lithography: reproducing photographs

Photography was invented in the late 1830s; by 1851 experiments had culminated in a light-sensitive lithographic stone from which a photographic image could be reproduced. As photography developed, it became possible to separate a full-colour image into three process colours (cyan, magenta, and yellow) and a fourth tone (black). Using these four process colours (known as CMYK), full-colour reproductions of halftone images were possible. Lithography, which made use of colour separation, registration, and multiple-roller cylinder presses, had become a sophisticated commercial print process.

By the beginning of the twentieth century, offset lithography in which the ink is transferred, or offset, from the printing plate to a rubber-covered cylinder before being printed on paper could lay down more colours more quickly than letterpress machines and was ideally suited to the reproduction of images. Its drawback lay in its reproduction of type. Letterpress, as the name indicates, was invented to reproduce words, through type, and had been adapted to print line and photographic halftones. Compositors and typesetters were as much a part of the letterpress process as printers and pressmen. By contrast,

Top A letterpress composition room of 1910 showing the compositors at work setting type by picking characters from the cases in front of them.

Above An unusual example of a letterpress book; the text is arranged in an expressive way by A. Soffici and was printed in Florence 1919.

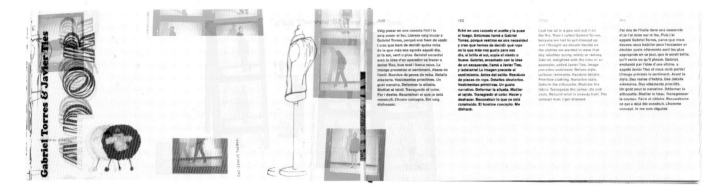

Above The Spanish catalogue *L'aparador* designed for the Museu Municipal Joan Abelló is printed using lithography. The design exploits the potential of lithography, making use of photographic halftones and overprinting the CMYK plates. The catalogue has text in four languages. These are printed solid using magenta for Catalan and French; black for Spanish; and blue for English.

lithography was principally a way of reproducing drawn and photographic images. Calligraphic lettering and engraving were reproduced lithographically throughout the nineteenth century, but books, being text-led, were not commonly reproduced using offset lithography until the 1960s, when the uptake of photo-typesetting enabled type to be transferred to a lithographic plate through a photographic negative.

Lithography: reproducing words, the separation of type and image

The period of book publishing from 1900 until the late 1960s saw considerable technical developments in both typesetting and photographic lithography. However, designers were often forced to consider text and image as separate elements because of the way each was reproduced. Letterpress represented the principal technology for reproducing words, and lithography and gravure the most precise way of reproducing images. This division saw books printed using combinations of processes for different sections. Designers had to plan the text and image elements of the page around the reproduction methods of the period, and this clearly affected every aspect of a book's layout.

Lithography: photosetting and the integration of type and image

Photosetting was first patented in 1894 by E. Porzsolt and William Freise-Greene, who exposed images onto a moving roll of light-sensitive paper with an electric spark. Not until 1946 was the technology sufficiently developed for commercial use, when the US Government Printing Office began to use the Intertype Fotosetter. Where letterpress had created type as an impression, photosetting was effectively creating type as an image. Since the principles of printing photographic images through offset lithography were well established, the potential for lithography to reproduce the type as well as the image was quickly realized and signalled a pivotal moment in the decline of the letterpress book. For the book designer this was a tremendous change: suddenly text and image could be considered in the same way, as both were to be reproduced using a single process. Pages were printed using four-colour offset lithography and the images and type could be fully integrated. Today the designer has, through digital setting, gained even more control over the integration of text and image and the manipulation of all the colour. The offset lithographic process has become the predominant method of printing books.

Lithography: the process, making the plates

Plate-making involves transferring the designed pages of a book either from artwork or from a digital file to the surface of the lithographic plate. The plates are thin sheets of aluminium, plastic, or paper, coated with a light-sensitive substance called diazo compound or photopolymer. The plates can be wrapped around the cylinder of the press. The texture of a lithographic plate is slightly granular to touch, which ensures that moisture can be trapped on its surface. At the time of writing, the process of plate-making is in transition. Some printers are continuing to make lithographic plates using a photographic mask, either positive or negative, and exposing the light-sensitive plate photographically in a darkroom. Others have invested in new technology that transfers the page image directly from the computer to the plate, a process known as CTP (computer to plate). In CTP, plates move through a platesetter containing a laser guided by the digital postscript file. The process is very similar to printing using a laser printer from a computer, and the finished plate emerges from the platesetter in much the same way as a paper copy.

On press

All lithographic presses are made up of many cylinders and rollers. The ink rollers form what is called an *ink pyramid,* moving the ink from the fountain to the plate, which wraps around a cylinder. A second cylinder, known as the *blanket cylinder,* is rubber-coated. This is in contact with the impression cylinder and becomes inked with a wrong-reading image. The third cylinder, known as the impression cylinder, has no ink but is used to trap the sheet between it and the blanket cylinder, imposing sufficient pressure to transfer the image from the blanket onto the paper.

Feeding the press

Sheet-feed presses lift the paper on tiny vacuum suckers into the press and then move it through either by a series of rollers, conveyer belts, or air beds. The printer can adjust the paper feed with movable stops so that the sheets meet the gripper edge square with 15mm for the clip to catch. The speed of the feed is controlled and relates to the speed at which the rollers are inked. The size of the plate and, therefore, the size of the paper that any rotary press can print on is determined by the circumference of the print cylinder; the sheet width is determined by the length of the cylinder. The larger the cylinder, the bigger its circumference and therefore the longer the plate. The longer the cylinder, the wider the plate.

Dampening the plate

Before inking, the lithographic plate must be moistened so that the non-image areas of the plate reject the ink. This process is called dampening the plate and involves rolling a very fine film over the surface of the rotating plate cylinder. The water is delivered to the plate via a series of rubber rollers linked to the dampening fountain (a reservoir of water and alcohol). A delicate balance has to be struck between sufficiently dampening the plate in order to prevent the

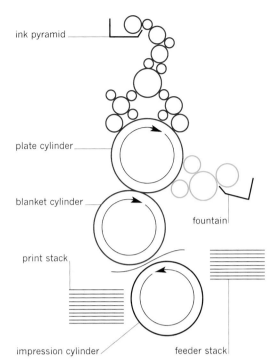

ink pyramid

plate cylinder

blanket cylinder

fountain

print stack

impression cylinder

feeder stack

Above This schematic diagram of a sheet-feed lithographic press shows a single ink pyramid for one colour (shown here in magenta), which feeds the ink down through a series of rollers to the plate cylinder. The fountain contains water, which is moved to the plate cylinder by another series of rollers and dampens the plate before the ink is applied. The ink sticks to the image areas of the plate but is rejected by the water on the rest of the surface. The inked image is transferred to the blanket cylinder and then onto the paper, which is pulled through the press from the feeder stack. The impression cylinder provides pressure between the paper and the blanket cylinder, ensuring the image is transferred evenly. Each of the CMYK colours is applied in the same way as the paper is moved through four sets of blanket and impression cylinders, reproducing halftone images and solid type in register.

Below Detail of CMYK progressives

Cyan

Yellow

Cyan/Yellow

Magenta

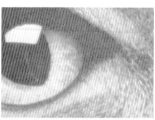

Cyan
Yellow
Magenta

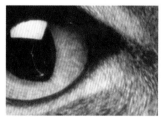

Black

Cyan
Yellow
Magenta
Black

ink sticking to the non-image areas, and over-wetting the plate, as the paper will absorb the moisture and stretch. The alcohol in the fountain lowers the water's surface tension, thereby reducing the paper's absorption of water and speeding up the drying process.

Inking the plate

The ink is stored in a reservoir, usually above the cylinder plate. A six-colour press printing four colours will make use of five plates, one for each of the colours plus the sealing varnish, which is stored in a separate reservoir. This type of press feeds one plate through a series of rollers. The speed of ink flow can be controlled and adjusted during printing, although even flow determines consistent printing. A densitometre (a handheld electrical instrument that measures the amount of ink on the paper surface as against the unprinted areas) is used to measure the amount of ink on the surface of the printed sheet and the printer scrutinizes the colour bar and registration before adjusting the ink flow. The ink is transferred from the reservoir via a blade to the rubber-faced rollers of the ink pyramid and moved from one roller to the next. This gradually creates an even film of ink across the surface of the rollers, which are in contact with the revolving plate cylinder.

Offsetting the image and printing the sheet

The inked plate has a thin film of ink adhering to the right reading image, which rolls off onto the blanket cylinder. The transfer of the ink image from plate to blanket cylinder is the 'offsetting' referred to in the process's name. The ink image on the rubber-coated blanket cylinder is a wrong reading and is rolled on to the sheet drawn towards it by the grippers. The impression cylinder applies even pressure behind the sheet and ensures the inked image is evenly transferred from blanket to paper. The printed image on the paper is now right reading. If the printing is single colour only, the sheet is released from the grippers into the printed paper stack. When the job involves several colours, the sheet is moved on through to a second blanket cylinder, where the next colour is overprinted in perfect registration. This process is repeated until all of the colours have been printed and the sheet is released to the paper pile.

Drying the sheet

The printer needs to preserve the quality of the print and avoid smudging and *setting off* (ink being transferred from one sheet to another). To avoid this, some presses blow-dry the sheets with hot air prior to stacking the pile. Others use a spray to seal the ink, preventing it from sticking to the sheet above it. Simpler litho presses may not have these more sophisticated features, so the printer interleaves the sheets (slipping a sheet of cheap plain paper between each printed sheet). This absorbs any set-off ink and keeps the backs of the printed sheets clean. So that the sheets on the pile are kept in alignment they are *jogged*. This is the mechanical equivalent of *hand knocking up*. Some web-feed presses frequently used for magazine and wire-stitched binding move the printed paper directly to the cutting and folding process without stacking.

Types of press

Offset lithographic presses are either sheet-feed (one sheet at a time), or web-feed (a continuous roll of paper). Printing speeds on both types of press have been raised to exceptional levels. Large sheet-feed presses can run at 12,000 sheets per hour – one sheet every 0.3 seconds – but their capacity is dwarfed by web-feed presses, which are capable of 50,000 sheets per hour (one every 0.072 seconds). The speed at which litho presses run has an effect on the quality of the print. To ensure high quality, books tend to be run at slower press speeds than newspapers, cheap brochures, or packaging, where high volumes of more than 100,000 per run are required.

Lithographic presses are typically either single-colour, two-colour, four-colour, or six-colour, although specialist presses have been built to deliver more selected colours at a single run. Single- and two-colour presses may be used for four-colour printing, with the sheet passing through the press in registration several times.

Intaglio printing: the origins of gravure

Intaglio print processes, including etching, engraving, and gravure, hold the ink in grooves below the surface of the plate. The gravure process is also known as rotogravure, which refers to the cylinders around which the plate is wrapped in a fashion similar to the offset litho press.

Making the gravure plate

The artwork for gravure printing, like that for the offset litho process, is likely to be digital and is made in exactly the same way for either print process. The CMYK colours are separated to produce four plates. The separations are converted into plates by a digital signal that controls a diamond-tipped engraver, which cuts into a copper plate. This process can also be realized using laser engraving, again driven from a digital colour separation. Making a gravure plate is significantly more expensive than making an offset litho plate and is specified by publishers for books with very long runs of several million or because of the very soft tones or exceptionally fine lines that can be printed using the process. The high cost has led to a decline in the number of printers working with the process. Attempts have been made to close the financial gap between the two processes by making photopolymer gravure plates, which use stainless steel and are as cheap as litho plates to produce.

Printing gravure

The image is printed by drawing out the ink that sits below the surface of the plate. Halftone images are broken down into a series of tiny dots. The larger or deeper the dot, the greater the volume of ink carried in that area of the plate. Large, deep dots give good ink coverage with almost no visible screen, while tiny dots create very subtle tones – a feature treasured by designers.

Gravure has twin qualities of continuous tone and consistency of ink lay throughout a run, which make it suitable for extremely high-quality printing, such as art photography, banknotes, postage stamps, coupons, and other

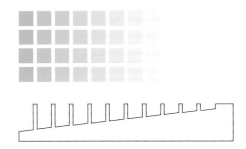

A schematic diagram of the cells on a gravure plate with equal area but different depths. The deeper the cell, the more ink it holds and therefore the darker the impression.

Circular cells with variable area and depth.

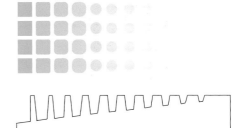

A combination of cell shapes with different area and variable depths produces very subtle graduated tones.

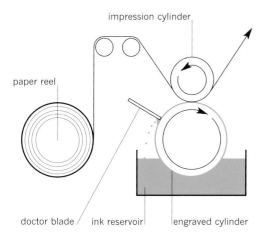

impression cylinder

paper reel

doctor blade / ink reservoir / engraved cylinder

Above Gravure presses are often web-feed. The paper is pulled from the reel and moved over the engraved cylinder. The engraved cylinder revolves through an ink reservoir and passes under the doctor blade, which scrapes excess ink from the plate's surface. The paper impression cylinder presses the paper onto the engraved plate cylinder to make the print.

Opposite This spread, titled 'The Heavens' from an early *Philips Atlas c.* 1900, was printed using the gravure process. The pages in older atlases were printed as map sheets on one side only, not as signatures as they are today. For this reason, the colour consistency throughout the atlas varies and the page reverse is blank. The colours are very soft but beautifully even.

security printing, and for cheaper mass-volume products such as catalogues, glossy magazines, wrapping, and wallpaper. Today, few general publishers use gravure, and expensive fine-art and photographic monographs are often the exception. However, many book designers have begun to renew their interest in gravure printing, as it lays the ink onto a page in a very soft and fine imprint that is different in character from lithography.

Stencil printing: screen printing

Stencil printing is any process in which the ink is forced through a mask to create the image. Screen printing uses a mesh screen, originally made of silk, areas of which are masked to prevent the ink from passing through, while the unmasked image area allows ink to pass through to the paper. The image on the screen is right-reading, like the printed image.

The origins of screen printing

Stencil printing is a very ancient process. The Romans, Chinese, and Japanese all made use of stencils to make patterns on tiles, ceilings, and cloth more than 1,500 years ago. The Japanese used a matrix of human hair, glued horizontally and vertically across the stencil. Hair was gradually replaced by silk threads, which, being very fine and yet strong, had similar properties. The stencil was laid over the mesh, often silk, and coloured ink dabbed through the pattern. Stencil printing continued in this form until the beginning of the nineteenth century, when it was realized that the stencil could be attached to a fabric screen, thereby making it more durable. Silk-screen stencilling then replaced the old silk stencil matrixes.

It was not until 1907 that the first patent was taken out for silkscreening that specified that the process involved a mesh screen and a squeegee for pulling the ink and driving it through the mesh. Screen printing can lay flat, opaque, or transparent coloured inks over one another. The amount of ink laid on the paper is far greater than with other print processes and so the saturation and vivacity of the colour has great appeal. Colour separations can be made and halftone photographic screens can be reproduced.

Preparing the screen

Today the screen is made of synthetic threads. These vary in width, mesh grade, and the number per inch in the weave, referred to as mesh count. If the mesh grade is fine and the mesh count high (many threads to the inch), the detail will be retained and subtle halftones can be reproduced. There are generally four mesh grades: S, the smallest, M, T, and HD, the thickest. Stencils can be cut in paper by hand, or using a knife plotter in rubylith, a red film from which a photographic positive can be made. Photographic stencils can be enlarged as negatives or positives using a copy camera or PMT (photo-mechanical transfer). The image is transferred to the screen either using a light-sensitive film or by covering the screen with a light-sensitive emulsion. The light-sensitive film is covered by the photographic negative, and the two are held together via vacuum suction and are exposed using ultraviolet light.

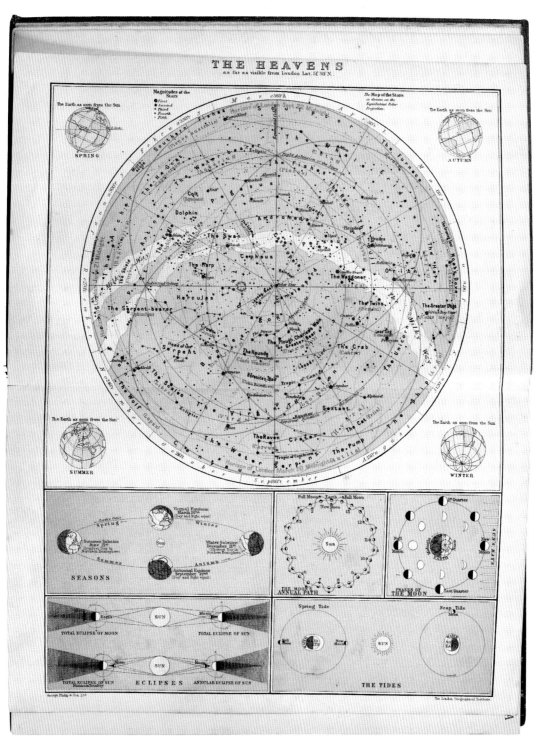

THE HEAVENS
as far as visible from London Lat. 51°30'N.

Right The book *Make Art Work,* printed by Artomatic, was designed to promote unusual uses of material. The grey-board page is screen-printed with three colours: blue, black, and white. The full-colour images and their supporting captions have been lithographically printed onto a crack-back (self-adhesive paper). The individual stamps have been tipped onto the baseboard.

The film is developed and hardened before being applied to the underside of the screen. It is then dried using warm air and the polyester backing peeled off leaving the right-reading image on the screen. The light-sensitive emulsion is exposed in a similar way, using ultraviolet light; the screen is exposed directly and, having been developed, the image area that was not exposed to the light is washed away. When the screen is clean and dried, it is ready to print.

Screen printing

A simple screen bed consists of a melamine-faced wooden bed through which tiny holes are drilled allowing a vacuum pump to pull down the sheet. Above the bed is a hinged frame in which the screen is locked. This frame is counter-balanced so that it will stay in the upright position while the printer positions the sheet. Some large frames have a squeegee, a length of wood housing a rubber blade, attached to the outside.

The screen is locked into place in the frame and lowered over the bed. The sheet fall (position of the paper on the bed in relation to the screen) is marked and then the frame is lifted again. The paper is positioned and the vacuum turned on to hold it in position. The frame is then lowered. The printer then pours ink onto the reserve at one end of the screen over a masked area. Then the printer places the squeegee behind the ink pool, manipulates the ink with little sideways movements across the whole of the rubber blade, and, pressing firmly down on the reverse of the screen, pulls the squeegee across the screen carrying the ink across the image area and squeezing it through the open screen mesh. The paper is then removed and placed in a drying rack.

Binding

This chapter introduces the basic stages of hand-binding a book. The order of these stages remains largely the same, although they are now undertaken by machines. We describe print finishes, cover materials, and binding techniques.

Traditional hand-binding processes

The techniques used for binding books were developed in the first century BC. The processes involved have remained largely the same since AD 400. Binding throughout Western Europe was undertaken by monks, who made up parchment, and later paper, books that had been copied or dictated from scripture. The process of writing and illuminating the book was slow, and books were both rare and extremely valuable. Bindings were very strong and often extensively decorated. The book as an artefact, as well as the message it contained, was highly prized by the Church and the aristocracy.

With the advent of printing in the West, binding increasingly became a secular activity and a commercial adjunct to the printshop. Letterpress printing increased the speed of book production, and this had a significant impact on the nature of binding. The highly decorated leather bindings of the monasteries were replaced by lighter, less decorative, bindings produced to reduce costs. Bookbinding remained a hand-craft, but by 1750 binders in England, France, Holland, Germany, and Italy were beginning to adapt the book's construction. Many books from this period are made with cords that are cut into the backs of the signatures and sewn with a smooth spine as opposed to the traditional approach of sewing to raised cords.

Type manufacture and printing technology continued to develop through the eighteenth century, as a result of technological development, increased profit margins, and an ever-growing literate public, which spurred on the drive for efficient book production. Binding, though a well-established business, continued to be a labour-intensive hand-craft.

The introduction of machine-binding

It was not until the nineteenth century that machines became part of the binding process. Machines were used for folding printed sheets into signatures, and large presses capable of exerting enormous pressure over a larger surface began to augment traditional wooden frames. This improved the binder's efficiency, as books could be pressed by the hundred rather than in single figures. Still, the characteristic form of bookbinding until the early part of the twentieth century remained hand-stitching. The adoption of mechanized perfect binding using glue and machine-stitching in the twentieth century finally made the book the product of industrial rather than craft manufacture. Hand-binding survives as a craft tradition for limited-edition publications, short runs, and the production of art objects. Single binding machines are capable of folding the printed sheets, collating, gluing, attaching covers, and cutting to size in a continuous process. Some designers and insightful publishers have showed a renewed interest in traditional hand-binding, and mechanical process have been developed to mimic some of the hand-craft finishes.

Binding the book

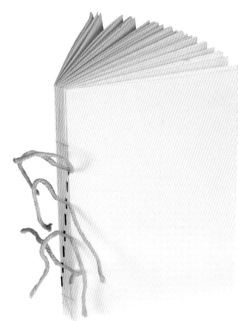

1 Folding the sheets

The flat printed sheets from the printer must be folded according to their imposition and made up into signatures. When hand-folding, a simple bone folder is used to crease the sheet; the folding machine undertakes the same task more quickly. The folds must be made precisely, as any inaccuracy of registration at this stage cannot be corrected later. This process is often termed 'folding to print', as the key relationship is that between the fold and the print rather than the fold and the edge of the sheet. The margins for each page should be the same throughout the signature. A misplaced fold has the effect of shortening one margin and lengthening another, leading to irregularities in the position of the print area in the bound copy.

Adding single leaves

Most books are made up of signatures of consistent size. Occasionally, however, additional sheets have to be incorporated. These might include a short signature – for example, four pages – or an individual leaf. The easiest way of adding single leaves is to 'paste in' – pasting along the edge of the leaf and attaching it to the appropriate signature. This slightly weakens the binding and occasionally causes cockling (where the paper bubbles) if the grain of the paper runs across the page and there is a high moisture content in the paste. The other, more expensive, alternative is referred to as guarding. A thin strip of paper 12 or 15mm wide is pasted to the edge of the leaf, folded vertically, and wrapped round the appropriate signature. The single leaf can now be sewn in with the signature.

2 Gathering and collating

The folded signatures must be put into the correct order, in a process known as 'gathering'. Piles of signatures are placed in order on a table, and one is gathered from each pile to make up the book block. Today, this is a machine operation. When a pile of signatures has been gathered, the order must be checked, or collated. The book becomes meaningless if a signature is missing, placed in the wrong sequence, or inverted. If collation marks are used today, they take the form of a small bar on the folded edge of the signature. Each successive mark is printed a fraction lower than the previous one. The set of incremental steps made by the marks makes collating easy, as any break in the step sequence indicates a missing signature.

3 Sewing

Sewing is the process of stitching the signatures together to make the book. The leaves in each signature are joined by vertical stitching tied off with kettle knots. The signatures are bound together by a series of tapes running across the back of the book around which the vertical stitching is threaded. This matrix of vertical stitching passing around horizontal cords or tapes prevents leaves moving in either direction.

Cutting back slots

In preparation for sewing, slots have to be cut in the back of the book to accommodate the tapes or cords that connect the signatures. The pressed book is positioned between strawboards and firmly held in a wooden laying press that resembles a vice. A set square is used to mark the position of the cuts. A tenon saw makes a very shallow cut – less than a millimetre – at each of the marked positions.

Pressing

Hand-bound books are pressed before sewing; machine-bound books are pressed afterwards. Pressing is used to give the book block solidity and firmness. If a book is well pressed, the folded signatures form a stable relationship with each other, and the leaves are likely to remain in alignment for the life of the book. The signatures must be 'knocked up' square (each signature must be positioned exactly on top of the previous one), as they cannot be repositioned effectively after pressing.

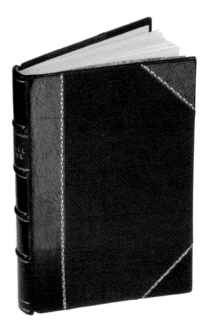

4 Trimming

A guillotine is used to trim the book to size: the blade descends onto a platen (flat metal sheet) to cut through the paper clamped beneath. The foredge of the book is cut first, followed by the tail and the head. In the past, some paperback books were not trimmed, only folded; the buyer had to open up the signatures with a paper-knife prior to reading. This practice has been revived by designers who enjoy the notion of the reader's involvement and the beauty of the rough foredge.

Rounding and backing

Hardback books that need to fall flat when open require an additional process called rounding and backing. Traditionally, large-format books such as atlases, lectern Bibles, and music scores are designed to lie flat. Other, smaller, books were also bound with this facility, but today many machine-bound books with square spines are designed to be read in the hand. Rounding is the process that removes the swell (the extra thickness added to the bound edge by sewing) at the back of the book. When hand-binding, a round-headed hammer is used to round the back of the book into a convex curve. As a consequence of rounding the back, the foredge takes on a concave curve. Backing involves clamping the book between wooden boards in a press and hammering the outer sections over to form a return and a recess in which the covers will sit. Rounding and backing can also be undertaken mechanically by a single machine, using mechanical rollers and often softening the back of the book with steam to make it more malleable.

5 Gluing

Hand-bound books are glued before trimming, and machine ones afterwards. The glue, which strengthens the binding, is worked into the back of the book and creeps between the sections. Excess glue is wiped away from the binding.

Cutting the boards

Cover boards come in many different weights and thicknesses. General binding previously used yellow strawboard, but this has now been largely replaced by greyboard. Where greater weight and strength is required, the denser and blacker millboard is used. The boards are smooth-faced but porous, allowing the paste to grip well to the face. It is important that the paste is applied evenly and does not have a high water content or the boards will warp. For machine production, specially adapted guillotines or rotary card cutters are used to cut the heavy book boards.

Treating the edges

The foredge of a book can be gilded prior to the boards being attached (see page 222).

Lining the backs

The lining is pasted down to the reverse of the cover either by hand or machine; the machine is also capable of applying the head and tail bands.

Fixing the endpaper

Endpapers line the back of the cover board and form the inside joint of the book. They may be plain, printed one side with a pattern, illustrated, photographic, or marbled. They are usually made of slightly heavier paper.

6 Pasting down

The cover material is cut larger than the book format to allow for the turnover on the inside cover. Leather covers involve additional hand-work. The edges of the leather must be pared thin to make it fold neatly around the cover board, and this is done with a shoemaker's paring knife. The leather is then pasted down onto the board and the overlap is turned in at the head and foot. The turnovers are fixed in place with temporary twine. If the book has raised bands, the definition can be drawn out with special nippers or grooved bandsticks. The book is then repositioned in a press and allowed to dry before the twine retaining the turnovers is removed. When this task is undertaken by machine it is referred to as 'casing in'; some machines are capable of casing in 2,000 books per hour.

Designing the foredge

Traditionally, many hand-bound books have the edges of the page finished with a colour, marbling, or, in the case of liturgical publications, gilding. Today, the majority of machine-bound books have no additional finishing to the edge of the page. Despite the additional cost, many designers have renewed an interest in this element of production. The burnished, gilded edge of a page is extremely smooth and, in addition to its decorative qualities, serves as a dust, light, and finger-grease seal, preventing discoloration of the pages.

Coloured staining can be applied to the edges of a book by sizing with alum water and then wiping on aniline water dyes. The choice of colour needs to be considered in relation to that of the board cloth.

Marbling is a multicoloured decorative edge, produced by transferring colour to the edge of the page. It gives each book an individual finish.

A book made of full-bleed images will affect the colour of the page edge. If the bleeds are of a uniform colour and the paper stock soft, the edge will take on the colour of the bleed. If the paper stock is less absorbent, the edge will be made up of alternating layers of ink and white paper and will appear as a lighter tint of the cropped pages. If the colour range of the full-bleed images is wide, the edge will take on an indistinct colour without a pattern. Recognizing the effect the full-bleed page has on the colour of the edge, designers can experiment with how the bleed is cropped.

Above The top left corner of every page in *Project M* (2000) has been folded over at an angle of 45°; text is revealed when the pages are fanned out.

Above right Stefan Sagmeister's book *Made You Look* (2001) has a small border bleeding off the right hand of every page. When the book is slightly bent, the foredge reveals the words 'made you look'. If the book is viewed from the back cover, three bones appear on the foredge printed full-bleed on the edge of the left-hand pages.

Below The finish of the foredge of each of these books has been carefully considered.

1 Yellow ink has been applied to the edge of a white page.

2 A red gilt finish has been applied to the edge of the page.

3 A traditional hand-marbled finish has been applied, giving each volume a unique foredge.

4 A matte black ink rolled onto the edge of a white page with full-bleed black margins produces an intense black edge here.

5 The rainbow bands here are created by printing a thin (4mm) strip on the surface of the page. Several signatures share the same coloured edge. The colour is less intense than rolling ink directly onto the foredge.

6 The foredge of Stefan Sagmeister's book *Made You Look* (shown opposite) combines silver gilting on the edge and a printed black border with white intervals on the surface of the page. These form type on the foredge that is just visible when the book is closed.

7 In much the same way as the Sagmeister book, an image is created on this foredge by printing a tiny full-colour border on the surface of the page. The image shows an American landscape when the book is closed.

1   2   3   4   5   6   7

Hand-finishing

Finishing refers to a set of processes completed after the book has been bound and cased, including embossing, lettering, decorating, and polishing. These were traditionally hand tasks and are all still performed by hand in library binding. For edition binding, these processes are carried out by machine.

Blind embossing is any impression made in the cover that does not contain ink or gilt infill. Hand tools are used to make the impressions. Blind-embossed lines, called fillet lines, can be of varying widths and can be rolled into the cover using a heated brass roller. These can be darkened and burnished using palette tools to create a two-tone cover detail. When the embossing is infilled with a metal this is referred to as gilt finishing.

Hand-lettering is a highly skilled task, as the impression created by a misplaced or slightly uneven letter cannot be repaired and the whole book is then devalued. Traditionally, the lettering is centred, though it can be aligned anywhere on the cover. The hand-lettering tools have wooden handles and a tip on which a single brass wrong-reading letter is raised. The range of fonts and sizes owned by most binders may be limited and restricted to letterpress bookfonts. These are specified in points or didots; some fonts consist only of capitals and numerals, while many do not include a full set of punctuation. If the designer wants to match the cover font with the text font inside the book, a stamp can be made to emboss the whole title as one element.

Machine-finishing

Today, the craft-based hand-finishing skills of the experienced binder have been replicated mechanically and augmented by new technologies, such as laser-cutting, to produce a huge range of cover finishes for mass-produced books. These include embossing, foil blocking, die-cutting, stamping, perforating, thumb indexes, laser-cutting, laminating, shrink-wrapping, and tipping in.

Embossing

Embossing produces an image raised above the surface of the paper. The image can be acid-photoetched or die-stamped into a hard plate, which creates a recess that the paper is forced into under pressure when placed on an embossing press. If the image has to be deeply embossed into the surface, additional heat is required. The acid-etched process is cheaper than hand-engraving, but produces a single or set of layered depths to the etching, whereas the skilled engraver is able to model delicate details within the type or image and, if embossed on fine paper, can achieve beautifully crisp results. Blind embossing uses no ink, only pressure, and raises the image above the surface. Single- or multicoloured engraving raises a printed image above the surface. Most boards and papers can be embossed, although Bible papers are the exception as they are simply too thin to endure the process.

Above The lavishly produced *Guide to Ecstacity*, illustrating the work of the architect Nigel Coates and designed by Why Not Associates, uses several machine finishes. The two-colour metallic blue and bronze boards have been debossed. The type is foil-blocked in two colours: metallic silver and matt black. The book is wrapped in a tummy band that resembles an airline ticket, overprinted on a thick matt stock and glued to the endpapers. A coloured book ribbon completes the impression of a high-quality publication.

Right A hand-engraved illustration of a bee shows the fine detail that a skilled engraver can realize through blind embossing. The forms within the image have complex curves that cannot be recreated by machine or etching. The deeper the cut in the engraving plate, the greater the definition on the paper. This image features very fine details that rely on appropriate press pressure and a substantial yet smooth-surfaced paper to retain the quality when reproduced. Hand-engraving is expensive but can provide an exquisite mark that could be used on a title page or chapter opener.

Far right This embossed crown has been foil-blocked and pressed twice to produce a burnished gold finish, in contrast to the very shiny metallic block on the *Guide to Ecstacity* cover shown on the previous page.

Foil blocking

When the embossing technique is used in conjunction with a metallic foil – gold, silver, platinum, bronze, brass, or copper – the embossed surface appears as a shiny metallic raised image. Heat and pressure are used to make the adhesive on the back of the foil stick to the paper.

Stamping

Stamping imprints the text or image below the surface. This, like embossing, involves making a die, which, for short runs (up to 1,000), can be of magnesium or zinc, or, for longer runs on heavier paper, is made of copper or brass. Blind stamping uses no ink. Infill foiling makes use of pressure and heat in much the same way as foil blocking.

Die-cutting

Die-cutting enables the printer to cut shapes out of paper or holes through paper. It is frequently used to cut the nets (flat shapes that, when folded, form three-dimensional boxes) in packaging and point-of-sale items. In publishing, the pieces that make up a pop-up book are die-cut. The die is very similar to a pastry-cutter. A toughened steel blade is set into a block of plywood. If more than one blade is required, these can be no closer than three millimetres to one another, defining the minimum cut width. The die is laid on a platen or letterpress bed, and the paper or card to be cut is pressed onto the die. When card is used it is cut in single sheets. Paper can be cut in small batches.

Laser-cutting

Laser-cutting is more expensive and slower than die-cutting, but is capable of exceptionally fine cuts. The width of the holes made can be equivalent to the thickness of the paper. This level of detail means that coarse-screened halftone images can be reproduced. Lasers can be used to cut the paper and board, and innovative designers have made use of this form of cutting on the pages of books and the covers. Lasers can also cut through an entire book up to 100 millimetres thick. As the price of laser-cutting falls, it is increasingly likely that this process will be incorporated in less expensive books.

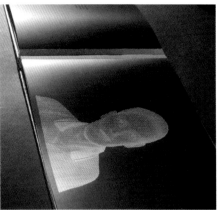
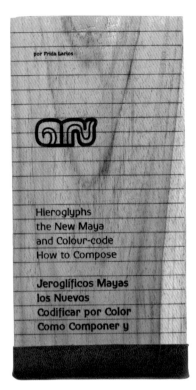

Perforating

Perforations are small holes or shapes through paper that enable it to be torn, like a sheet of stamps. These can be cut into a sheet using perforating rules. The rule consists of thin strips of metal with raised teeth that are set in a chase and laid on a platen press or letterpress machine. The paper is pressed onto the rule and the teeth puncture the paper with a line of small, neat holes. Laser-cutting can be used to perforate many sheets simultaneously.

Paper drilling

Paper drilling is used to cut holes through several sheets of paper at the same time. Loose-leaf ring-bound file pages use simple pillar drills. Drilling holes for spiral binding is performed by machines with multiple bits. As with wood drills, a range of hole widths specified in millimetres or inches can be cut.

Thumb indexes

These are usually found in frequently used works of reference such as dictionaries, encyclopedias, and Bibles. The thumb cut is a semicircle slightly larger than the average thumb that is cut into the foredge of a book. The cut is made through all the pages up to the indexed page, allowing the reader very quick access. For example, a Bible could be opened at the end of the Old Testament, with the thumb cuts on the left-hand foredge referring to the books in the Old Testament, and those on the right identifying the books of the New Testament. The cut is made down to the exact page and has to be done after the signatures are bound together. Small tabs of thicker card, or even leather, can be tipped in at the thumb point to strengthen the page. Today another approach to making section dividers is to use die-cut tabs with labels that extend beyond the foredge.

Top left A series of laser-cut portraits of philosophers designed by Oskar Bostrom. A coarse halftone dot screen has been used to guide the laser in cutting the circles. The screen works in negative, unlike print, as the largest circles produce the lightest tones.

Top centre Hannah Dumphy's book *Sheffield* (2003) uses laser-cutting to produce the imagery and some of the text, although each of the pages is made of very fine-gauge stainless steel. The choice of material echoes the content, as the English city of Sheffield is the home of British steel and the portraits are of retired cutlery workers or *blades*. A similar effect can be achieved by screenprinting an acid resist onto a metal surface and etching the holes by dipping in acid. This process is known as photoetching, and can only be used with metal pages.

Above Frida Lariou's book *Jeroglificos Mayas los Nuevos Codificar por Color Como Componer y* shows how a laser can be used effectively to heat-engrave type and a logo into the surface of a thin teak sheet.

Cover finishes

A variety of cover finishes can be applied to the cover of a plain-faced or image-cover. The designer should consider the material aspects of the cover as thoroughly as the image and typographic elements.

Laminating

Laminating a cover adds additional scuff protection. The lamination is usually a clear plastic film that is stretched over the cover and bonded to its surface using heat and pressure. Lamination is usually applied to printed surfaces and is likely to bubble if bonded to plain greyboard. It should not be used with screen-printed images or metallic inks, as the heat-sealing disturbs the surface.

Tummy bands and corner flags

A tummy band, or belly band, is a sheet of paper wrapped around the book. This can be broken before the book is opened or, alternatively, it can be folded and even tipped down onto the endpapers on the inside covers. Sometimes it is used to announce the contents or a new edition, but, increasingly, designers are seeing this feature as yet another indicator of quality production.

Corner flags are small triangles of paper that are folded but not permanently attached to the top right-hand corner of a book to announce a new edition, a significant date, and so on. They allow the publisher to add additional information to the cover after the book has been bound. The flag can be removed and discarded after sale.

Dust-jackets

Dust-jackets are folded sheets of paper that were originally designed to protect the binding prior to sale but have become an integral part of case-bound books. They give the designer the opportunity to wrap a four-colour image around a case-bound cloth book. Simple jackets are strips of paper, the same height as the cover, that are folded around the spine and have flaps of varying width that are tucked into the book between the endpaper and the flyleaf. These jackets are inclined to tear, as the cut edge of the paper is exposed. An alternative, more durable, approach makes use of a larger sheet. The sheet is divided approximately into three horizontally, each outer section being half the height of the central section, which is the height of the book. The outer sections are folded inward, so that the strip is now double thickness and has the folds at the head and foot. When it is wrapped around the book, it creates a far more substantial jacket.

Dropping in

'Dropping in' is a term used for adding any loose additional material into a book before it is shipped. This could include publisher's promotional material, a postcard seeking the reader's name and address details, or an erratum slip apologizing for an error or misrepresentation.

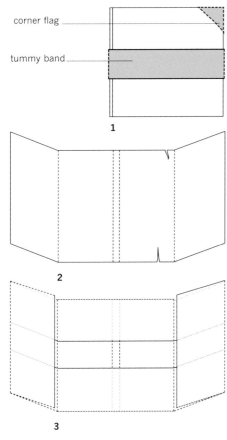

corner flag

tummy band

1

2

3

1 The tummy band is a strip of paper wrapped around the book and tucked inside the covers, while the corner flag is a triangle of paper folded over the edge of the cover.

2 A simple dust-jacket is made up of a single sheet of paper folded around the book with the flaps tucking inside the front and back covers. The cut edge of the sheet is exposed to wear and easily becomes torn.

3 A thicker and more durable dust-cover is made by folding a larger sheet so that the head and foot have a folded as opposed to a cut edge.

Tipping in

This is the process of pasting in additional illustrations by hand. This was a common practice when type was printed by letterpress and images lithographically. A letterpress caption was printed on a blank page and the appropriate lithographic image, printed on a separate sheet and trimmed to size, was tipped in above it. Four-colour books printed offset lithographically have removed the need for this form of tip-in, but designers' interest in attaching separate elements to pages and covers for aesthetic reasons has ensured that the practice continues. Pop-up books nearly always involve some hand tip-in work to glue the various moving elements to the card pages.

Lenticulated images

A lenticulated image creates an impression of movement as the eye moves across the page. They are frequently used in kitsch postcards but can be incorporated into books as tip-ins or pasted onto the front of covers. An object is drawn or photographed from several positions. The sequential images are then divided into strips, which are positioned alternately to make a single image. The lenticular lens is a series of triangular prisms made from thin plastic strips, which is bonded on top of the image. As the eye moves across the image, alternate parts are visible and the image appears to change.

Left A lenticulated image of the Eiffel Tower has been tipped in on the front cover of this book of Parisian photographs.

PARIS in 3D

From stereoscopy to virtual reality 1850-2000
In association with the Musée Carnavalet, Museum of the History of Paris

Above The cover of *The Art of Money* by David Standish features a holographic strip that, like the detailed engravings, reflects the nature of banknote design and security printing.

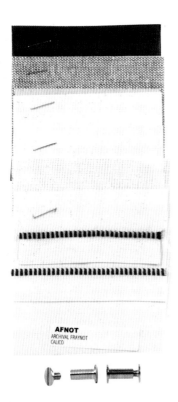

Above The functional strength and tactile qualities of binding and cover materials can be felt and considered in relation to the weight of the paper, size of the page, style of the type, use of colour, and content of a book.

Holographic images

These images appear to have a three-dimensional quality. When the viewer moves his or her eye across the page, the image appears to turn, as though the viewer were walking around a three-dimensional object. Holographic images are difficult and expensive to create. They are frequently used in security printing, but have also been successfully used as book and magazine covers. The image cannot be of a moving object (or living creature), as any movement during the process of laser capture will destroy the holographic potential. More than 300 laser images are recorded onto a minute ridged and grooved sheet. The object must be the same size as it is to appear in the final hologram: the present maximum size is a 150-millimetre square. Colour cannot be used within the object, but the viewer is aware of a spectrum of colours appearing to emanate from the hologram as the eye moves around it.

Binding materials

A huge variety of cover materials is available for binding, all of which offer the designer different finish qualities. It is useful to build up a collection of sample bookbinding materials, cover cloths, book ribbons, boards, and headbands.

Leather covers are associated with high-quality binding and are produced in a wide range of colours, weights, and finishes. Morocco is the binder's term for goatskin, which is pleasant to touch and pliable and does not easily soil. Pigskin is traditionally more suited to heavy binding as it is less pliable, while sheepskin is cheaper but more inclined to split. Today many manufacturers produce artificial skins resembling leather that provide a cheaper alternative for mass-produced books.

Cloth-cover, woven fabrics are usually called greige (pronounced 'gray'). The fabric is bleached to remove all impurities before being impregnated with starch or pyroxylin. The starching process, traditionally referred to as sizing, gives the fabric a stiffness and resistance to creasing, but it is inclined to absorb moisture in a damp atmosphere. Starched cloth is cheaper than pyroxylin-impregnated cloth. Pyroxylin is a type of liquid plastic that is stronger than starch and has waterproofing qualities. Pyroxylin cloth is versatile and can be finished in many different ways.

Cover materials

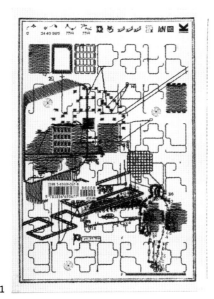

1

2

3

4

1 The vinyl back cover of *Pathfinder a/way/ through/swiss/graphix* (2002) is machine-embroidered with black cotton to create a series of barely legible words and patterns.

2 The illustrator Laura Carlin (2004) bound her book *Le Berét rouge* in red felt with a stalk protruding from the cover.

3 *Bent Ply* by Dung Ngo and Eric Pfeiffer (2003) is a book that celebrates the way plywood has been used in interiors and furniture. The plywood boards are glued to the stiff cloth cover.

4 *Spoon* (2003) is a book that features contemporary product designs. The metal cover is bent like a spoon and embossed with the title.

Above *Soon: Brands of Tomorrow* by Lewis Blackwell (2002) uses a conceptual approach to the cover finish. Thermoreactive ink responds to the heat of your hand when touched, changing the black cover white to reveal the type as though the cover itself were a portal to the future.

Paper covers

Paper coverings are less expensive than either leather or woven fabrics and can be divided into three types: paper, reinforced paper, and synthetic fibres.

Paper is the weakest of all cover materials in its unfinished form, but can be strengthened by coating the surface with acrylic, vinyl, or pyroxylin. Binding papers are classified either by weight, specified in grams and pounds, or by thickness, specified in 'points'. The paper points have no relationship to the typographic system of measurement; there are 1,000 paper points to the inch. Characteristically, paperback novels use covers of between 8 and 12 paper points in thickness.

Reinforced paper contains additional elements to add strength. These can be polymers or resins added during the manufacturing process, in addition to coatings of pyroxylin. These papers are used in larger-format paperback books in paper point thicknesses of 14, 17, 20, 22, and 25. Thinner reinforced papers are used as coverings on case-bound books, where the thickness is characteristically between 8 and 10 paper points.

Synthetic papers are made from acrylic fibres, spun into threads, and then bonded together in hot presses to produce sheets or rolls of grainless paper, which is therefore less likely to tear. The sheets can be coated and have a very high natural whiteness, making them ideal for four-colour printing.

Styles of binding

For sales purposes, books are often divided into hardbacks and paperbacks (also known as softbacks). These common terms do not differentiate the styles of binding, but only make reference to the cover material. For the purpose of binding, the styles can be broken down into library binding, case or edition binding, perfect or adhesive binding, and loose-leaf binding.

Library binding

While any book may be found in a library, this term refers to a particular approach to binding that is designed for longevity and heavy use. Library binding is characteristically undertaken by hand. The covers are often millboard rather than the lighter grey- or strawboards. The vertical stitching runs the length of each signature and is tied into the saw cuts with kettle knots. Over time, individual binders have developed many different sewing patterns, but most thread the stitching around the cords or tapes. These may be raised above the spine as bands. The cords are laced through holes in the boards that extend beyond the page and are glued to the cover. The cover material can be leather or cloth. The book is rounded and backed. On a library-bound copy, the heavy boards do not run quite into the joint but form a French groove (a gully running vertically down the cover of the book that is formed by the cover material extending beyond the cover board to make a hinge). The edge of the pages may be gilded and the title hand-stamped into the cover.

Opposite
1 *KEN,* a small book in part written and designed by Lucy Choules, takes the form of a folded map and cover rather than a bound book.

2 A perfect-bound book of paper samples designed by North makes use of a paper cover that has perforations running around the spine on to the back cover.

3 Substantial pig rings (a ring that can be opened and passed through a series of holes in a page) have been used to bind the loose folded sheets for this thick catalogue for the Royal College of Art Degree Show, 1990.

4 A book about the florist McQueens uses a simple paperback cover that is stitched through from the front.

Case-binding

Case-bound books are sometimes still produced by hand but have become the main form of machine-produced hardback. This type of binding is often referred to as edition binding. The case is made up from three sections of board: front cover, back cover, and spine. The sections are stitched together in both hand and machine versions, though machine-sewn books are not stitched down the length of each signature but in short sections. The back may be square or rounded and backed. The board may be covered with cloth or a printed paper and is glued to the book by a strip of crash or muslin. The end-papers are pasted down over the lining of the grey coverboard. The case may overlap the book leaves in the form of a square or be cut flush without an overlap. The title is printed, machine-embossed, or hot-stamped to the cover, which may be wrapped in a protective dust-jacket. Many of the hand-finishing processes associated with case-binding have been replicated by machine: square, foil embossing, edge-finishing, adding headband, and book ribbons can all be performed mechanically. The appearance and production values are extremely high for what is a mass-produced product.

Perfect binding

Perfect or adhesive binding is the binder's term for a paperback binding. This is the fastest and cheapest method of bookbinding. Neither the binding nor covers are stitched, relying on the adhesive for strength. The pages are glued to a strip of muslin and then to the cover. The cover material is usually heavier than the book and does not require endpapers. Paperback books are cut flush (the covers do not extend beyond the book), but, confusingly, perfect-bound books can have a hard cover.

Concertina books or broken-spine binding

Concertina books, often described as Chinese or French binding, can be bound with a wrap-around cover that enables the pages to be opened like a concertina so that they can be viewed as a single sheet. In this case, the cover is a single folded card or cloth-covered board that makes up back cover, spine, and front cover. The concertina pages are glued to the inside back cover but not to the inside front cover. Concertina books of this type may also be described as having a broken-spine binding.

Paperback bindings

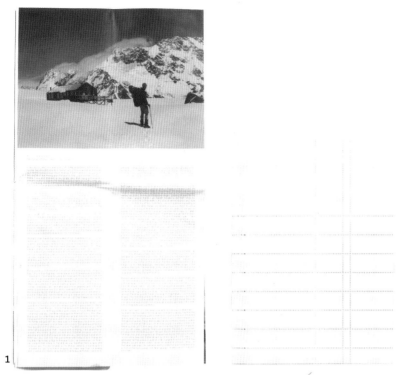

1

2

3

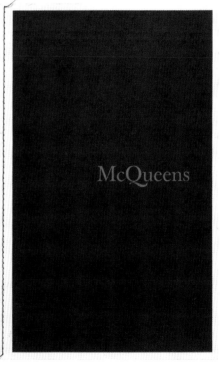

4

Experimental hardback bindings

1 Matilda Saxo's design and binding of the clas-sic book by Robert Louis Stephenson, *The Strange Case of Dr Jekyll and Mr Hyde*, has a single short fold down the centre of each page. These are supported by a thicker board attached to the front and back covers. The short central fold is about the width of a conventional column interval and is printed in green but rises vertically. The physical form of the book reflects the narrative of the main character's split personality.

1

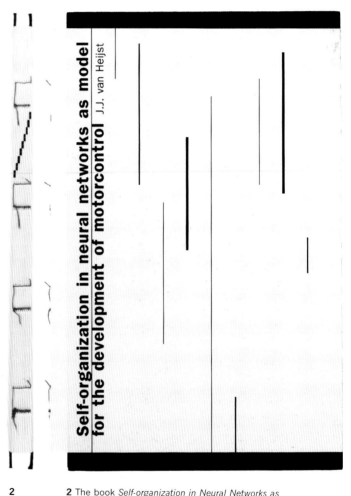

2

2 The book *Self-organization in Neural Networks as Model for the Development of Motorcontrol* uses hard covers, machine-stitching, and gluing, but has no spine panel, revealing the raw red stitch-ing on the spine – perhaps reflecting the neural networks of the title.

3 Designer Francesca Prieto took the poems of Nicanor Parra and set them in a small hardback landscape book with a dust-jacket. Each page featured broken fragments of the poems set at a strange angle. Only when the pages are removed from the book, folded, and slipped into one another, is a polygon created, making the poems readable. This imaginative binding reflects the nature of the poetry, which advocates left-wing ideas but was written under a right-wing regime. It could therefore not be published in its entirety, but had to disguise its real content.

3

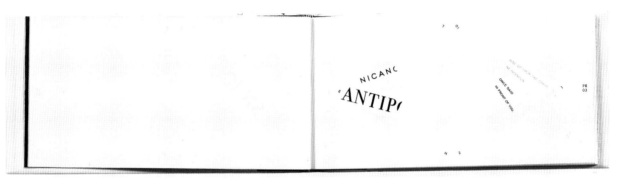

4 The binding of *Gordon Matta-Clark,* a book of the sculptor's work, has a panel cut out of the spine, revealing the machine-stitching. Matta-Clark's work involves cutting holes through floors of disused buildings and photographing the results from many angles. The cutaway case binding of the book reflects this process on a smaller scale: the buildings and the book are subjected to the same kind of 'carving'.

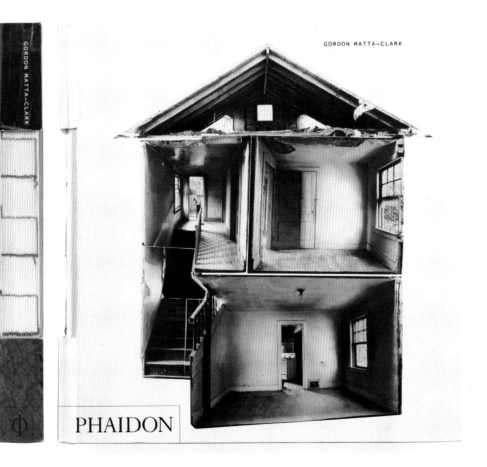

4

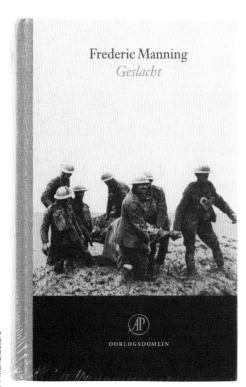

Above A Dutch hardback copy of Frederic Manning's *Geslacht* is shrink-wrapped to protect the cloth binding and to prevent the soft matt printed cover from scuffing.

Saddle-wire stitching

This is the printer's term for stapling. It is principally used to bind magazines, pamphlets, and catalogues. Thin publications can be saddle-stitched, while those with greater bulk have to be side wire-stitched. In either case, the book is not made up of sections but is collated as a single signature.

The saddle-stitched booklet, once collated and folded, is hung over a saddle at the centre spread and wires are punched through from the back. The wires are automatically turned over and the pages are secured. The booklet is then trimmed flush top, bottom, and foredge.

Books of greater thicknesses have be wire-stitched from the side. Side wire-stitching does not allow the book to be opened flat but to be read in hand. The greater the number of pages, the less each spread can be opened without damaging the book and an extra allowance may have to be made in the gutter. To hide the stitches, these books are often finished with covers that are glued directly to the back.

Spiral binding

Spiral-bound books allow the page to lie absolutely flat and are often used for manuals that readers may have to read when their hands are full. The leaves are individual, rather than signatures, and are drilled on the binding edge with a series of holes that match the pitch (angle of the screw thread) and the width of the spiral binding. The spiral wire is rotated through the holes and turned over at either end to prevent the leaves slipping off.

Loose-leaf binding

Loose-leaf binding is often associated with stationery binding, ring files, and Filofaxes, but is used within commercial publishing as well. The style allows the reader to remove a particular piece of information so that the whole book does not have to be carried. In part-work publishing (series sold in monthly or weekly issues that build into a complete work), a file is used to store the collection of magazines. The holes can be round or square-cut depending on the binding mechanism. In legal publishing, loose-leaf is used to update a work: new or replacement material can be added as the law changes.

Shrink-wrapping

Shrink-wrapping seals books into a polythene or cellophane tube from which the air is sucked out and the ends heat-sealed. This will protect vulnerable elements of the book from being damaged. Most pop-up books are sealed in this way to prevent potential buyers playing with the copy on the shelf. Many bookshops open a single copy as a sample.

Additional material

Styling the text

Many publishers devise a set of text conventions that all editors and designers work to. These guidelines are often referred to as a 'house style', and may affect both the visual and linguistic detailing of the text. Some publishers will develop style guides that are pertinent for a particular type of book or series; others allow individual editors to develop the detailing strategy in relation to the title, its potential readership, and the market. Some writers have a very particular view of the way the text detailing is presented, so it is important that the designer has agreed detailing conventions with the editor prior to starting the layouts. In a previous book, *Type & Typography*, Phil Baines and I developed a set of typographic styling guidelines that were based on a mixture of visual considerations and language usage. I am very grateful to Phil for allowing me to adapt these guidelines for this book. The guidelines were based on our own evolving practice (which includes work for several large publishers in Britain and the US); there is no single universal style manual either for editorial or typographic detailing. However, the most widely used reference books are *Hart's Rules for Compositors and Readers* and Judith Butcher's *Copy-editing* for editors, authors, and publishers in the UK, and *The Chicago Manual of Style* in the US. I hope these guidelines will prove helpful. Any system needs adapting to circumstance, but editors and designers should strive to present information consistently.

Below A spread from *The Chicago Manual of Style* shows the complexity of language usage and, on the right-hand page, describes differences between British and American style.

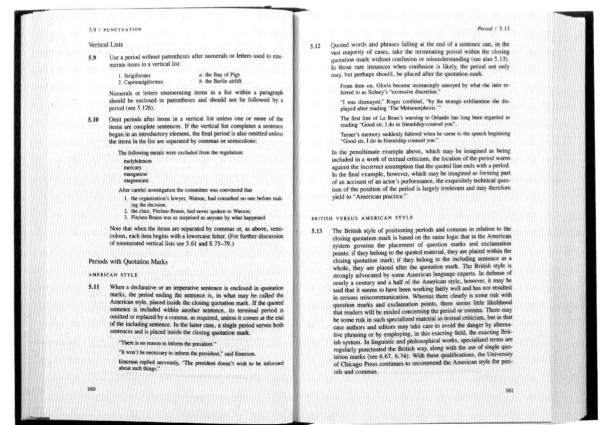

Abbreviations

The Rev Malcolme Love

Abbreviations for dimensions do not need a full point, nor should they be pluralized:

51cm not 51cms

In abbreviations for 'page' and 'circa', common British practice is to use a period without a following space ('c.' is italicized):

p.245   *c.* 1997

The abbreviations for 'that is' and 'for example' can look too spotty if used with full points; an alternative used in the UK is to omit the periods and simply italicize them, but this is not common practice in the US:

ie not i.e.   *eg* not e.g.

Acronyms

These are names derived from sets of initials that are pronounced as words in their own right. Once established as the standard term of reference, they can be treated as a normal name with an initial cap only.

Where are the Nato headquarters?

Ampersand

The abbreviation for 'and' is derived from the Latin 'et', whose characters can still be seen in some versions of the character.

& (Bembo)

Today its use is generally confined to lists, where it saves space, and to company names where it clearly indicates a particular rather than a general relationship:

Smith & Jones
not Smith and Jones

Annotation and labelling

Labelling should generally form a secondary level of information to support the illustration, diagram, or photograph. The size and weight of type and leader lines should be considered in relation to the weight (or colour) of the line used within the image: generally, leader lines should be lighter in appearance than the illustration or image to avoid confusion. There is generally no need to box or underline labels.

Apostrophe

This is used to indicate that a word is possessive or that there is a missing letter:

It's Peter's book.

The correct character (sometimes known as a 'smart quote') should always be used, not a prime.

Peter's not Peter's

Bibliographies

Books, articles, and web addresses should be listed as suggested below. In academic work, editors will insist on having the author's surname first: a possible compromise may be to use small caps to emphasize the surname. Some publishers also omit the publisher (which doesn't seem very helpful). When giving page references, use p. (without a following space) for a single page, and pp. for more than one.

Phil Baines & Andrew Haslam, *Type & Typography*: Second edition, London, Laurence King Publishing 2005

Brackets and parentheses

An afterthought, a subordinate clause, and references can all be contained within parentheses (round brackets):

book parts (2, 3, & 4) relate to ...

square brackets are used to denote an omission:

'He [Martin] owned a flat.'

Capitals ~ appearance of

When setting text in capitals, some adjustment needs to be made to their spacing – by using tracking – to avoid the letters looking too crowded: typefaces are generally spaced for combined upper- and lower-case usage. Certain words will need more work than others depending on the particular character combinations involved.

CAPITAL LETTERS no tracking: cramped

CAPITAL LETTERS with tracking: elegant

If setting on several lines, care should also be taken with the leading to ensure that the space between lines looks larger than the space between words.

CAPITAL LETTERS NEED SPECIAL TREATMENT

The use of capitals is a complicated issue. The rule in English is that all proper names should begin with a capital, and there is the common practice that within titles all words other than 'the', 'and', 'of', etc., should also start likewise. However, the latter practice can make titles look ugly and in many cases old-fashioned.

Q Do Initial Capital Letters Really Make Headings Clearer?

A No, initial capital letters do not make headings clearer.

A further problem today arises when companies who use lower-case only (or all caps) as part of their identity want them always to appear like that in print. There is no reason for this: their name is different from their signature and should be set in a standard style.

Column, page, and paragraph endings

Never end or begin a column or page with a single line of a paragraph (the normal minimum is two or three lines), and try to avoid ending a paragraph with a single word.

A single word at the end of a paragraph is known as an 'orphan', and a word or group of words at the top of a page that don't run to the full column width is called a 'widow'. There are a number of solutions.

1 If the setting is ranged left, paragraphs can be 'massaged' by a judicious use of soft returns.

2 If the copy is newly written, the author or editor should usually be able to write (or cut) a few words.

3 If there are pictures within the column, some subtle resizing can save copy changes.

4 If these fail, as a last resort leave the column or page a line short. A consistent spatial relationship between the elements on the page is far more important than whether the pages line up across the foot of the spread.

Contractions See abbreviations

Dashes

For parenthetical clauses use a dash not a hyphen. Two kinds of dash exist:

an en dash

—

and an em dash

——

Their names indicate their length.

En dashes with a space either side are the norm today in Britain and are nearly always better than em dashes with sans-serif typefaces:

The reason – which Phil doesn't agree with – is that it looks out

of place.

Em dashes often look more bookish and tend to work better with older typefaces. They should be used without a space either side. This is the standard American style:

The reason—which Phil doesn't agree with—is that it looks out of place.

If using different typefaces within a piece of work, it would be acceptable to use a different style of dash for each: the main guide is to be consistent.

Never use hyphens for this role. Hyphens simply indicate broken or compound words. An en dash is also used within ranges of dates and page numbers, where it is employed without a space either side:

1938–2005   pp.27–37

En dashes are also used in compounds where the two parts are equal: the dash can either mean 'and', as in 'Arab–Israeli conflict', or 'to', as in 'the London–Brighton race'. Where the first part of the compound is not a complete word, a hyphen should be used, as in Anglo-Asian.

Dates

As with many details in this chapter, British and US usage differs. British style is to use cardinal numbers (1, 2, 3, etc.) and in the following order:

14 February 1938

US style uses cardinal numbers as follows:

February 14, 1938

When speaking of a date in running text, however, US style may use an ordinal number ('on the 14th of February'), while UK style would be more likely to maintain cardinal number usage.

Decimal points

Although a full point is often used for this purpose, a decimal point exists in every font and is often far clearer:

78·5cm not 78.5cm

See also figures and mid-point

D**rop caps** Derived from the manuscript tradition, this device is often used at the beginning of a chapter, article, or paragraph. Careful attention to space is required to integrate these decorative details with the rest of the paragraph. The cap letter can be any number of lines deep but will integrate well with text if it is positioned on a baseline rather than hanging in space above a white 'pool'. In this example, the drop cap is three lines deep and its top has been aligned visually with the x-height of the main text.

Ellipsis

. . .

The ellipsis, with a space either side, is used to denote omissions in the text, or text trailing off. Instead of typing three full points with spaces, the special ellipsis character should be used.

Endnotes See references

Figures ~ kinds of

There are two kinds, lining:

1234567890

and non-lining: 1234567890

In the vast majority of fonts, all figures are designed with identical character widths to enable tabular matter to align correctly: when setting dates, the 1 may need to be kerned (see pages 79–80)

Within text, it is best to use non-lining figures if available:

The book was published in 1974.

not The book was published in 1974.

But use lining figures with capitals:

PELHAM 123 not PELHAM 123

Note that not all typefaces have both versions.

With the older PostScript fonts, suppliers of 'classic designs' often produced a regular font and a matching expert set that contained non-lining figures (and often small caps and an assortment of ligatures and fractions). Newer designs, such as Meta or Swift, had a version called caps or SC, which had a similar font layout.

Fonts produced in OpenType format with its extended character set can now come with both sets of figures as part of one individual font file.

~ quantities and monetary units

When dealing with quantities, it is usual to indicate thousands with a comma, except in dates:

1,000 not 1000

When dealing with monetary units, particularly in financial work, figures should be set ranged right or aligned on the decimal point:

£34,710·00

1,341·90

Note also that different countries may have different ways of showing decimals and thousands.

English usage is:

3,128·50 but in French it would be 3.128,50

See also mid-point.

Folios

This is the correct term for page numbers. If the document needs to be referred to, it needs folios. Position them where they can be seen clearly – never near the back margins – and in a way that suits the style of the document. They rarely need to be larger than the text size. They are often placed next to the running head/foot.

In the past, books used to have two sets of numbers: lower-case roman (i, ii, iii, etc.) was used for the prelims, and arabic (1, 2, 3, etc.) for the book proper. Today, it is more usual to use arabic throughout but not show them on either blank or display pages.

Footnotes See references

Fractions

Only basic fractions are built into the ISO standard character set, and these are not accessible on the Mac keyboard. However fractions can be created manually by sub- and super-scripting the appropriate number then taking it down by a few points. Alternatively there is the 'Make Fraction' option available in Quark.

Quark-made fractions 19⅓ x 4¾ in

Full points (stops)
See abbreviations and sentence endings

Hanging punctuation

This facility of some layout programs allows punctuation to extend beyond the confines of a text column width in order to present an even visual edge. This is useful for occasional headline and display use.

Hyphenation & justification (H&Js)
See page 81

Hyphens

—

A hyphen is not a dash (see dashes). A hyphen only ever indicates broken or compound words:

What a lovey-dovey couple

Initials

Initials for people's first names should be evenly spaced, not grouped as a separate item from their surname. Unless otherwise requested by the client, they do not need full points:

F P Haslam not F.P.Haslam

Qualifications do not need full points:

Peter Haslam MEd

See also small caps

Intercaps

Generally, this is a contemporary way of shortening compound names and omitting the hyphen.
As the capital has an important function it must be respected:

OpenType

(Occasionally they provide an excuse for gratuitous bad spelling, *eg*, QuarkXPress.)

Italics

Italics originated as typefaces in their own right, but modern-day practice has placed them firmly in the role of an accompaniment to roman. In this they have three main purposes.
1 They denote the titles of artistic works, whether books, newspapers, paintings, or plays;
2 They indicate foreign words and phrases (unless they have become accepted as part of the language: a good up-to-date dictionary will provide guidance here);
3 They can also denote a particular tone of voice (but can become irritating if used too much for this purpose).

Ligatures

In printing terms, a ligature refers to two or more characters that touch. In linguistic terms, these are usually vowels such as:

Æ æ Œ œ

These are combined for phonetic reasons, although the creation of keyboard symbols for umlauts, circumflexes, etc., have pretty much made their use obsolete. Their use in English is generally reserved for lending a period flavour or for the accurate rendering of archaic texts.

Typefaces have been developed that overlap consonant pairs, the two most common being fi and fl:

fi   fl

fit not fit

If running a spell-check on a document, it is best to do this before inserting ligatures, because the dictionaries in some programs do not recognize them. In some faces and in expert sets, further ligatures for ffi and ffl also exist.

Marginal notes See references

Omissions See ellipses

Ordinal numbers

1st, 2nd, 3rd, etc.
In British and American English these are generally avoided in running text by spelling the word out:

twentieth-century boy

Page numbers See folios

Paragraphs

A paragraph is a unit of thought and as such, one needs to be distinguishable from another. The paragraph may be shown in a variety of ways. Raw copy from a typist will invariably come with line spaces, but the typographic norm is to use a simple indent. A value equal to the leading – the dominant vertical increment of measure – is a suggested minimum. The first paragraph in a chapter or section does not need an indent.

Do not use tabs when you want an indent, since a tab becomes a character in the text. Instead, use a formatting instruction, which can be altered or cancelled more easily.

Parentheses See brackets

Primes

ʹ   ʺ

In general typographic use, these are a leftover from the typewriter keyboard, where they were used both as apostrophes and quotation marks – showing no difference between open and closed. They should never be used instead of properly designed 'smart' apostrophes or quotation marks.

The prime is now generally used to denote feet and inches. If both metric and imperial dimensions are used, it is preferable to use abbreviations:

a 2m (6ft. 6in.) plywood sheet

Proof correction marks

In the days when the boundaries between the editorial, design, and typesetting processes were more clearly delineated, a set of commonly understood proof correction marks enabled all parties to communicate clearly and succinctly about corrections and alterations to the copy. Despite the apparently seamless nature of much of today's design environment, that need for communication still exists. Different countries have their own standard marks; all are a form of shorthand and use marks both within the text and in the margins. The marks shown opposite are from the British Standard (5261: 1975).

Basic marks

Insert ⟨	subtract or delete /	error ✗
add ⟨	subtract ↑	queries ⓘ
superior ⟨	inferior ⟨	leave alone ✓

Typestyle

marginal mark	text mark	as corrected
⊔⊔	<u>italicize</u>	*italicize*
⊔	romanize	romanize
〜〜	<u>embolden</u>	**embolden**
≡	<u>caps</u>	CAPS
≠	NOT CAPS	not caps
=	<u>small caps</u>	SMALL CAPS
≠	no sc	no sc

Spacing, character, and line errors

marginal mark	text mark	as corrected
⟨	add⟨space	add space
↑	c./2000	c. 2000
⌒	clo⌒se up	close up
	[reposition]	
Ⴎ	trⴎaspose	transpose
w.f.	Wrong font Swift	Swift
	then. Make new para	
	lines ⌐ transpose	transpose lines
	run ⟩ on	run on
	take back now	take back now
	take over now	take over now

Punctuation marks

No word space is used before punctuation marks, but characters with ascenders or overhangs may need some tracking before a closing bracket or a quotation mark.

In running text, punctuation has an important role to play in conveying the intended meaning:

2-6 Catton Street, London

but in display setting – for title pages, for example – line breaks, space, or general arrangement can often take its place:

2-6 Catton Street

London

Quotation marks and quotations

' ' " "

British style is generally to use single quotes, both for quotations and to denote particular usage of certain words. Double quotes create spotty holes in the text and should only be used for quotes within quotes.

'I liked it when the car went "beep, beep" suddenly.'

American style is to use double quotes rather than single quotes, and single within double:

"I liked it when the car went 'beep, beep' suddenly."

In either case, use quotation marks (sometimes called 'curly' or 'smart' quotes) not the typist's version ('primes'). Note also that British style is to place the punctuation mark within the quotation mark only if the quote is a complete sentence, while American style is to place the punctuation mark within the quote marks in every case.

For quotations of more than four lines, it is better not to use quote marks at all, but to set the text differently, for example in a slightly smaller size and indented.

> The book is the greatest interactive medium of all time. You can underline it, write in the margins, fold down a page, skip ahead. And you can take it anywhere.
>
> Michael Lynton in the *Daily Telegraph* 19 August 1996

References

In non-fiction and academic writing, there is often a need to refer to works cited within the text.

The 'parenthetical citation' method is one of the least invasive methods of citing sources, with only the bare essentials used and no need for additional notes (foot, side, or end) on the page.

Parenthetical citations include only the author's surname, the date of the text being referred to (if there is more than one publication by a particular author) and the page reference for the text or ideas being quoted or paraphrased. They are included in the text immediately following on from the material to which they refer, for example:

from doing so'. (Tracy p.11) The function of …

Footnotes (see page 108) would be needed when, in addition to citations, there is the need to make further comment separate from the main text. This requires annotation in the main text and then a position and typographic style for the note itself. Notes can sit alongside the text (shoulder-notes), below the text (footnotes), be placed at the end of individual chapters, or removed to the back of the book (endnotes). If there are only a few notes on each page, they can be cued by using the standard reference characters in this order:

but for copious references or when the notes follow the chapter, superior ('superscript') numbers placed at the end of the relevant phrase or sentence are far clearer. These are not part of a standard font but are created in the page layout program and may need some adjustment to balance visually with the text.

cast iron; enamelled steel;[14] and

Running heads/running feet

Like folios, running heads or feet are necessary in longer documents. The usual book style is to have the book title on the left-hand page and the chapter title on the right. It is often useful to group the folio and running head together. Variations to the content and position of both these elements can be made to suit particular circumstances, but they should always be consistent with the contents page.
See also folios

Sentence endings

The common typing practice of using two spaces at the end of each sentence creates white holes in the texture of a text. A single space following the full point is all that is required to allow the punctuation mark to do its work.

sentence creates white holes in the texture of a text. A single space following the full point is all that is needed.

Small caps

Small caps are capitals designed with a height approximately that of the lower-case x-height. If available, they are useful for emphasis in bibliographies, for academic qualifications, in post or zip codes, and for an additional level of heading or subheading. Never use computer-generated versions, which simply take the capitals and reduce them: they look too light:

Wendy Baker MA (RCA)
not Wendy Baker MA (RCA)

Most suppliers of 'classic fonts' produce a matching expert set that contains small caps as well as non-lining figures and an assortment of ligatures and fractions. Many contemporary faces, such as Meta or Swift, have a version called caps or SC with a similar font layout.

Soft returns

These are used for turning over overhanging words in ranged-left copy, or for forcing turnovers in justified copy without creating a new paragraph.

Temperature

This is indicated by the degree symbol. When two units of measurement are being used, or where there may be confusion, use initials to clarify. If the numerals are non-lining, small caps look better. A full point is unnecessary.

the April average is 61°F (15°C), but not this year.

Word space

The space between words is defined by the type designer or manufacturer, but can be adjusted with the page layout program. Where something more prominent than a normal word space is needed, use an en space (usually the width of the figure 0).

British and US Macintosh keyboard legend for ISO Latin set 1

Note that although typefaces designed for this set have 256 possible character positions, not all of them are accessible from the Mac keyboard. In addition, only characters not shown on the keys themselves are listed below. Where characters have more than one function, the information is duplicated.

Accented characters

Å [Shift] [Alt] [A]

å [Alt] [A]

Á [Alt] [E] [Shift] [A]

á [Alt] [E] [A]

À [Alt] [`] [Shift] [A]

à [Alt] [`] [A]

Â [Alt] [I] [Shift] [A]

â [Alt] [I] [A]

Ä [Alt] [U] [Shift] [A]

ä [Alt] [U] [A]

Ã [Alt] [N] [Shift] [A]

ã [Alt] [N] [A]

Ç [Shift] [Alt] [C]

ç [Alt] [C]

É [Alt] [E] [Shift] [E]

é [Alt] [E] [E]

È [Alt] [`] [Shift] [E]

è [Alt] [`] [E]

Ê [Alt] [I] [Shift] [E]

ê [Alt] [I] [E]

Ë [Alt] [U] [Shift] [E]

ë [Alt] [U] [E]

Í [Alt] [E] [Shift] [I]

í [Alt] [E] [I]

Ì [Alt] [`] [Shift] [I]

ì [Alt] [`] [I]

Î [Alt] [I] [Shift] [I]

î [Alt] [I] [I]

Ï [Alt] [U] [Shift] [I]

ï [Alt] [U] [I]

Ñ [Alt] [N] [Shift] [N]

ñ [Alt] [N] [N]

Ó [Alt] [E] [Shift] [O]

ó [Alt] [E] [O]

Ò [Alt] [`] [Shift] [O]

ò [Alt] [`] [O]

Ô [Alt] [I] [Shift] [O]

ô [Alt] [I] [O]

Ö [Alt] [U] [Shift] [O]

ö [Alt] [U] [O]

Ø [Shift] [Alt] [O]

ø [Alt] [O]

Õ [Alt] [N] [Shift] [O]

õ [Alt] [N] [O]

Ú [Alt] [E] [Shift] [U]

ú [Alt] [E] [U]

Ù [Alt] [`] [Shift] [U]

ù [Alt] [`] [U]

Û [Alt] [I] [Shift] [U]

û [Alt] [I] [U]

Ü [Alt] [U] [Shift] [U]

ü [Alt] [U] [U]

Ÿ [Alt] [U] [Shift] [Y]

ÿ [Alt] [U] [Y]

Accents

acute
´ [Alt] [E] (GB) [Shift] [Alt] [E] (US)

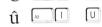

breve
˘ [Shift] [Alt] [>]

circumflex
^ [Shift] [Alt] [N] (GB) [Shift] [Alt] [I] (US)

dotless i
ı [Shift] [Alt] [B]

dieresis (umlaut)
¨ [Alt] [U] (GB) [Shift] [Alt] [U] (US)

grave
` [Alt] [`] (GB) [Shift] [Alt] [`] (US)

macron
¯ [Shift] [Alt] [<]

overdot
˙ [Alt] [H]

ring
° [Alt] [K]

tilde
~ [Shift] [Alt] [M] (GB) [Shift] [Alt] [N] (US)

Apostrophe
' [Shift] [Alt] [}]

Apple
(on system fonts)
 [Shift] [Alt] [K]

Bullet
• [Alt] [8]

Copyright
© [Alt] [G]

Dashes

em dash
— [Shift] [Alt] [-]

en dash
– [Alt] [-]

Decimal or mid-point
· [Shift] [Alt] [9]

Diphthongs
Æ [Shift] [Alt] ["]   æ [Alt] ["]
Œ [Shift] [Alt] [Q]   œ [Alt] [Q]

Ellipsis
… [Alt] [;]

En space
ie 500 units wide
[Alt] [Space]

Fraction bar

'Whole fractions' cannot be accessed on the Mac. Use the solidus (not the 'virgule' or forward slash) as the bar when creating your own

/ [Shift] [Alt] [!₁]

Ligatures

fi [Shift] [Alt] [%₅]

fl [Shift] [Alt] [^₆]

In some faces and in expert sets further ligatures for ffi, ffl exist; positions are usually specific to each particular manufacturer.

ß [Alt] [S]

Eszett (the German 'double s', although it is actually a separate letter and can change the meaning of words)

Mathematical & other symbols

American number symbol (GB)

[Alt] [#₃]

ascii circumflex

^ [Alt] [I]

approx/equal

≈ [Alt] [X]

degree

° [Shift] [Alt] [*₈]

delta

Δ [Alt] [J]

division

÷ [Alt] [?/]

epsilon

∑ [Alt] [W]

greater than or equal to

≥ [Alt] [>.]

infinity

∞ [Alt] [%₅]

integral

∫ [Alt] [B]

less than or equal to

≤ [Alt] [<,]

logical not

¬ [Alt] [L]

lozenge

◊ [Shift] [Alt] [V]

mu

µ [Alt] [M]

not equal to

≠ [Alt] [+=]

omega

Ω [Alt] [Z]

ordinal a

ª [Alt] [(₉]

ordinal o

º [Alt] [)₀]

partial difference

∂ [Alt] [D]

per thousand

‰ [Shift] [Alt] [E] (GB) [Shift] [Alt] [R] (US)

Pi

∏ [Shift] [Alt] [P]

pi

π [Alt] [P]

plus or minus

± [Shift] [Alt] [+=]

solidus (fraction bar)

/ [Shift] [Alt] [!₁]

square root

√ [Alt] [V]

Mid- or decimal point

• [Shift] [Alt] [(₉]

Monetary symbols

Cent

¢ [Alt] [$₄]

Euro

€ [Alt] [@₂]

Florin

ƒ [Alt] [F]

Pound sterling (US)

£ [Alt] [#₃]

Yen

¥ [Alt] [Y]

Punctuation marks

open Spanish exclamation mark

¡ [Alt] [!₁]

open Spanish question mark

¿ [Shift] [Alt] [?/]

Quotation marks

' [Alt] [}]] , [Shift] [Alt] [}]]

" [Alt] [{[] " [Shift] [Alt] [{[]

Guillemets (used pointing out in French and Italian; in German they point in)

‹ [Shift] [Alt] [#₃] › [Shift] [Alt] [$₄]

« [Alt] [|\] » [Shift] [Alt] [|\]

open Spanish quotation marks

‚ [Shift] [Alt] [)₀] „ [Shift] [Alt] [W]

Reference marks

dagger

† [Alt] [T]

double dagger

‡ [Shift] [Alt] [&₇]

paragraph (pilcrow)

¶ [Alt] [&₇]

section

§ [Alt] [^₆]

Registered trade mark

® [Alt] [R]

Soft return

this creates a new line without it giving a new paragraph format

[Shift] [Return]

Temperature

degree

° [Shift] [Alt] [*₈]

Trademark

™ [Shift] [Alt] [@₂]

Further Reading

I: What is a book?

Alan **Bartram**, *Five Hundred Years of Book Design*, London: The British Library, 2001.

Robert **Bringhurst** and Warren **Chappell**, *A Short History of the Printed Word*, Vancouver: Hartley & Marks, 1999.

Harry **Carter**, *A View of Early Typography up to about 1600*, London: Hyphen Press (reprint), 2002.

Lois Mai **Chan**, John P. **Comaromi**, Joan S. **Mitchell**, and Mohinder P. **Satija**, *Dewey Decimal Classification*, New York: Forest Press, OCLC Online Computer Library Centre, 1996.

Martin **Davies**, *The Gutenberg Bible*, London: The British Library, 1996.

Geoffrey Ashall **Glaister**, *Glaister's Encyclopedia of the Book*, London: British Library, and New Castle, Delaware: Oak Knoll Press, 1996.

Christopher de **Hamel**, *The Book: A History of the Bible*, London: Phaidon, 2001.

Norma **Levarie**, *The Art and History of Books*, London: British Library, and New Castle, Delaware: Oak Knoll Press, 1995.

Margaret B. **Stillwell**, *The Beginning of the World of Books, 1450 to 1470*, New York: Bibliographical Society of America, 1972.

II: The book designer's palette

Phil **Baines** & Andrew **Haslam**, *Type & Typography*, London: Laurence King (revised edition), 2005.

Andrew **Boag**, "Typographic measurements: a chronology," *Typographic Papers 1*, University of Reading, 1996, pp.105–21.

Hans Rudolf **Bossard**, *Der typografische Raster (The Typographic Grid)*, Zürich: Niggli, 2000.

Robert **Bringhurst**, *The Elements of Typographic Style, Version 2.4*, Vancouver: Hartley & Marks, 2001.

Bruce **Brown**, *Brown's Index to Photo Composition Typography*, Minehead: Greenwood, 1983.

Christophe **Burke**, *Paul Renner: the Art of Typography*, London: Hyphen Press, 1998.

David **Crystal**, *The Cambridge Encyclopedia of the English Language*, Cambridge: Cambridge University Press, 1995.

Kibberly **Elam**, *Grid Systems*, New York: Princeton Architectural Press, 2004.

Michael **Evamy**/Lucienne **Roberts**, *In sight: a guide to design with low vision in mind, examining the notion of inclusive design, exploring the subject within a commercial and social context*, Hove: Rotovision, 2004.

Steven Roger **Fisher**, *A History of Reading*, London: Reaktion Books, 2003.

Bob **Gordon**, *Making Digital Type Look Good*, London: Thames and Hudson, 2001.

Denis **Guedj**, *Numbers: the Universal Language*, London: Thames and Hudson, 1998.

David **Jury**, *Letterpress, New Applications for Traditional Skills*, Hove: Rotovision, 2006.

Robin **Kinross**, *Modern Typography a Critical History*, London: Hyphen Press, 1991.

Willi **Kuntz**, *Typography: Macro- + Micro-Aesthetics*, Zürich: Niggli, 1998.

Le Corbusier, *The Modulor and Modulor 2*, Basel: Birkhauser Verlag AG, 2000.

Ruari **McLean**, *How Typography Happened*, London: British Library, and New Castle, Delaware: Oak Knoll Press, 2000.

Josef **Müller-Brockmann**, *Grid Systems in Graphic Design (Raster Systeme für die visuelle Gestaltung)*, Zürich: Arthur Niggli (revised edition), 1996.

Gordon **Rookledge**, *Rookledge's International Type Finder*, selection by Christopher Perfect and Gordon Rookledge, revised by Phil Baines, Carshalton, Surrey: Sarema Press, 1990.

Luciene **Roberts** and Julia **Thrift**, *The Designer and the Grid*, Hove: Rotovision, 2004.

Emil **Ruder**, *Typographie: Ein Gestaltungslehrbuch/ Typography: A Manual of Design/Typographie: un manuel de création*, Zürich: Niggli (7th edition), 2001.

Fred **Smeijers**, *Counter Punch: Making Type in the Sixteenth Century, Designing Typefaces Now*, London: Hyphen Press, 1996.

Jan **Tschichold**, *Die neue Typographie: Ein Handbuch für Zeitgemäss Schaffende*, Berlin: Brinkmann & Bose, 1987; English edition *The New Typography: a Handbook for Modern Designers*, translated by Ruari McLean, with an introduction by Robin Kinross, Berkeley and Los Angeles: University of California Press, 1995.

— *The Form of the Book; Essays on the Morality of Good Design*, edited by Robert Bringhurst, translated by Hajo Hadeler, London: Lund Humphries, 1991.

Wolfgang **Weingart**, *My Way to Typography: Retrospectives in Ten Sections, Wege zur Typographie Ein Rückblick in zehn Teilen*, Baden: Lars Müller, 2000.

III: Type and image

Jaroslav **Andel**, *Avant-Garde Page Design 1900–1950*, New York: Delano Greenidge Editions LLC, 2002.

Phil **Baines**, *Penguin by Design: A Cover Story*, London: Allen Lane, 2005.

Alan **Bartram**, *Making Books: Design in Publishing since 1945*, London: British Library, and New Castle, Delaware: Oak Knoll Press, 1999.

Jacques **Bertin**, *Semiology of Graphics Diagrams, Networks, Maps*, Madison, Wisconsin: University of Wisconsin Press, 1983.

Derek **Birdsall**, *Notes on Book Design*, New Haven: Yale University Press, 2004.

Jeremy **Black**, *Maps and Politics*, London: Reaktion Books, 2000.

Kees **Broos** and Paul **Hefting**, *Dutch Graphic Design, a Century*, Cambridge, Massachusetts: The MIT Press, 1993.

Henry **Dreyfuss**, *Symbol Sourcebook: An Authoritive Guide to International Graphic Symbols*, New York: John Wiley (paperback), 1984.

Michael **Evamy**, *World Without Words*, London: Laurence King Publishing, 2003.

Roger **Fawcett-Tang**, *The New Book Design*, London: Laurence King Publishing, 2004.

— with Daniel **Mason**, *Experimental Formats: Books, Brochures, Catalogues*, Hove: Rotovision, 2004.

— *The New Book Design*, London: Laurence King Publishing, 2004.

— *Experimental formats: Books, Borchures, Catalogues*, Hove: Rotovision, 2001.

Mirjam **Fischer**, Roland **Früh**, Michael **Guggenheimer**, Robin **Kinross**, François **Rappo** et al., *Beauty and the Book/60 Jahre Die schönsten Schweizer Bücher/Les plus beaux livres suisses fêtent leur 60 ans/60 Years of the Most Beautiful Swiss Books*, Berne: The Swiss Federal Office of Culture, 2004.

Steven **Heller**, *Merz to Emigre and Beyond: Avant-garde Magazine Design of the Twentieth Century*, London: Phaidon, 2003.

Richard **Hendell**, *On Book Design*, New Haven: Yale University Press, 1998.

Jost **Hochuli** and Robin **Kinross**, *Designing Books: Theory and Practice*, London: Hyphen Press, 1996.

Allen **Hurlburt**, *Layout: The Design of the Printed Page*, New York: Watson-Guptill, 1977.

John **Ingledew**, *Photography*, London: Laurence King Publishing, 2005.

Michael **Kidron** & Roald **Segal**, *The State of the World Atlas*, London: Pan Books, 1981.

Robin **Kinross** (ed.), *Antony Froshaug, Documents of a Life, Typography and Texts*, London: Hyphen Press, 2000.

Carel **Kuitenbrouwer** (guest editor), *De best Boeken 2001/The Best Dutch Book Designs of 2001*, Amsterdam: CPNB, 2002.

Ellen **Lupton** and Abbot **Miller**, *Design Writing: Research Writing on Graphic Design*, London: Phaidon Press, 1999.

Ben van **Melick**, *Wertitel/Working title, Piet Gerards, grafisch ontwerper, graphic designer*, Rotterdam: Uitgeverij 010 Publishers, 2003.

Paul **Mijksenaar** and Piet **Westendorp**, *Open Here: The Art of Instructional Design*, London: Thames and Hudson, 1999.

Ian **Noble** & Russel **Bestley**, *Experimental Layout*, Hove: Rotovision, 2001.

Jane **Rolo** and Ian **Hunt**, *Book Works: A Partial History and Sourcebook*, London: Bookworks and the ICA, 1996.

Rebecca **Stefoff**, *The British Library Companion to Maps and Mapmaking*, London: The British Library, 1995.

Edward R **Tufte**, *The Visual Display of Quantative Information*, Cheshire, Connecticut: Graphic Press, 1983.

— *Envisioning Information: Narratives of Space and Time*, Cheshire, Connecticut, Graphic Press, 1990.

— *Visual Explanations: Images and Quantities, Evidence and Narrative*, Cheshire, Connecticut: Graphic Press, 1997.

Daniel Berkeley **Updike**, *The Well-Made Book, Essays and Lectures*, edited by William S. Peterson, New York: Mark Batty, 2002.

Howard **Wainer**, *Graphic Discovery: A Trout in the Milk and other Visual Adventures*, Princeton: Princeton University Press, 2005.

John Noble **Wilford**, *The Mapmakers*, London: Pimlico (reprint), 2002.

Further reading

Type and image *(continued)*

Richard Saul **Wurman**, *Information Anxiety 2,*
Indianapolis: Que, 2001.

IV: Manufacture

Michael **Barnard** (ed.), *The Print and Production
Manual,* Leatherhead, Surrey: Pira International,
1986.

Alastair **Campbell**, *The New Designers' Handbook,*
London: Little Brown, 1993.

David **Carey**, *How it Works, Printing Processes,*
Ladybird Book series, Loughborough: Wills and
Hepworth, 1971.

Poppy **Evans**, *Forms, Folds, Sizes: All the Details
Graphic Designers Need to Know but can Never
Find,* Hove: Rotovision, 2004.

Kōjirō **Ikegami**, *Japanese Book Binding: Instructions
From a Master Craftsman,* translated and
adapted by Barbra B. Stephan, New York:
Weatherhill, 1986.

Arthur W **Johnson**, *The Manual of Bookbinding,*
London: Thames and Hudson, 1978.

Tim **Mara**, *The Manual of Screen Printing,* London:
Thames and Hudson, 1979.

Alan **Pipes**, *Production for Graphic Designers,*
London: Laurence King Publishing (4th edition),
2005.

Wayne **Robinson**, *Printing Effects,* London: Quarto,
1991.

Keith A **Smith,** *Volume 1: Non-adhesive Binding:
Books Without Paste or Glue,* New York: Keith A
Smith, 2001.

Rick **Sutherland** and Barbra **Karg**, *Graphic
Designers' Colour Handbook: Choosing and Using
Colour from Concept to Final Output,* Gloucester,
Mass.: Rockport, 2003.

Harry **Whetton**, *Practical Printing and Binding: A
Complete Guide to the Latest Developments in all
Branches of the Printer's Craft,* London: Odhams
Press, 1946.

— (ed.), *Southward's Modern Printing,* Leicester: De
Montfort Press (7th edition), 1941.

... Additional material

The Chicago Manual of Style, Chicago: The Chicago
University Press, 15th edition, 2003.

Geoffrey **Dowding**, *Finer Points in Spacing and
Arrangement of Type,* Vancouver: Hartley &
Marks (second edition), 1995.

*Hart's Rules for Compositors and Readers at the
University Press,* Oxford: Oxford University Press
(39th edition), 1993.

R L **Trask,** *The Penguin Guide to Punctuation,*
London: Penguin, 1997.

Glossary

An illustrated glossary of basic book terms is shown in Part I, pp.20–21.

Alignment The positioning of type in relation to the vertical edge of the column (see justification).

Ascender The element of a lower-case letter that projects above the x-height.

Axonometric drawing A drawing system in which three facets of an object are represented in a single drawing, top, left, and right. The facets are presented at 45°.

Baseline grid The lines on which letters sit.

Beard Part of the body of metal type that extends below the x-height of the type.

Blad A small section of a book that is printed and simply bound prior to production. It is used to visualize the page design, cover, check reproduction quality, and as a marketing tool by the publisher.

Chinese binding A concertina-folded book; an alternative term for French binding.

CMYK The abbreviation for four-colour printing using cyan, magenta, yellow, and black (black being referred to by printers as *key*).

Co-edition A book that is published by more than one publisher, *eg* a book written in English and published in the US may be translated, published, and distributed in German and Spanish by other publishers.

Codex Historically, a manuscript text bound in book form – as opposed to a scroll.

Colophon A production list at the back of the book that states the title, fonts used, method of printing, etc.

Colour gamut The range of colours that can be seen in the spectrum, or reproduced through CMYK process or RGB.

Colour separation The process of dividing full-colour images into cyan, magenta, yellow, and black.

Compositor The person who sets type, traditionally by arranging individual metal characters.

Continuous tone A tonal range that can be reproduced in full, *eg* 1% to 100%.

Corner flag A small triangular piece of card or paper that is folded over the top right-hand corner of a book carrying promotional information.

Debossing Type or image that is pressed into the surface of the page or cover using a metal plate and great pressure.

Descender The part of the lower-case letter that projects below the baseline.

Didots A measurement of type devised by François Ambroise Didot in *c.* 1783 and used widely throughout Europe (although not in Britain).

Directional An arrow or word that links a caption to an image, e.g. left, right, etc.

Dry proof Proofs produced without a lithographic process, e.g. photographic or digital proofs.

Duotones Images that are made up of two separated halftone screens printed in selected or *special* colours.

Dust jacket Protective paper cover that wraps around a hardback book.

Embossing Type or image that is raised above the surface of the page and is created by squeezing the paper between a male and female form.

Endmatter A catch-all term for any material that is not part of the narrative or body of the book, *eg* appendixes, glossary, picture credits, acknowledgments, index. Sometimes referred to as *subsidiaries*.

Endnotes Notes on the main text printed all together at the end of the book.

Endpapers The leaves of paper that are glued to the front- and backboards of a hardback book to strengthen the joint between the boards and the book block. They are often decorative.

Factorial grids Grid systems that rely on subdividing columns and intervals by whole numbers rather than dividing lengths into decimal points.

Flatplan A schematic diagram of all the pages in a book, used by editors and designers to organize chapters and colour sections.

Foil blocking A debossed text or image used on a cover board that is in-filled with a metallic foil.

Folio 1 The number used to identify one side of a page, often referred to as the page number. **2** A paper format resulting from folding a sheet of paper once.

Footnotes Notes on the main text printed in the tail margin of a page.

French binding A book made without conventional signatures but made from concertina-folding a sheet. Sheets may be joined together by glue tabs prior to binding.

Frontispiece An illustration facing or preceding the title page.

Frontmatter A catch-all term for any material that is not part of, and is positioned prior to, the narrative, *eg* title page, contents, preface, introduction *etc*. Also called *preliminary matter* or *prelims*.

Full-bleed An image that is printed without a margin, running off all page edges.

Gatefold A page with a format that extends beyond the foredge of the book, but is folded into the book block at the foredge, which performs the same function as the hinge of a gate. When unfolded, it has nearly twice the surface area of the page. A double gatefold consists of two gatefolds on adjacent pages unfolding to the left and right to create a surface area nearly four times that of the page.

Golden section The division of a straight line, plane figure, or sheet of paper etc., such that the relationship between the smaller and the larger is the same as between the larger and the whole. In algebra, this proportion can be expressed as $a : b = b : (a + b)$. Its approximate decimal value is $1 : 1 \cdot 61803$.

Gravure printing An intaglio method of printing in which the image and text are etched into a copper plate. The ink sits below the surface of the plate and is drawn out of the recesses when pressed against the paper.

Greyboard Stiff board produced in a variety of weights and thicknesses used for covers in hardback bindings.

Grid A matrix of horizontal and vertical lines that divides the page into columns and intervals and helps the designer position the image and text elements of the page in relation to one another to create a sense of visual coherence.

Half-title The title of the book printed on the page preceding the title page.

Halftone A screen that breaks down the continuous tone of a photographic or drawn image into tiny dots or lines of different widths so that they can be reproduced in print.

Hand-setting The process of arranging type into words by selecting hot-metal individual characters from the type case by hand.

Histogram A term often loosely used to describe bar charts, measuring frequency within class. In mathematical terms, a histogram records frequency and density.

Hot-metal type Type cast on a mechanical composition system. Molten metal is forced into a female mould, where it cools and solidifies into type as either a line or an individual type character.

Ideogram A symbol that represents an idea as opposed to an object or person (see pictogram).

Imposition The arrangement of pages on either side of a printed sheet that makes up a signature.

Incunabula Books printed before AD 1501. Used more widely to refer to the early years of typographic printing following Gutenberg's invention *c.* 1455.

Intaglio printing A type of printing in which the ink sits below the surface of the plate in tiny cells; when the paper is pressed onto the plate the ink is drawn out of the cells onto the paper.

Interval The space between two columns of type on a page.

Isometric A drawing system in which three facets of an object can be represented in a single drawing, top, left, and right. The facets are presented at 30°.

Justification Alignment in which the left and right edges of a column of type run vertically and parallel down the page; as a consequence the inter-word space varies from one line to the next. Alternatives are *ranged left*/unjustified, with the type running vertically down the left edge of the column only, or *ranged right*.

Keyline A line that defines the perimeter or edge of an illustration or piece of text conventionally reproduced in black (printers referring to black as key), but now more commonly used to describe a fine line reproduced in any colour.

Leader line A line that links a caption label or numeral to an element of an illustration.

Leading In metal setting, strips of lead inserted between the lines of type to increase the vertical spacing. In digital setting, the space between baselines.

Leaf A sheet of paper in a book, often loosely referred to as a page although its two sides (recto and verso) are also individually called pages.

Lenticulation A method of reproducing an image so that, when viewed from different positions, it appears to move.

Letterform The shape of a hand-drawn or type character.

Letterpress The first form of typographic printing, usually from metal or wooden letters or stereotypes.

Linocut A method of relief printing in which the image or text is cut wrong-reading into a sheet of lino.

Modernist grid An approach to grid systems that divides the text area into a series of equal picture fields. These are exactly subdivided by baselines. Often the width of column intervals matches the space between the picture units.

Modular scales Numeric scales in which the increments are proportionally related to one another, eg a Fibonacci series.

Moiré pattern A swirling or circular pattern formed by overlaying two or more screens. It is often undesirable, as it interferes with the image, but can be used as a creative element within a page designs producing a striking effect.

Octavo (written 8vo) A paper size derived from folding a sheet with three right-angle folds to produce 8 leaves and a 16-page signature.

Orthographic drawing A drawing system that describes three-dimensional form by presenting a series of related scale elevations, each of which is depicted from a viewpoint square to the object.

Overprinting The printing of one colour over the top of another, using two or more plates.

Ozalid A trade name for a paper coated with diazo compounds used for producing dry proofs prior to printing.

Page One side of a book leaf.

Pantone matching system A trade name for an extensive set of printing inks with over 1,000 colours, pastels, and metallics, which enable special colours to be matched to CMYK equivalents.

Parchment The split skin of a sheep or goat used as a writing material. An alternative term for vellum in English.

Pastedown Half of an endpaper pasted to the inside of a greyboard cover of a book.

Photoetching The process of preparing a metal plate by covering the area's non-etched surface with an acid resist, then dipping the plate into acid to form a recessed image.

Pica Unit of typographic measurement, consisting of 12 points.

Pictogram A symbolic image or sign that represents an object or person; a visual noun.

Pilcrow (¶) A graphic symbol (possibly medieval in origin) that represents a new string of connected thoughts.

Planographic printing Any method of printing where the ink sits on the surface of the plate. The paper is pressed onto the surface to make the impression.

Quadtones Images that are made up of four separated halftone screens printed in selected or special colours.

Quarto (written 4to) A paper size derived from folding a sheet with two right-angle folds to produce 4 leaves and an 8-page signature.

Recto 1 The front of a sheet or leaf. **2** The right-hand page of a spread.

Registration The process of ensuring that all the colours on a sheet are positioned correctly in relation to one another.

Relief printing A method of printing where the ink passes from the raised surface of the plate to the paper.

RGB Abbreviation for red, green, blue; the light or additive colours used in computer and television screens.

Roman numerals Numbering system sometimes used for folios in the frontmatter: i/I = 1, ii/II = 2, iii/III = 3, iv/IV = 4, v/V = 5, vi/VI = 6, vii/VII = 7, viii/VIII = 8, ix/IX = 9, x/X = 10, xi/XI = 11, ... l/L = 50, c/C = 100.

Rubric Red initial letter traditionally added by hand to a printed text. A drop or enlarged cap at the beginning of a chapter paragraph may be referred to as a rubric if printed in a second colour.

Scatter proofs A set of non-sequential proofs taken from different sections of the book as a check on consistency of image and colour reproduction.

Shoulder-notes Notes on the main text printed in the vertical margins of the page.

Show-through Ink printed on the reverse of the page that is visible from the front side. This is often undesirable as it can interfere with the text or image, but can also be used creatively to give a sense of depth.

Side story Separated independent text that is positioned in a side column and covers in greater detail an issue identified in the main text.

Signature Section of a book made up from a folded sheet to create pages when guillotined. Signatures are built up in 2, 4, 8, 16, 32, 64, or 128 pages.

Source-notes Notes indicating the origin of the author's information; they may be positioned as footnotes, shoulder-notes, endnotes, or at the ends of chapters.

Stencil printing A method of printing using a screen that masks areas not to be printed and allows ink to pass through the cut-out areas of the stencil to the surface of the paper.

Storyboard A way of visualizing an entire book page by page in drawn form.

Superprint Two or more different tints of one colour printed together.

Swatchbook Collection of paper, board, or colour samples produced by a company.

Throwout A long page folded at the foredge or head of a book that unfolds to reveal several other pages.

Tipping in Pasting into the book additional paper elements.

Trapping The amount of overlap added to the lighter colour when reproduced next to a darker colour so that the two touch without a gap.

Tritones Images that are made up of three separated halftone screens printed in selected or special colours.

Tummy band Strip of paper wrapped around a book.

Verso 1 The reverse of a sheet or leaf. **2**, The left-hand page of a spread.

Wet proofs Proofs made on press.

Woodcut A method of relief printing in which the image or text is cut wrong-reading into a block of wood.

Wrong-reading Text flipped so that the letters and reading direction are reversed (mirror image), as on a printing plate.

X-height The height of the main part of the lower-case letters measured from the baseline to the top of the lower-case x.

Index

*Page numbers in **bold** refer to picture captions*

A

AA Book of the Car **116, 136**
Aftermath:Kuwait 1991 **190**
Alfabeto Sobre La Literatura Infantil (Atxaga and Hidalgo) **156**
Alice in Super Pop-up Dimensional Wonderland (design: Robert Sabuda) **208**
Antipoems: Nicanor Parra (design: Francesca Prieto) **237**
The Art of Money (Standish) **230**
authors 13, 14, 22, 26, 28

B

Baines, Phil **150**, 240
Bent Ply (Ngo and Pfeiffer) **231**
The Bible **7**, 12, 106, **107**, 227
Biesty, Stephen **134**
Bill, Max 53
Billy Liar (Waterhouse) **163**
binding
    boards **221**, 233
    covers 219, **221**, 228
    design relationship 222, 230
    dropping in 228
    embossing 224, **225**, 226–7, **231**, 234
    endpapers **221**, 234
    experimental **236, 237**
    finishing 224, **225**, 226–7
    foil blocking **225**, 226, 234
    foredge design **221**, 222, **223**, 233
    hand-binding 219, **220, 221**, 233, 234
    hardbacks 233, **236, 237**
    history 6, 219
    leather **221**, 230
    loose-leaf **234**, 239
    machine-binding 219, **220, 221**, 234
    materials 230, **231, 232**, 233
    paperbacks 233, 234, **235**
    process 220–1
    rounding and backing **221**, 233, 234
    sewing **220**, 233, 234, **236, 237**, 239
    shrink-wrapping **238**, 239
    stamping 226, 233, 234
    styles 233–4, **235, 236, 237, 238**, 239
    thumb indexes 227
    tipping in 229
Bird Recognition (Fisher) **118**
Birdsall, Derek 43, 64, **73**, 165
Blago (design: Gordon Davey) **208**
Bollmann, Hermann **127**
Book of the Dead (Hunefer) **10**
books
    commercial value 9
    components *see* parts of a book
    creating 13, 22
    defined 8–9
    format *see* format of books
    future of 12
    history 6–8
    influence of **11**, 12
    manufacture *see* binding; paper; pre-production; printing
    marketing 14, 17
    selling 9, 19
Bosshard, Hans Rudolf **55**
Bostrom, Oskar **227**
Brown's Flags and Funnels **112**
Brunelleschi, Filippo 129

C

Capital magazine 58, **59**
The Chicago Manual of Style 240
Chicks on Speed **41**
Circus (Calder) **157**
The City: Problems of Planning (design: Derek Birdsall) **165**
Collins Guide to Insects **113**
Collins' The Night Sky **122**
Colores digitales para internet y otros medios de comunicación (Zwick, Schmitz and Kuedhl) **104**
columns 21, 39, **55**, 56, 62, 71, **72**
The Communist Manifesto 12
A Complete Course of Lithography (Senefelder) 210
Copy-editing (Butcher) 240
covers 20, 100, 160
    advertising **164**
    back covers 20, 100, 161, **164**
    binding 219, **221**
    boards 20, **221, 225**, 233
    brand promotion 165
    cloth 230, **231**
    conceptual 165
    corner flags 228
    cover finishes 228
    designing 160, 162, 165
    developments in 160, **162, 163, 164**
    documentary 165
    elements of 161
    endpapers 162, **221**, 234
    expressive 165, **167**
    flaps 160, 161
    formats 160
    front *vs.* back 161
    images **169**, 224, 229–30
    ISBN numbers 100, 161
    laminated 228
    leather **221**, 230
    lining **221**
    materials **231, 232**, 233
    paper 233
    photographic **163, 166, 167**
    publisher's marks **161**, 162
    spines 161, 162, **170, 236, 237**
    title sequence 162
    tummy-bands **225**, 228
    turnover 191, **221**
    types of 162, 165
    typographic designs **170**
    vinyl **231**
    wood **231**
    wraps 160–1, **169**
    see also dust-jackets
Cranbrook Academy of Art Handbook 2002 (design: Catelijne von Miiddlekoop and Dylan Nelson) **70**

D

Der Typografische Raster (Bosshard) **55**
design
    analytical approach 25, 42
    approaches 23–7
    art directors' role 16, 22, 27
    conceptual approach 27
    documentation approach 23–4
    expressive approach 26, 42
    styling the text 240
designers
    approaches to design 23–7
    design brief 28, 160
    interpretation 26, 110
    role in publishing process 16
Diamond Sutra (Buddhist text) **10**
Die Kunst der Typographie (Renner) 46
Dirty Dublin (design: Orala O'Reilly) **154**
A Dog's Life (Fanelli) **156**
Dries van Noten book **155**
Duotones, Tritones and Quadtones (Clark) **180**
dust-jackets 160, 228, **237**

E

editorial structure
    annotation 105
    captions 105–7
    chapter openers 101, 104
    colophons 109
    contents 100, 102–3
    design brief 28, 160
    endnotes 108
    flatplans **101** *see also under* layout of a book
    folio numbers 6, 100, 102–3, **104**
    footnotes 108
    glossaries 109
    headings 104
    indexes 100, 109
    layout 101, 140 *see also* layout of a book
    quotations 104
    running heads 104
    shoulder-notes 108
    source-notes 101, 108
    styling the text 240
    verse numbers 108, **109**
    visual hierarchies 104
Een Huis Voor de Gemeenschap (van Heeswijk) **148**
El arte de amar (Fromm) **177**
The Elements of Typographic Style (Bringhurst) 32
Encyclopaedia Britannica 71
Erni, Hans 53
Eye magazine **175**

F

Faust (design: Typeaware) **152**
Fibonacci series 30, **31, 32**, 44, **51, 53**, 74, 88–9
For Sale: an Explanation of the Market Economy (Mølhave) **25, 137**
format of books 21, 30
    choosing 30
    chromatic scale 32
    content-linked 39, **40, 41**, 50
    de Honnecourt's diagram 44
    Fibonacci series 30, **31, 32, 51**
    golden section 30, **31**, 32, 33, 44
    landscape 21, 30
    Modulor 33
    page size 39
    paper size 39
    portrait 21, 30
    rectangles 43–4, **45**, 46, **47**, 48, **49**
        rational and irrational 33, **38**
    square 30
Frutiger, Adrian **87**, 91, 94
Fugle i Felten **112**
Full Moon (Holborn and Bradford, design: Michael Light) **149**

G

Gerstner, Karl 58, **59**
Geslacht (Manning) **238**
Gill, Eric **73**
golden section 30, **31**, 32, 33, 44, 74
Gordon Matta-Clark **237**
Grafisch Theatre **169**
Grid Systems in Graphic Design (Müller-Brockmann) 53, **54, 61**
grids 42
    appropriated 68
    asymmetric 42, **55, 144**
    baseline 21, 39, **50**, 56, 57, 84–5
    cartographic grids 67
    characters per line 21
    columns 21, 39, **55**, 56, 62
    content-linked 68
    de Honnecourt's diagram 44
    deadline 21
    developmental 68
    factorial 62, **63**
    folio stand 21

frames 43
functional approach 43
gatefold 21
geometric basis 42–9
grid fields 58
grid squares 64–5, 67
images 21, 53, **54**, 58, 60, 69, **147**
interval 21
interval sequences 62, **63**
margins 21, 39, 43, **50**, 56
measurement basis 50, **51**, 53
metric quadrat system 64, **65**
modernist 53, **54, 55**, 56–8, **59**, 60, **61, 146**
modular scales 50, **53**, 88
multi-layered 58, **59**
multiple 58
organic 68
parts of 21
picture units 21, 58
point quadrat system 64
proportional scales 50, **51**, 88–9, 90
proportioning 43
rectangular division 43–4, **45**, 46, **47**, 48, **49**
root rectangles 48, **49**
running head stand 21
in sequential chronology 67
shoulder 21
symmetrical 42, 43, 53, 77–8, **144**
text boxes 43, **50**
throwout 21
title stand 21
type size 56, 57, 58
typographic elements basis 62–7
units 21, 46, **47**, 56–7
without grids 69–70, 150
Guide to Ecstacity (Coates, design: Why Not Associates) **103, 225**
Guillermo de Osma: Galeria catalogue **170**
Gutenberg, Johannes 7–8, 12, 71, 210

H
'*Ha, daar gaat er van mij*' (design: Jan Middendorp) **155**
The Handbook of Sailing (Bond) **133**
Hart's Rules for Compositors and Readers 240
Haslam, Andrew **27, 105, 141**, 143, 240
Haynes Car Manuals **128**
Heraldry Sources, Symbols and Meaning (Neubecker) **124**
Het Beste Van (Schippens) **154**
Hewlett Packard printer manual **130**
Hoefler, Jonathan 82
How To (McKnight-Trontz) **131**
The Human Body (Pelham and Miller) **201**

I
I Was Hitler's Prisoner (Lorant) **163, 164**
illustrations *see* images
images
    in binding process 229
    box plots 115
    caption lists 107
    captions 105–7, **145, 150**, 229
    charts 110, 114–15
    in children's books 156–7
    on covers **169**, 224, 229–30
    diagrams 110, **113**, 123–5, **130**, 131, **132, 133**
    embossing 224, **226**
    framing **147**
    full-bleed **147, 148**, 222
    geographical projections 119–20, **121**
    graphic schedules 117, **118**
    graphs 110, 114, 116–17
    in grids 21, 53, **54**, 58, 60, 69, **147**
    holographic 230
    for identification 111–13

ideograms 136
labels 107, **111**
in layouts **144, 145**, 146, **147**, 148–51
lenticulated 229
line and tone 172–3
linking with text 76, 106–7, **144, 145, 146**, 148, 150–1
maps 67, 119–20, **121**, 122, 177
Marey Schedule **118**
notational systems 139
pictograms 136, **137**
plate numbers 105
printing 211–12, 215–16, 229
scatter plots 117
star maps 122, **216**
statistical presentation 110
symbols **25**, 136, **137**
tables 138
three-dimensional *see* three-dimensional representations
time lines 117, **118**
timetables 117, **138**
as wall charts **147**
see also photographs
The Importance of Being Earnest (Wilde, design: Tania Conrad) **152**
Internet 12, 19, 94
ISBN numbers 9, 100
Isotype system 136

J
Jeroglificos Mayas (Lariou) **227**

K
Kelmscott Chaucer (Morris) **93**
KEN (Choules) **234**
Korean books production 8

L
Ladybird Book of Sailing and Boating **133**
L'aparador (Museu Municipal Joan Abelló) **212**
Law, Liza **208**
layout of a book
    books on visual culture 154–5
    children's illustrated fiction 156–7
    comic books **147**
    digital files 140
    extending the page 149
    flatplans **101**, 140–1, 143, 189
    framing images **147**
    graphic novels **147**
    image-driven 146–9
    individuality 150
    layers 151
    in multilingual publishing **145**
    passe-partout **147**
    photographic books 158–9
    preparation 140
    scripts 152
    storyboards **142**, 143
    text and image files 140
    text and image linking 76, 106–7, **144, 145, 146**, 148, 150–1
    text-driven 143–5
Le Berét Rouge (Carlin) **231**
Le Corbusier 33
Le Modulor books (Le Corbusier) 33
Le Petit Prince (Saint-Exupéry) **157**
Lego model diagrams **132**
L'exil et le royaume (Camus) **72**
Little Red Book (Mao Zedong) **11**, 12
London College of Printing catalogue 1998 **169**
The Lore of Flight (BDD Promotional Books) **105**
The Lore of Ships (A.B. Nordbok) **106**
L.S. Lowry: A Biography (Rohde) **103, 104**

M
Made you Look (Sagmeister) **222, 223**
Make Art Work (Artomatic) **218**
Make it Work! series (design: Andrew Haslam) **27, 105, 119**, 143
Mallart, Bruno **169**
Manuale tipografico (Bodoni) 93–4
manufacture of books *see* binding; paper; paper engineering; pre-production; printing
Mapping Sitting – On Portraiture and Photography **148**
Mar Adentro screenplay **102**
margins 21, 39, 43, **50**, 56
Mattotti, Lorenzo **169**
McQueens **234**
Mein Kampf (Hitler) **11**, 12
Mmm … Skyscraper I Love You (design: Tomato) **26**
modernist approach
    grids 53, **54, 55**, 56–8, **59**, 60, **61, 146**
    typeface 94, **95**
    typographical conventions 74–5, 77
Morris, William 78, 92, 93
Müller-Brockmann, Josef 53, **54**, 57, **61**
Mr Lunch (Siebold and Walsh) **157**
Musical Notation (Gandra) **139**
My Way to Typography (Weingart) **55, 170**

N
Nederlands Postzegels (Boom) **151**
Neurath, Otto 136
The New Typography (Tschichold) 53, 94
New York Notebook (Rosenwald) **96, 170**
No Logo (Klein) **40**
Notes on Book Design (Birdsall) 64
Nudes in Budapest (Cotier) **159**

O
Observer's Book of Ships **111**
OMTE Stolen **188**
On ne copie pas (Douzou and Bertrand) **69**
Ordinary Citizens, the Victims of Stalin (King) **24**

P
pages
    contents page 100, 102–3
    defined 7
    die-cut 149
    double-page spread 21, 42
    extending 149
    fly leaf 20
    foot 20, 21
    in format selection 39
    gutter 21, 39
    head 21
    height and width 21, 30, 39
    landscape 21, 30
    numbering 100, 102–3, **104**, 105
    organizing 187–90
    portrait 21, 30
    recto 21
    short 149
    single pages 21
    verso 21
Pantone Matching System (PMS) 176, 182, 184
paper
    bulk 196
    calliper 196
    colour 198
    costs 191, 198
    in design 191
    finish 197
    grain 197
    history 6–7
    opacity **151**, 197, 198
    paper-making 7
    selecting 191, 196–8, **199**

surface 198
weight 196
see also paper engineering; paper sizes
paper engineering
  cubes and cylinders 204, **205**
  die-cuts 200, 204, 206
  folds 200, 201
    angled **202**
    pillar and buttress **203, 204**
    short and long **202**
    square parallel **202**
    symmetrical ridge **203**
    triangular prism **203**
  gluing 200, 201, 202, 203, 229
  90° structures 201, 202, **208**
  180° structures 201, 203, 204, **205**
  procedure 201
  pull-tabs 200, 201, 207
  terms 200
  tip-ins 200, 229
  tip-ons 200, 203
  wheels and rotation 206
paper sizes
  A-series 39, 191, 192
  B-series 192
  British 39, 191, 194–5
  C-series 192
  DIN (Deutsches Institut für Normung) formats
    39, 191
  folio 6, **194**
  in format selection 39
  history 191
  imperial 39, 191, 194–5
  ISO (International Organization for
    Standardization) formats 39, 191, 192
  North American 39, 191, 193
  octavo 6–7, **194**
  quarto 6
Paris in 3D **229**
parts of a book
  binding 100
  book block 18, 20
  endmatter 101
  endpapers 20, 100, 162, **221**, 234
  fly leaf 20
  foot 20
  foredge 20, 21, **40, 221**, 222, **223**, 233
  frontmatter 100
  head 20, 21
  head band 20
  hinge 20
  leaves 6, 20, 21
  pastedown 20
  signature 20
  spine 20, 100, 161, 162, **170**, 196, **236, 237**
  tail 20
  turn-in 20
  see also covers; pages
Pathfinder a/ way/ through/ swiss/ graphics 231
Penguin books **161, 162, 163, 164**
A Penguin Special: Russia (Pares) 163
Philips Atlas **216**
photographs
  on covers **163, 166, 167**
  in design **24**
  in format selection 39, **40**
  formats **60**
  framing **147**
  in grids 60, **61**
  in layouts **148, 149,** 158–9
  plate numbers 105
  printing 211–12, 215
Piatti, Celestino 53
Pic-a-Drink (Singer) **137**
Poet's Pub (Linklater) 163
Pohadky (Hesse) **173**
Pollicino (Perrault) **156**

Portraits (Avedon) **159**
pre-production
  colour 176–80
    colour systems 176, 182, 184
    full-colour *see* full-colour reproduction
      below
    page organization 189–90
    printing effects 178–80
    single colour 176
    two-colour work 177
  defined 172
  design relationship 172, 177
  digital technology 174, 182–3
  full-colour reproduction 181–4, 211
  line and tone 172–3
  organizing the pages 187–90
  proofing 185–7
  reproduction defined 172
  scanning 182–3
  screens 174–5, 183
Printed MatterDrukwerk **169**
Printers' Imposition (Avis) **189**
printing
  colour printing effects 178–80
  CTP (computer to plate) 213
  digital technology 212, 213, 215
  full-colour reproduction 181–4, 211
  gravure 212, 215–16
  hand-composing 210, **211**
  history 7–8, 210
  images 211–12, 215–16, 229
  intaglio 210, 215–16
  letterpress printing 210, **211**, 212, 219, 229
  lithography 210–15, 229
  movable type 8, 12, 210
  photographs 211–12, 215
  photosetting 212
  planographic 210–15
  processes 210, 213–14, 215–16, 218
  relief 210
  screen **210,** 216, 218
  stencil 210, 216, 218
  woodblock 8, **10**
Project M **222**
publishers
  house style 240
  marks **161,** 162
publishing roles 13–19

Q
Quotations from Chairman Mao Zedong **11,** 12

R
RAC *Manual* (design: North Associates) 60, **61**
Raster Systems (Bosshard) **38**
Raw Creation: Outsider Art and Beyond (design:
  Phil Baines) **150**
Room at the Top (Braine) **163**
Royal College of Art Degree Show 1990 catalogue
  234
Ruder, Emil 53

S
Sci da manuale (Kobold) **132**
Self-organization in Neural Networks **236**
Senefelder, Aloys 210
Services and Prayers for the Church of England
  (design: Derek Birdsall) **73**
Sheffield (Dumphy) **227**
The Silence (Peress) **40**
The Small Garden (Brookes) **107**
Soffici, A. **211**
Soon: Brands of Tomorrow (Blackwell) **232**
Speakerman, Eric 143
Spoon **231**
Stadium und Arenen **127**

Starn, Mike and Doug **158**
The State of the World Atlas (Kidron) **120**
The Strange Case of Dr Jekyll and Mr Hyde
  (Stephenson, design: Matilda Saxo) **236**

T
Tankard, Jeremy **90**
This Sporting Life (Storey) **163**
three-dimensional representations
  axonometric drawings 126, **127,** 129
  concertina folds **208**
  cross-sections 134
  cutaway drawings and models **134,** 135, **201**
  drawing programs 129
  exploded drawings **128,** 129
  holographic images 230
  orthographic drawing 126, **127**
  perspective 129
  pop-up books 200, 201, 202–5, 207, **208,
    209,** 229
  schematic drawings 135
Times Atlas **67,** 71, 120, **121**
Tokyo subway maps **113, 125**
Touching North (Goldsworthy) **40**
Tripitaka 8
Tschichold, Jan 30, 53, 94
Tulipa (Blok, design: Willem van Zoetendaal) **158**
type
  digital 80–1, 82, 86, 95, 96
  fonts 90, 94
  history 7–8
  ISO Set 1 90
  metal 79–80, 81, 83, 86, 87
  movable 8, 12, 210
  type design 80, 81, 82
  typeface **73,** 82–3, **87, 90,** 91, 92–6, 98
  type families 90–1
  type size 56, 57, 58, 86–91, 104, **170**
  weight 91, **152**
Type and Typography (Baines and Haslam) **118,
  124,** 240
Type at Work (Balius) **102**
typographical options
  alignment of text 76–8, 81, **82, 144, 145, 146**
  colour 92
  column depth 71, **72**
  contrast 92
  for covers **170**
  em square 64, 74, 79, 80, 81
  hierarchy 92
  H&J settings (hyphenation and justification)
    77, 81, 82
  horizontal space 21, 64, 74, 75, 77, 78–83
  hyphenation 76, 77, 81
  inter-word spacing 75, 77, 78, 79–82
  paragraphs 72–5, **150**
  vertical space 83–5
Typographie (Ruder) **54, 170**
Typography: Macro- + Micro-Aesthetics (Kunz) **91,
  95**

V
The Visual Display of Quantitative Information
  (Tufte) 110
Volkswagen Maggiolino (Batazzi) **135**

W
Weingart, Wolfgang **170**
Why Not Associates **103**
Witch Zelda's Birthday Cake (Tatcheva) **41**
Wright, Frank Lloyd **209**

Y
Ydry, Charles 117

Acknowledgments

Students and staff, both past and present, have all unwittingly contributed to the writing of this book. Particular thanks to the MA Communication Design students at Central Saint Martins who allowed me to feature their books, all the MACD staff for their support, especially: Danny Alexander, Andrew Foster, John Ingledew, Sadna Jaine, Val Palmer, Gary Powell, Ros Streeton and Mike Smith. Many people have offered encouragement: Wendy Baker, Blue and Blaise Baker-Haslam, Karl Henry and Ian Noble at the London College of Printing. Others have offered specific help: Pat Dibben (librarian at CSM), my brother Martin Haslam, the Rev. Helen Matthews for lending a collection of liturgical books, Andrew Boag, Nick Nienham (letterpress technician at CSM) for letterpress setting, Ollie Olsen and Malcolm Parker at CSM for lending print production material, Wyvern Bindery for binding the book in Part IV and Phil Baines for use of material we originally wrote for *Type & Typography* in Additional Material. Thanks to Danny Alexander for initial photography and to Martin Slivka for photography. I am very grateful to all the the staff at Laurence King who have helped in the making of this book, particularly Laurence King, Jo Lightfoot (Commissioning Editor), Anne Townley (Developmental Editor), Nicola Hodgson (Copy Editor) and the very patient and extraordinarily supportive Emily Asquith (Senior Editor) and Peter Kent (Picture Researcher and permissions).

Dedication

To my dad, Peter Haslam, 14 April 1938 – 28 Feburary 2005, he will never read this book but was the inspiration for so much of it. He could not walk past a bookshop without crossing its threshold.